Strangers and Pilgrims

Strangers

and Pilgrims

From *The Castle of Perseverance*
to *King Lear*

EDGAR SCHELL

The University of Chicago Press

CHICAGO AND LONDON

EDGAR SCHELL is Professor of English at the University of California, Irvine.

The University of Chicago Press, Chicago 60637
The University of Chicago Press, Ltd., London

Library of Congress Cataloging in Publication Data

Schell, Edgar.
    Strangers and pilgrims.

    Includes bibliographical references and index.
    1. Pilgrims and pilgrimages in literature.
2. English drama—Early modern and Elizabethan,
1500–1600—History and criticism.   3. English drama—
17th century—History and criticism.   4. Moralities,
English—History and criticism.   I. Title.
PR635.P45S3   1983   822'.2'09353   82-20207
ISBN 0-226-73673-3

for Chris and Tory, and for Deb

CONTENTS

CONTENTS

ACKNOWLEDGMENTS

Part of chapter 1 of this book appeared originally in a slightly different form under the title "On the Imitation of Life's Pilgrimage in *The Castle of Perseverance*" in the *Journal of English and Germanic Philology,* volume 67 (1968), pages 235–48. I want to thank the copyright holder, the Board of Trustees of The University of Illinois, for permission to reprint it here. Part of chapter 2 first appeared under the title "*Scio Ergo Sum:* The Structure of *Wit and Science*" in *Studies in English Literature 1500–1900,* volume 16 (Spring 1976), pages 179–99. I am grateful to William Marsh Rice University, owner of the copyright, for permission to reprint it.

The Regents of the University of California, through the Humanities Institute, have twice provided grants that enabled me to take time off from teaching to study and write.

Stories of petty intrigues among university faculties are part of popular folklore, but I have found that one of the continuing pleasures of literary scholarship has been the open generosity of my colleagues. Joanne Kantrowitz, Travis Bogard of the University of California at Berkeley, and Robert Montgomery and Alexander Gelley of the University of California at Irvine have commented on various parts of my manuscript. Frank Lentricchia, now at Rice University, provided help and encouragement just when they were needed. And I especially want to remember here a late friend and colleague at the University of California at Irvine, Howard Babb, to whom my debts are past recounting.

Irvine, California
November 1982   E. T. S.

Dearly beloved, I beseech you as strangers and pilgrims, abstain from fleshly lusts, which war against the soul.

[1 Peter 2:11]

These all died in faith, not having received the promises, but having seen them afar off, and were persuaded of them, and embraced them, and confessed that they were strangers and pilgrims on the earth. For they that say such things declare plainly that they seek a country. And truly, had they been mindful of that country from whence they came out, they might have had opportunity to have returned. But now they desire a better country, that is, an heavenly: wherefore God is not ashamed to be called their God: for he hath prepared them a city.

[Hebrews 11:13–16]

Thus is man's whole life a pilgrimage, either from God, as Cain's, or from himself, as Abel's.

[Samuel Purchas, *Purchas, His Pilgrimes*]

INTRODUCTION

On the Imitation of Action and the Pilgrimage of Life

The discussions that follow are concerned with five plays from the Middle Ages and the Renaissance: *The Castle of Perseverance,* John Redford's school play *Wit and Science,* an anonymous play about Richard II that has been given the title *Woodstock,* Ben Jonson's *Volpone,* and Shakespeare's *King Lear.* Each of them is related to the form of didactic theatrical allegory called the morality drama, and the last three are also prominent examples of the major categories of Renaissance secular drama: history, comedy, and tragedy. Taken together, the discussions of these plays might be said to make up a skeletal history of the English morality through close examinations of plays that exemplify its major types and illustrate their evolution, or devolution, when the principles around which they were constructed were pursued in secular dramatic forms. But excellent comprehensive histories of the morality drama have already been written—most recently by Robert Potter, earlier by Spivack and Bevington, still earlier by Farnham and Mackenzie.[1] What concerns me here is something much more particular.

That is the persistence during the two hundred years that separate the *Castle* from *King Lear,* in a variety of dramatic forms and genres, of a single action involving a character who perverts his natural inclinations and loses thereby his own identity. In each of the essays that follow I concentrate on one play, describing its narrative and thematic structures, trying to give an account of the relationships among its parts, and trying to speculate, at least, about the reasons why its elements have been given their particular forms. Each essay, that is, attempts to define the action of one play and to consider the ways in which that action has been imitated. But the argument that threads its way through all of the essays concerns the various ways in which the central action that concerns me—the universal form of man's pilgrimage through his temporal and spiritual lives—was imitated and reimitated, at first in transparent allegory, later in ways

1

that sought to harmonize the competing claims of a sequence of literal events with that universal form by reshaping historical facts into virtual truths, and finally in ways that called into question whether those competing claims could be reconciled at all.

The terms "imitation" and "action" and the Aristotelian poetic to which they refer have been interpreted so variously by modern critics that, at the risk of belaboring what may be obvious to many readers, I want to explain what I understand by them.[2] Also, because it may seem naïve to read allegories from an Aristotelian perspective, I want to explain why that does not seem altogether foolish to me.

THE IMITATION OF AN ACTION

In the portion of the *Poetics* that has survived, Aristotle talks mainly about tragedy; but the larger scope of his original inquiry is suggested in the preliminary chapters that deal with the imitative arts in general and in particular with those whose medium is language. Arisotle's definition of tragedy in chapter 6 of the *Poetics* is explicitly presented as a deduction from what he has already said about the characteristics of mimetic poetry, and we can find in his earlier chapters the outlines of a more comprehensive poetic.

In chapter 4 Aristotle argues that poetry derives from two natural instincts in men, one an instinct for rhythm and harmony, the other an instinct for imitation. Both instincts survive and flourish in men's actions because their pursuit is pleasurable, rhythm and harmony for the senses, imitation for the mind. It is by imitating, Aristotle says, that children learn their first lessons about the world and how to live in it, and as they grow they continue to find pleasure in imitating and observing the imitations of others because "the act of learning" is itself naturally pleasurable. What men learn by imitating—recognize might be a better word, since for Aristotle learning is discovering the categories to which things belong—is to make sense of experience. They discover the moral and personality types to which individual characters belong, and they discover the logical processes of cause and effect that make single events intelligible.

The peculiar pleasure of mimetic poetry lies in those discoveries. One learns from mimetic poems, but not the separable lessons of Platonic or Horatian imitations, not the facts of life or the maxims of morality. What one learns or recognizes is simply the intelligible order of the poem itself, which in turn imitates the intelligible order of an experience. And mimetic pleasure is the feeling of that recognition.

What distinguishes poets from historians, who also deal with the experiences of men, is chiefly their capacity to create that sort of pleasure. History, by which Aristotle means chronicle history, is simply one damn thing after another, but facts in their temporal order are not the province of poetry: "It is not the function of the poet to narrate events that have actually happened, but rather events such as might occur and have the capability of occurring in accordance with the laws of probability or necessity."[3] So poetry is more philosophical than history because poets have the advantage over historians of being freed from the opaque tangles of reality itself. They are free to treat men's actions as if they were fully intelligible, to let us see through apparently discrete events to the logical tissues that make them part of an enveloping and illuminating process.

Because Aristotle takes mimetic pleasure to be the end to which a poem is made, he takes plot to be, as it were, a poem's soul. By plot Aristotle does not mean either the separable story or the exciting manipulation of events, neither fable nor intrigue. What he means is the part of the poem that corresponds directly to mimetic pleasure on one side and to action, which we will take up in a moment, on the other. That part of the poem is the "arrangements of the incidents" in a certain and significant order, with a beginning, a middle, and an end (chap. 6). So the killing of Duncan, part of the story of *Macbeth,* is not part of what Aristotle would call the plot of Shakespeare's play—though it provides the occasion for several incidents that are part of the plot—just as the killing of Laius is not part of Sophocles' plot for *Oedipus Tyrannus.* For plot is the design of a narrative, the principle of arrangement that determines which incidents will be included and which will not, where they will be placed, which will be emphasized and which muted. Plot is not literally a poem's soul, because a poem is a made object and not a natural body; but it serves the same function the soul serves in a natural body. It is the informing principle from which everything else takes its shape: character, thought, diction, rhythm—even spectacle, though Aristotle seems to regard spectacle as something that belongs merely to the unpredictable arts of the theater and not properly to poetics.[4]

Plot in turn takes its form from what Aristotle calls action. "Action" is in one respect a puzzling term in the *Poetics* because Aristotle uses it in at least two different senses. The meaning of the broader of them, as in Aristotle's comment at the beginning of chapter 2 that "artists imitate men involved in action," seems clear enough: art deals with what men do rather than what they are. But as it appears in the definition of tragedy ("the imitation of *an* action"), the term has a narrower, even a technical, meaning. While Aristotle never defines action in the narrower sense, we can infer its meaning from his discussions of plot, which is its perceptible form. "Tragic plot is an imitation of action," he tells us (chap. 6). And since a plot is the intelligible form of a narrative, it would appear that action is the intelligible form of the experience imitated by that narrative, whether it is drawn from life or history, from myth, or simply from the imagination of the poet. Whatever the original mode of the experience, its action in this technical sense is merely latent until it is perceived by a poet, whose recognition of the way that separate events compose one intelligible whole is his initial and most important creative act. The first form of action in this technical sense is thus an intellectual form. Action is a conception of order. While poetry in general draws on life and history and myth for its materials, what the maker of an individual poem imitates by means of these materials is his own understanding of their intelligible form. So a single myth might yield dozens of actions. That is why Aristotle is relatively indifferent to the sorts of mimetic errors that trouble Plato in the *Republic.* For where Plato worries about whether a poem mirrors external reality accurately, the important transactions in Aristotle's *Poetics* lie between the poem and its maker. Errors of fact in the details of medicine and other disciplines, or faulty descriptions of the way that horses run, are for him merely accidental errors, annoying, perhaps, but not central to the art (chap. 25). What is central is the poet's illumination, through the sensuous materials of his art, of the intelligible form he has perceived. It is here that the most vexed of Aristotelian terms, catharsis, becomes important.

Until recently the catharsis clause has usually been taken to be Aristotle's answer to Plato's complaint in the *Republic* that, attractive as it may be, poetry cultivates emotions, such as pity and fear, that are not suited to citizens of strong and well-ordered communities. Readers who take the word catharsis to mean purgation, on the model of Aristotle's use of it in the *Politics,* have understood him to be saying here that, far from cultivating such emotions, tragedy expels them. Other readers have understood the concept of catharsis in light of Aristotle's discussion in the *Nicomachean Ethics* of emotional health as a mean between excess and defect, and have interpreted the catharsis clause to mean that tragedy purifies the feelings of pity and fear by bringing them within bounds and attaching them to their proper objects, showing what sorts of things ought properly to be pitied and feared.

Readings of the catharsis clause that see it as involved in some way with the capacity of tragedy to transform the feelings of its audience have spoken in important ways to the real feelings of readers of tragedy, as expressions like "tragic exaltation" or "tragic calm" attest. And the psychology of catharsis as the transformation of feelings has generated a literature all its own, independent of the *Poetics*. In the context of the *Poetics*, however, such readings of the term leave Aristotle radically confused. For while he promises at the beginning of chapter 6 merely to bring "together the definition of [the] essence [of tragedy]" from what has already been said, he has not said anything about purging or purifying emotions in his discussion of the general characteristics of poetry. Moreover, the notion that catharsis has to do with transforming emotions provides a goal for tragedy different from the goals of all other forms of poetry, which have been said to aim at the pleasure that comes in the act of learning, and this suggests that tragedy is different in kind from all other forms of poetry.

More recently, classical scholars have begun to insist that the proper objects for catharsis are not the emotions of pity and fear but rather the tragic events themselves, and they suggest that tragedy in Aristotle's view ought to be understood to aim at "the catharsis of pitiable and fearful incidents."[5] H. D. Goldstein, for example, would take catharsis to mean purification in the sense of pruning away irrelevancies and would understand the catharsis clause to mean simply that tragedy orders its "pitiable and terrible materials to serve the form of the poem."[6] That seems to be what Aristotle himself has in mind in chapter 8 when he reminds us that not everything that happened to Odysseus is germane to a unified action and when he praises Homer for keeping out of the *Odyssey* incidents like Odysseus' wandering on Parnassus and his feigned madness because there is no probable relationship between them. Leon Golden comes at the same point from a different direction by arguing that in ancient Greek the word catharsis meant purification in an intellectual as well as a physical sense, so that the catharsis clause might be taken to mean simply that tragedy makes sense of its pitiable and fearful incidents by clarifying the relationships among them.[7] According to these views, then, tragedy is like all other kinds of narratives in imitating the intelligible form of an experience with the aim of making it as clear as possible, and it differs from other kinds merely in the sort of experience it imitates and in the manner of its imitation.

Those are the assumptions I will be making in the essays that follow. I do not intend to pepper my discussions with Aristotelian terms but simply to assume that all the plays I will be talking about are organized so as to imitate the significant forms that make individual events intelligible and that all of the parts of the plays—character, thought, diction, spectacle—are shaped toward that end. It is clear that an Aristotelian poetic does not raise all the questions that might be raised about any narrative, and it is also clear that none of the playwrights I discuss here set out self-consciously to write Aristotelian plays. Jonson aside, there is no reason to believe that any of them knew the *Poetics* at all. But then there is no reason why they should have known it. Theories of poetry are of use to critics, not poets. While they are often couched in the language of composition, as the *Poetics* is, they are essentially theories of how to read poems, not of how to write them. What Aristotle provides for me, then, is not a historical hypothesis about how the plays were written. It is simply an articulated and disciplined critical approach that seems especially congenial to a body of philosophical plays, particularly since what interests me about those plays are certain similarities in the forms of their plots. What I will be arguing is that, for all their differences in style and in the details of their fables, the *Castle, Wit and Science, Woodstock, Volpone,* and *King Lear* imitate significantly similar actions.

IMITATION IN DIDACTIC ALLEGORIES

The *Castle* and *Wit and Science* are not ordinarily thought of as mimetic plays. They are didactic allegories. And *Woodstock, Volpone,* and *King Lear* all share characteristics of didactic allegories. That fact is important because Aristotelian critics have tended to argue that didactic allegories are different in kind from the sorts of poems Aristotle had in mind and thus that to approach them by way of the *Poetics* is inappropriate because the *Poetics* is likely to suggest the wrong sorts of questions to ask about them.[8] That is true if, reading the catharsis clause to mean that tragedy transforms the feelings of its audience, one then assumes that all mimetic narratives have the same general goal of raising and transforming feelings; for a plot that is shaped toward an emotional effect is obviously different in kind from one designed to make a moral doctrine clear and persuasive, just as a wooden table is different in kind from a wooden chair. But the difference is not quite as distinct if we take the goal of mimetic poetry to be simply the imitation and clarification of the intelligible form of an experience. Insofar as both aim to make sense of their incidents by relating them to the universal categories to which they belong, there is no difference in kind between mimetic narratives and allegories. Both yield naturally to the sort of analysis that seeks to discover the internal relationships between the action that shapes a narrative and the characters and events that give it substance. But there are important qualitative differences.

The most important of these differences is rooted in the concept of mimetic pleasure. The distinguishing feature of poetry for Aristotle, and the end toward which poems are made, is poetry's capacity to provide the kind of pleasure that comes in the act of learning. Mimetic pleasure is not a feeling of satisfaction at having learned something. It is rather the feeling of learning *itself*. That is a slight but important distinction because it accounts for Aristotle's indifference in the *Poetics* to the quality and the content of what is learned. While Aristotle insists that poetry is more philosophical than history, he never suggests that the value of a poem is related to the value of its philosophical content. When he does speak about the differences in narratives in qualitative terms, it is simply to say that complex plots are more pleasurable than simple ones and that events that are surprising but turn out to be related according to probability or necessity to what has gone before are particularly effective (chaps. 11 and 16). That is to say, if I understand him correctly, that the most pleasurable narratives are those in which learning is most active, in which we are required to follow the logic of plots that veer off in unexpected ways or to make inferential leaps across the gap between the unexpected and the inevitable. While mimetic pleasure is not proportionate to the philosophical value of what we learn, then, it does seem to be loosely proportionate in Aristotle's view to the amount of intellectual activity a narrative demands of its readers.

If that is so, we can understand why the kind of narrative Aristotle envisions in the *Poetics* is realistic in the ordinary sense of that term; it is realistic because, however any particular narrative was actually constructed, the peculiar intellectual pleasure at which mimetic narratives aim begins in a world of mere events and proceeds toward the illumination of the tissues that connect them into a single intelligible process. Mimetic poems reach out from experience toward the universal categories that make sense of it. So an epistemological puzzle, an initial illusion of mere facticity, is an integral part of the special form of pleasure provided by mimetic poems. And I suspect that Sophocles' *Oedipus Tyrannus* came so often to Aristotle's mind as an illustration because he saw in it a sort of metadrama, which, beginning in a world of mysterious and discrete particulars and proceeding toward their clarification, imitated what he understood to be the poetic act itself.

It is here that didactic allegories differ most sharply from mimetic poems. For while they share the same structural principles, being designed to clarify the moral forms of action, they are relatively less tactful in demonstrating the sense they make out of experience. They pursue more aggressively and more explicitly the illumination of conceptual categories, moral doctrines, and principles of moral psychology, and they merely exemplify them by means of characters and events that have the status of metaphors. Thus, where mimetic poems reach from experience toward ideas for illumination, didactic allegories reach from ideas toward experience for illustration. And to the extent that their fables are treated simply as rhetorical signs pointing toward their themes, and not as the substantial activities of substantial characters, didactic allegories do not allow for the peculiar pleasure of seeing through particulars to the universals that illuminate them, although they may allow for the complementary pleasure of recognizing in particulars examples of universal forms.

The distinction between mimetic narratives and allegories is thus a matter of balance, a matter of the relative prominence of the conceptual structure that organizes a poem. The peculiar balance of didactic allegory is unmistakable in *The Castle of Perseverance,* which is made up almost entirely of universals, with only brief and discontinuous forays into the everyday world of particulars. Its central character is Humanum Genus, and he inhabits a fictional world composed of the personified elements of every man's moral situation: God; the World, the Flesh, and the Devil; the Seven Deadly Sins and the Seven Moral Virtues. If the *Castle* allows at all for the perception of relationships between particular events and the universal Christian moral categories that give them meaning, it does so in the special and relatively painful fashion of a sermon. Each member of the audience / congregation is encouraged to make a personal application of the moral paradigms presented onstage, to find in his own experience particular analogues of Humanum Genus' commitment to the World in his youth, or his lack of moral perseverance in his old age, and to amend his life accordingly.

That is also true of *Wit and Science,* which dramatizes the false and true stages of Wit's courtship of the Lady Science so that the budding wits entrusted to John Redford's charge might discover the educational paradigms relevant to their own experience. And it is true of every other morality play, for every morality play aims to influence the behavior of its own audience. But *Wit and Science* also includes a skein of particular events that runs parallel to the educational doctrines it preaches, and thus it begins to allow for mimetic pleasure as well as moral illumination. The metaphors of *Wit and Science* are more substantial than those of *The Castle of Perseverance,* sustained in longer narrative lines, and they are developed sufficiently to make up a self-contained fable that is from time to time logically independent of Redford's thesis.

Of course in *Wit and Science* the balance between the romantic fable and the pedagogical theme is still clearly struck in favor of the theme. The center of the play's dramatic gravity clearly lies in John Redford's classroom. And when Idleness paints Wit's face, we do not say, "I see how Wit's face came to be dark"; we say, rather, "I see that the wit is dimmed when it is idle." But the balance point is different in a play like *Woodstock,* which gives individual names to its characters and much greater substance to the fable in which they act. There, with characters and events taken from history and arranged so as to illuminate the significant form of Richard II's political career, we need to attend to such matters as consistency of character, clarity and adequacy of motivation, and the question of whether one event follows another in a recognizably probable order. For *Woodstock* is clearly the sort of play Aristotle had in mind, an imitation of "men involved in action" with the aim of clarifying the form of their experiences. Where *Wit and Science* gives the substance of a romantic fable to the principles of education, then, *Woodstock* goes in just the other direction and gives intelligible dramatic form to the substantial events of history, so that through its performance we come to understand the internal logic of Richard II's fall from kingship to tyranny.

The form to which *Woodstock* reduces the actual events of Richard's reign in order to reveal their logic is an adaptation to historical materials of the form of the morality drama. Richard Plantagenet is a substantial historical character, and the play treats him like one. But the anonymous playwright, bent on interpreting the processes of history by Christian paradigms, has sharpened and highlighted the implicit resemblances between Richard's actual political dilemma and the universal moral dilemma of all men. As a dramatic character, Richard has been shaped along the lines of the universal moral type Mankind, newly come to his kingdom and forced to choose between two sets of counselors, one of which would draw him toward political responsibility, the other to self-indulgence. Around the dramatic center of Richard's character the playwright has re-formed and placed other actual historical persons so as to clarify the underlying shape of his tragic reign. Richard's turbulent uncle Thomas of Woodstock has been unhistorically cast as the chief spokesman for political responsibility, while the royal favorites, Bushy, Bagot, and Greene, have been set, equally unhistorically, to play Woodstock's vicious opposites. And as Richard reenacts the moral progress of Mankind, turning from his uncles, putting himself under the guidance of his favorites, and sliding toward the loss of his crown, we are enabled to see the actual events of his reign (such as his assumption of the throne *in propria persona,* or the arrest and death of Woodstock) as stages in a single political process whose universal form is the moral life of Mankind.

Much the same statement might be made about Volpone and King Lear, for the particular acts of each, as different as they are, are universalized by being related, in ways we shall examine, to the form of the moral pilgrimage of Mankind. Both the Venetian grandee and the pagan king are more sharply individuated than Richard is, and their stories are more densely literal than his. But both follow the spiritual course of Mankind's journey as they pursue their separate ends, and the significant forms of their experiences are revealed with reference to that journey.

THE STRUCTURE OF A MORALITY PLAY

G. R. Owst has argued that morality plays grew out of the illustrative dialogues used by medieval preachers to vivify their sermons.[9] Whether that is historically accurate or not, it is true that the voices of different characters in morality plays are often resolvable into a single voice that sounds a good deal like that of a preacher. What one hears in a morality play is often not the expression of a discrete character or even a discrete moral quality, like anger or greed; it is rather what anger or greed might be imagined to say if it were impersonated by someone anxious to make clear how anger and greed ought to be judged. So morality characters are not simply personifications; they are personifications located and defined—enacted, as it were—by their bustling and omnipresent authors. For example, when Covetous welcomes Mankind to his scaffold in *The Castle of Perseverance,* he promises to teach him all the wisdom of the world and then adds, in a formulaic phrase that echoes one spoken by Mankind's Good Angel, that the world's wisdom "fadeth as a flode" (836; cf. 353). Thus, even as we hear Covetous urge Mankind to seize the World, we hear the preacher who speaks through him warning us of its futility. A more extended example of the morally and dramatically complex voices of morality characters appears a few moments later when Mankind, having embraced all of the Seven Deadly Sins, obligingly steps forward to point out to us how foolish he has been and how painful his end will be:

> Mankynde I am callyd be kynde,
> Wyth curssydnesse in costys knet.
> In sowre swettenesse my syth I sende,
> Wyth sevene synnys sadde beset.
> . . . .
>
> My prowd pouer schal I not pende,
> Tyl I be putte in peynys pyt,
> To helle hent fro hens.
>
> [1238–46]

And then, when he has anatomized his soul and predicted its end, he turns back into the play to take up again his course for hell. At such moments, however we imagine the origin of the morality drama, I think we are helped in reading the plays by a critical postulate, first made a half-century ago, that morality plays are essentially sermons embodied, tacitly fleshing out the preacher's abstract propositions in all the sensuous languages of the theater. That is not to say that we ought to think of morality plays as dramatized sermons in Owst's sense or in the sense in which the phrase *sermo corporeus* has begun to trouble modern critics of the plays.[10] To be sure, morality plays are not constructed around the principles of organization of medieval sermons. And they generally deal with only the most commonplace doctrines. But that is often true of sermons as well, which exhort as much as they explain, and which, far more often than they teach, simply recall for their listeners the moral principles they already know. I mean simply that morality plays satisfy the same rhetorical impulse that produces sermons: the impulse to urge a moral proposition to an audience immediately present; but they satisfy it not just in words but in sights and sounds and movements and colors.

Bernard Spivack has pointed out that morality plays are generally constructed so as to unfold the logic of such propositions. Each play is built, he writes, around a "sequential thesis in fulfillment of an instructive purpose, which maintains itself throughout the whole reach of the plot and in every part of it."[11] The action of *The Interlude of Youth* (c. 1513), to choose a brief example, clearly derives from such a thesis. It might be stated in this form: The natural vanity of youth leads to sins that inhibit charity; but the cultivation of humility frees charity, causes youth to abstain from self-indulgence, and leads ultimately to salvation. In conformity with that thesis, the play begins with Youth's mocking rejection of Charity's appeal that he attend to the needs of his spirit. Instead Youth calls for Riot, his "brother." Riot leads in Pride, and Pride in turn introduces Youth to his sister, Lechery. When Charity tries to prevent Youth from going off to a tavern with his new companions, Riot and Pride bind him in chains. While they are offstage, Humility enters and frees Charity from the bonds of Riot and Pride. And then, when Youth returns, swollen with pride, Humility persuades him to give up his companions and to take the name Good Contrition. At the end of the play, informed now by charity and humility, Youth promises that when he sees "misdoing men, / Good counsel I shall give them / And exhort them to amend" (768–70).

Other morality plays might be as fully, if not as economically, described as straightforward embodiments of the terms of particular moral propositions. But there is also another structural principle at work in the morality drama, a pattern of action common to almost every morality play, whatever particular moral proposition it develops. This pattern has been described and accounted for in different ways by different readers,[12] but essentially it is the expression of a shape and rhythm common to the lives of all men according to Christian moral theology, which holds that all men are born into sin and that all men are offered by grace the capacity to grow toward salvation. The significant form of any man's life is the record of how he fulfills that capacity. So morality heroes, embodying for rhetorical ends the moral dilemma of all men, are caught in a state of fragile innocence, inclined toward virtue but open to vice. At first they pursue folly to its dead end in frustration or despair, and then they turn to show how men may be recovered from their errors by cultivating the virtues that correspond to and correct their follies. That is to say, they are seen always in spiritual transit, in motion between heaven and hell. And the acts they perform are always imagined as stages in a moral process that is at once narrow and pointed in its explicit terms and universal in its form.

That form also shapes a number of medieval and Renaissance poems written during the heyday of the morality drama. These poems imagine human life in terms of the ancient biblical figure of spiritual transit, the pilgrimage, and they imitate that conception of the significant form of human life by means of a fable about a journey through a symbolic landscape. What I want to show initially, partly through the remainder of this Introduction and partly through my essays on *The Castle of Perseverance* and *Wit and Science,* is that the plays and poems share a common perception of the significant form of Christian moral life. I do not intend to suggest that the poems were the sources for the plays or anything of the sort[13] but merely that both imitate, in the different ways appropriate to poetry and drama, the same action. Of the dozens of pilgrimage allegories written during this period,[14] three in particular will allow me to describe more fully the action I have in mind. They are *Parabola I,* an allegory based on the parable of the Prodigal Son, which may have been written by Saint Bernard of Clairvaux; *The Pilgrimage of the Life of Man,* written originally in French by Guillaume de Deguileville and translated into English by John Lydgate; and *Reason and Sensuality,* another translation by Lydgate, whose mind, as Prince Hal said of Poins', "keeps the roadway" better than any man's.

The Action Imitated: The Pilgrimage of
the Life of Man

The figure of life as a journey is not peculiar to Christianity. It is one of that stock of universal images, born out of the facts of the human condition, that are common to many religions. Man lives in time, and we naturally imagine life as a passage through time. But while it is not peculiar to Christianity, the figure of life's journey is peculiarly apt in Christian thought, as it is in any system of thought that posits a normative goal for man's life or assumes that qualitative distinctions will be made among men after they have passed "through nature to eternity." Under such assumptions, man is not merely an aimless traveler through time; he is, rather, a pilgrim journeying toward a goal he shares with other men. Thus the author of the Epistle to the Hebrews, looking back on the Judaic image of men as "strangers and

sojourners" with God (Gen. 23:4), finds in the image itself evidence
that

> These all died in faith, not having received the promises,
> but having seen them afar off, and were persuaded of
> them, and embraced them, and confessed that they were
> strangers and pilgrims on the earth. For they that say such
> things declare plainly that they seek a country. And truly,
> had they been mindful of that country from whence they
> came out, they might have had opportunity to have
> returned. But now they desire a better country, that is, an
> heavenly: wherefore God is not ashamed to be called their
> God: for he hath prepared them a city.
>
> [Heb. 11:13–16][15]

Because it catches up fundamental Christian assumptions about
the nature of life, the figure of the pilgrimage has been used in a wide
variety of ways in Christian rhetoric, narrow and exclusive as well as
universal. It has provided authors of contemplative treatises with a
language by which to mark out the stages through which the devout
may gain illumination,[16] while it has served moralists as a metaphor
for the spiritual processes enacted by all men, whether these lead to
heaven or to hell. Here the pilgrim is one of the "numerus electorum";
there he is everyman, for "man's whole life [is a] pilgrimage, either
from God, as Cain's, or from himself, as Abel's."[17]

In the central tradition of Christian thought through the Middle
Ages and most of the Renaissance, the tradition articulated by Saint
Thomas Aquinas and racapitulated near its end by Richard Hooker,
man, like all creatures, was understood to be connaturally attracted
to what was best for him. His first knowledge of virtue was thought to
come to him *per inclinationem,* though in practice his natural
inclinations might be overlain and obscured by passions or by the
manifold accidents of daily experience. But those individual impedi-
ments aside, there was understood to be, in man himself, "first a
tendency toward the good of the nature he has in common with all
substances, secondly...a bent towards things which accord with his
nature considered more specifically, that is in terms of what he has in
common with other animals," and finally an inclination to the things
that correspond to his peculiar nature as a man.[18] The first leads him
to preserve himself, the second to perpetuate his kind, and the third to
seek his maker. For as Grace Dieu explains to the Pilgrim in
Lydgate's allegorical *Pilgrimage of the Life of Man,* the very
construction of man's being draws him toward God: "Thow off

God...art thymage and creature," she tells him, and therefore "to hym off verray right certayn / Thow must resorte and tourne ageyn, / As by mevyng natural / Ageyn to thyn orygynal" (12251–54).[19]

Thus the sense that his life is a pilgrimage is bred into every man's bones. Preachers may exhort him to the spiritual discipline of the journey with images of the jeweled towers of Revelations, or threaten him with the fires of hell, and the accumulated wisdom of the church may guide and comfort him along the way, but even without preachers and churches he is moved toward his end by connatural knowledge. Lydgate, following Guillaume de Deguileville, makes the point most literally by locating the beginning of the Christian pilgrimage in the womb itself. There, "shut up clos" for nine months, the Pilgrim has a vision of the Gates of the New Jerusalem. He does not realize what he sees or understand it—his knowledge comes by inclination—but he is powerfully moved to seek it out. And the first ten thousand lines of the *Pilgrimage* are given over to explicating the resources the Church provides for every pilgrim's journey.

The initial stage of life's pilgrimage is treated more economically in *Reason and Sensuality,* which seems at first a less clerkly poem than it turns out to be. Here the pilgrim is a nameless Young Man, lying in bed on a May morning (the poem is, on one level, a courtly romance), when Nature appears and chides him for not being out and doing. Like Grace Dieu, she reminds the Young Man that he was made in the image of God and warns him that

> sithe thow art semblable
> To goddys that ben pardurable,
> Thow owest wel to do thy peyne
> Thy self fro vices to restreyne,
> Knowyng the grete dignyte
> Wheche god a-bove hayth yove to the,
> Which thou shuldest never cesse
> In vertu al wey to encresse.
>   [569–76][20]

What distinguishes him in particular, Nature tells him, is his rational soul, "by whech of ryght, with-oute shame, / Of a man he bereth the name" (725–26). That is why in the course of his life he must subordinate his sensual desires and "oonly by reson him governe, / Lyst that he whiche wer grete shame, / Be depryved of hys name" (762–64). In order to develop his understanding of himself and his place in her scheme, Nature sends the Young Man off on a journey

"rond thys worlde in lengthe and brede...that thow maist com-
prehende / The mater and thy selfe amende, / To preyse the lorde
eternal, / The wheche made and caused al" (519–28), warning him at
the same time to keep always to "the weye of reson, / The whiche...
doth a man to heven lede" (844–46). Like the Pilgrim, then, the
Young Man of *Reason and Sensuality* is sent off on the journey of his
life by the prompting of his own nature.

Nature's warnng that he may be "depryved of his name"—that is,
lose his identity as a man—if he does not subordinate passion to
reason brings us into the second stage of the pilgrimage, during which
the pilgrim is deflected from the proper course of his life and wanders
into what Saint Bernard called "the land of unlikeness." Because man
has reason, he must have free will—the one would be meaningless
without the other, Saint Thomas said[21]—and, being free to choose, he
may choose not to be reasonable and so not to be himself. Thus man
is peculiar among all the rest of creation in being born to the necessity
of achieving and maintaining his own nature. Beasts cannot fail to be
beasts as long as they live, but men may cease to be men when they
turn from reason. Reason in the *Pilgrimage* promises the newly
tonsured priests that as long as they follow her guidance "ye shall be
men"; but she warns that, when they stray from her, "ye may avaunte
(& that a-noon) / That ye be bestys & unresonable" (2046–48). The
pilgrim's journey along the way of reason, then—the way that leads
ultimately to heaven—is also a journey toward the perfection of his
own nature, and it always involves the possibility that he may lose
himself.

Neither the Pilgrim nor the indolent Young Man in *Reason and
Sensuality* is able to hold to the guidance of reason. Both are undone
by the rhythm of life itself. Each is at first too young to be provident,
too impatient to take a long view of goods and evils.[22] While each is
connaturally inclined to follow reason, it is difficult to know always
what reason directs, because its promptings are obscured by the
forces to which man subjected himself in the Fall. Thus Reason warns
Lydgate's Pilgrim, as he starts out on his journey, that she will often
be hidden from him by clouds. And when in the course of his journey
he encounters his Youth, his reason becomes beclouded. The
Pilgrim's Youth is personified in a girl feathered all over like a dove.
She seems to him altogether beguiling, fresh and lusty, a pearl beyond
price. Because she is given only to pleasures, this feathery Youth is
impatient with solemn talk, especially the sort that insists that the
pains of life cannot be avoided. There is no need to listen to Grace

Dieu, she tells the Pilgrim (Grace Dieu has urged him to restrain the impulses of his body and to keep always in the forefront of his mind the image of Christ on the Cross); Grace Dieu, she says, is like the nightingale, whose song is always "occy, occy...go sle thy selfe" (12688–90). It is far better to seek pleasure and ease.

Thus when the Pilgrim comes to the first of life's crossroads, where the paths of Labour and Idelnesse diverge around the hedge of penance, his Youth urges him toward the "large & pleyn and esy" path of Idelnesse. His own instincts, on the other hand, incline toward the way of Labour. Tugged at on one side by his own connatural knowledge of what he ought to do and on the other by the desires of his Youth, the Pilgrim exemplifies what Saint Bernard, at the end of *Parabola I*, speaks of as the first stage of man's pilgrimage: "Primo enim est egens et insipiens":[23] man is at first in need, yearning to be completed, and foolish. And of course it is folly that prevails, both in *Parabola I* and in the *Pilgrimage*. The Pilgrim follows his Youth along the way of the world into a nightmarish land inhabited by the Seven Deadly Sins. Lydgate's treatment of the creatures of that land, their forms all grotesque perversions of human forms, locates it in the spiritual country Saint Bernard calls in *Parabola I* "the land of unlikeness" *(regio dissimilitudinis)*.

Parabola I draws on a good many narrative strains in the Bible, but essentially it is a conflation of the story of Adam's fall from paradise with the parable of the rescue of the Prodigal Son from the far country of his exile. Adam and the prodigal are fused in the figure of Filius Regis, who has been installed by his father in the Paradise of Good Conscience and promised all the treasures of his father's glory if he does not leave it. There he is protected and instructed by the Laws and the Prophets, just as the Pilgrim is protected and instructed by Grace Dieu. But Filius Regis has free will *(liberum arbitrium)* and he comes to desire a knowledge of good and evil. And so he leaves the Paradise of Good Conscience to wander "per valles curiositas, per campos licentiae, per nemore luxeriae, per paludes voluptam carnalium, per fluctus curarum saecularium." As he wanders he is seized by an old man (the *vetus homo*), bound in the cords of worldly concupiscence, put on the ship of false security, and transported to the land of unlikeness. In the immediate terms of the fable, the land of unlikeness is the far country to which the Prodigal Son wandered and from which Filius Regis is recovered and restored to his father in the latter part of the poem. But the larger significance Saint Bernard attaches to the figure provides a gloss on a long-lived poetic and theatrical trope to which I will be returning often in the essays that follow, as I try to establish connections among such things as Richard II's masquing, the disguises of Volpone, and Lear's crown of wildflowers.

The figure of the land of unlikeness came to Saint Bernard from Saint Augustine's *Confessions,* where it refers to the state of man in life, hovering between being and non being.[24] As Saint Bernard uses it, however, the figure takes on more pointedly moral significance as an image of the effects on the forms of men's souls of the choices that they make. Saint Bernard understood the statement that man was made in the image of God to mean that man's will was made as free as God's own: "it is in the free will above all else," he wrote, "that there seems to be impressed a kind of substantial image of the eternal and unchangeable Godhead."[25] The natural object of man's will is God himself, its creator and original. But, being free, man's will may turn from God, as the will of Adam did in his fall; and, when it does so, man's will becomes disfigured. Still free even in perversity, man continues to bear God's image, but that image is no longer like its original. Man becomes, as it were, a parody of himself, alienated from God and from his own proper form. In the most general sense, the place of his alienation is the earth, to which all men were exiled in Adam's fall. And the moral imperative to which all men on earth are born is to grow in charity, to realign their wills with God's, so as to regain their lost likeness. But every man is free by his very nature— Saint Bernard's terms and emphases are different but his thought runs parallel with Saint Thomas'—to intensify his exile, to further disfigure himself, by pursuing worldly delights, as Filius Regis pursues them through the valley of curiosity and the groves of luxury, by the pools of carnal pleasure and the rivers of worldly care, into the far reaches of the land of unlikeness.

That is the figural country into which the Pilgrim's Youth leads him when he comes to the age of discretion. It is beyond the domain of Reason, who has warned the Pilgrim that she will not remain where the Seven Deadly Sins are established, and thus it is a country where man is no longer himself. So, in describing the Sins, Lydgate shows us how they distort the human form along the lines of the perverse inclinations they embody. Avarice has six arms, the better to snatch and grasp. Wrath bristles all over with nails, like a hedgehog. Gluttony, "olde...hydows and owgly off hyr look," has two bellies. She tries to strangle the Pilgrim, and he escapes from her only to be seized by Venus, who is not the beautiful goddess of classical mythology but an ugly old hag. None of the Sins appear as delightful temptations to which the Pilgrim might succumb; they are all rendered under their ultimate moral aspects, *sub specie aeternitatis,* as monsters that seek to destroy him. Venus rides on a "swyn savage," her clothes "defouled with donge and clay." And when she seizes the Pilgrim, she ties him to the back of her pig and whips him until she is distracted by another, wealthier, traveler.

Venus also appears in *Reason and Sensuality,* but here she is treated very differently because *Reason and Sensuality* is a less ascetic poem than the *Pilgrimage,* concerned more immediately with the quality of man's life than with the ultimate fate of his soul. Indeed, the whole sequence in which life's pilgrim comes to the age of discretion, *egens et insipiens,* and passes into the land of unlikeness is treated differently; for where the point of view of the *Pilgrimage* is fixed in eternity, the point of view of *Reason and Sensuality* is nominally set close to the point of view of its central character. In the *Pilgrimage,* Lydgate is careful always to present the Pilgrim's experiences as encapsulated within their ultimate moral categories, so that we always understand the significance of what is happening to him even though we may not understand how it came to happen. But in *Reason and Sensuality,* following the anonymous author of *Les Echecs Amoreux,* Lydgate acknowledges that in the midst of experience the surfaces of things are often opaque and beguiling and that only rarely can we see through them to the larger moral structures from which they take their meanings. *Reason and Sensuality* is thus most often descriptively rather than analytically psychological, making us aware of the real and blinding delights of *amoure courtoise,* however dangerous they may be *sub specie aeternitatis.* So its Venus is astonishingly beautiful.

Soon after the Young Man sets off on the journey of his life along the way of reason, he is "dislogggyd" from his way (976). Nothing in particular happens to deflect him. It is merely what the preachers call "curiosity." He is beguiled by the sensuous pleasures of a broad meadow dotted with pools and streams, so beguiled, indeed, that "al my lyf which passyd was, / Was clene out of my remembraunce" (970–71). In the meadow he comes upon Mercury, Venus, Juno, and Pallas and is offered the opportunity of making for himself the judgment of Paris. Someone has supplied a Latin gloss (Ernst Sieper thinks it was either Lydgate himself or someone who knew intimately the conditions of his poem)[26] to explain that the episode signifies that the Young Man has come in his journey to the age of discretion:

Per istam fallacium trium deorum clare significatur quod
Iuvenis cum venerit ad annos discrecionis sibi potest
proponi triplex modus vivendi, vel triplex vita, scilicet
contemplativa, activa et voluptuosa, de quibus potest
eligere illam que sibi magis placuerit sua libera
voluntate etc.

[opposite line 2071]

He chooses Venus, of course, over Pallas (the contemplative life) and
Juno (the active life), and Venus offers him the most beautiful woman
in the world, "yif thou thy purpose nat remewe / My tracys fethfully
to sewe" (2205–6). But the Young Man hesitates for a moment,
remembering Nature's warning that he must follow the path of reason
if he is to be faithful to his nature as a man. Like Filius Regis, *egens et
insipiens,* or the Pilgrim at the crossroads, pulled between his
instincts and his Youth, the Young Man hangs "as yet in ballaunce,"
reason and sensuality in equipoise. The balance is tipped when Venus
claims to be Nature's junior partner, "necessarie to hir honde," and so
gives the Young Man a strategy to rationalize yielding to sensuality.
And when he promises to be ruled by her, Venus sends him off to the
Garden of Pleasure, where Idleness keeps the gate and Cupid and
Deduit jointly rule.

The Garden and its surroundings are nothing like the broad plain
of the world in the *Pilgrimage.* With the point of view of the poem
aligned with the point of view of the Young Man, it is all made to
seem fresh and delightful. It is "lyke," he says, "the Romaunce of the
Rose." Indeed, much of the description of the Garden is taken from
Guillaume de Lorris' opening section of the *Roman:* the paintings on
the wall around the Garden, which depict the qualities that bar men
from pleasure; the small wicket through which one enters; the idyllic
natural scene, with birds singing angelic harmonies; the Well of
Narcissus, with its crystal bottom in which one can see into all the
corners of the Garden. Guillaume de Lorris himself is there, along
with all the personifications of sensuous pleasure he had found, and
the Young Man is as delighted with his first impression of the Garden
as Guillaume had been. But before he reaches the Garden, while he is
still approaching it through the Forest of Chastity, Lydgate has
Diana anatomize and explicate its pleasures in such a way that the
reader can recognize, though the Young Man does not, that the
Garden is located in the figural country of the land of unlikeness.

The pleasures of sensuality are all double-faced, Diana warns the
Young Man. They are "debonayre unto the syght, / Lusty, fresh, and

amerouse, / But in werkyng venymmouse" (4058–60). Serpents lurk under the flowers of the Garden; its trees are hollow and conceal dragons. The beautiful music in the Garden is really made by Sirens, "monstres of a treble kynde, / Ffyssh and foule, but hede and face / Meke as a mayde ful of grace, / But venym in the tayl behynde" (3648–51). And while the waters in its wells may seem "most fresh and colde / Upon the tonge..., / Wonder lusty of tarage, / That never... noon to forn / No welle unto thy plesaunce / Havyng so moche suffisaunce / Outwarde as in apparence" (3810–17), rather than slake thirst they increase it. Everything in the Garden is turned from its proper end and form, she says, although all may seem natural on the surface. The drinks that Venus serves to men there are like the drinks that Circe served to Ulysses' crew, by virtue of which they

> Ytourned weren to lyknesse
> Of bestys and, makid bestial,
> Lost hir reson natural.
> Thynke wel thereon, this was the fyn,
> Somme were asses, somme swyn,
> To foxes fals and engynous,
> And to wolves ravynouse,
> And yet wel wors peraventure.
> [3424–31]

The Garden of Pleasure is thus the place that Nature had warned the Young Man against at the beginning of his pilgrimage, the place where men are "depryved of hir name." But he is so caught up in sensual folly that the promptings of Nature have gotten turned around in his mind, and he selects from them only those that serve his pleasures at the moment. He blithely tells Diana that Nature herself sent him to Venus' Garden, for "she bad me, as I kan report: / 'Go se the world' and me disport, / And theryn oonly me delyte: / Goon aboute and vysite / Places which that be Iocounde" (4511–15). Indeed, he goes on to say, turning Nature's teleological scheme upside down, that visiting the Garden of Sensual Pleasure "semeth a maner destane, / The which, in sooth, no man may fle" (4759–60).

The Young Man's blithe inversion of Nature's scheme suggests the second stage in Saint Bernard's spiritual ages of man: "Primo enim est egens et insipiens; postea, praeceps et temerarius in prosperis." When things seem to be going well, man is rash and thoughtless, brushing aside the restraints of reason in favor of the immediate goals of his will. So the Young Man tells Diana that she may have her opinions of the Garden but that he is resolved to trust his own. Beneath all its delights, the Garden may be "ful of blak derknesse,/ Of sorwe, and of wrechidnesse,/ Yet fynaly, how every yt be,/ I shall assayen and go see" (4751–54).

While the broader moral perspective Diana provides is explicitly dropped when the Young Man leaves the Forest of Chastity and enters the Garden, it is implicitly retained in the ironies that play around his idealizing descriptions of everything that he sees there, so that we are steadily kept aware of his naïveté and of the fragility of the pleasures that seem to him firm and stable. For example, Dame Beauty, who seems to be the woman Venus promised to him, challenges the Young Man to a game of chess. She chooses "such as hir lyst" of the chess pieces, which he thinks "she sholde of duete" (6005–6), leaving him the rest. Among her pawns are Youth, Beauty, Simplicity, Bounty—all the qualities suitable to young lovers—and the Young Man describes each and explains with wide and guileless eyes how each is related to the virtues of women. Youth carries a crescent moon, symbolizing that youth "varieth ofte of corage" (6166), but women, he says at great length, "chaunge never...they be so perfyt and enter / And stable in her sykernesse" (6174–93). The pawn Simplicity reminds him that women suffer all with silent humility, and he assures his readers that "ther ys no man that wyl sey nay / That hem hath preved at assay" (6271–72). At the end of his description of the pawn "Port and Manere" he urges readers who would keep a secret to "tel yt a woman boldely, / And thow maist truste feythfully / Thow shalt never here yt more" (6365–67). All of the commonplaces in medieval satires of women are blandly, though pointedly, recalled and blithely dismissed. Women are said to be deaf to flattery, indifferent to money; they care nothing for fancy clothes, and they never envy others who are better dressed. They are unfailingly obedient, and to prove it the Young Man appeals to "her husbondys / That knowe best experience / Of her mekeness and pacience" (6584–86). Lydgate's translation breaks off here in the middle of these descriptions, with the Young Man about to play their game, but it seems clear that he is too illusioned to win it and that he will inevitably be disillusioned.

The stage of thoughtless prosperity is muted in Lydgate's *Pilgrimage*. What it emphasizes instead is the third of Saint Bernard's spiritual ages of man, the state of fear and trembling in adversity *(trepidus et pusillanimus in adversis)*. Because the poem looks at the Pilgrim's wandering in the land of unlikeness from the point of view of eternity, what it sees is not the transient illusions of one who does not really believe that he is in danger but rather the fearful bewilderment of one who feels himself lost in a nightmare. That life in the secular world has the quality of a bad dream is due, I suspect, to the brief the poem's author, Guillaume de Deguileville, *moine de Chaalis,* holds for the cloistered life. Carried away from reason by his Youth, the Pilgrim stumbles through a round of error, never wholly committed to the sins that snatch at him, and not their suitor, but steadily feeling himself alienated from grace and "disconsolat off al vertu, / Only for lack of Grace Dieu, / That was whylom to me friendly, / Whom I ha lost through my folly" (19679–82). He no longer has any sense of how to get to the New Jerusalem. To escape the nets that Satan has spread over the plain to trap unwary pilgrims, he plunges into the Sea of the World. He is briefly caught up on Fortune's wheel and dropped back. He takes refuge on an island but finds there only the monstrous superstitions of Astrology and Geomancy. Conspiracyoun comes from the Sea with her hounds to attack him, and when he escapes from her he is beaten by Worldly Gladness. At length, driven to take refuge on a rock in the middle of the Sea, lost and frightened, and, like Filius Regis, "trepidus et pusillanimus in adversis," the Pilgrim prays to God to "brynge me throgh thy grete myght / Into the way I may go ryght" (21699–700). And immediately on this cry for help, Grace Dieu appears in the Ship of Religion to rescue the Pilgrim from the far country of his exile and carry him off to the "Castle" of the Cistercians, the monastic order to which both Deguileville and Saint Bernard belonged.

Once in the Castle, the Pilgrim carries on his spiritual journey in more direct and literal terms. This section of the poem is a good deal like the ending of *Parabola I,* where Filius Regis, recovered from *regio dissimilitudinis,* is installed in the Castle of Sapience. There he completes the last of Saint Bernard's spiritual ages: he becomes "providus, et eruditus, et perfectus in regno caritatis." So, too, Lydgate's Pilgrim is prepared by the monastic disciplines of the Cistercians to grow in charity. Obedience binds him in her cords; he is inspired by Hagiography, instructed by Lady Lesson, and given a vision of paradise by Orison. His spiritual education is interrupted when the Castle is besieged by the enemies of man. The point of this repeated motif[27] (we will see it again in the *Castle of Perseverance* and find it dimly echoed in *King Lear*) would seem to be that even those who have committed themselves wholly to the religious life need always to be vigilant against the spiritual assaults of the world. But when Age and Sickness come to the Pilgrim, and Misericord leads him to the "fermerye," Grace Dieu assures him that he has reached his goal: "Thow art come to the wyket," she tells him, "(Which is gynnyng of thy labour), / Thow beheld in a myrrour / Whan thow wert ful tendre of age, / At gynnyng of thy pylgrymage" (24800–804). Then Death swings his scythe.

Once allowance is made for its secular emphases, the French romance *Les Echecs Amoreux,* Lydgate's source for *Reason and Sensuality,* ends in a quite similar way. The Young Man whose pilgrimage to maturity the poem imitates is not perfected in the domain of charity, of course, but he is perfected in his knowledge of how to live his earthly life in accordance with his nature. After he loses the chess game of love to Dame Beauty, the Young Man is urged by Amor to challenge her to another match. But Pallas Athene breaks in on his erotic fancies like a secular grace, surprising the Young Man, who has forgotten that time passes and brings reason with it. Pallas provides him with traditional remedies against erotic love, taken from Ovid, and instructs him at great length and in practical detail in how to live the contemplative and active lives according to reason. In this poem, in spite of his active will, the Young Man is recovered from the land of unlikeness by the natural rhythm of life itself.

These three poems—*Parabola I, The Pilgrimage of the Life of Man,* and *Reason and Sensuality*—exemplify what I want to call the action of life's pilgrimage. For all their differences in point of view, in fable, and in the scope of their themes, they share a common sense of the significant form of Christian life. At the beginning the Pilgrim, Filius Regis, the Young Man—mankind in general, since these are typifying characters—is incomplete: made in God's image, he has fallen generically away from God and so from himself. He needs to grow spiritually, to perfect himself in charity and in reason, so as to perfect his identity as a man and to reclaim his lost heritage. He knows by inclination what he ought to do; that knowledge is bred in his bones. But he does not do it. *Egens et insipiens* because his spirit was fractured in the Fall, he settles for immediate sensuous pleasures, further disfiguring himself in the metaphorical land of unlikeness, where his very identity as a man is imperiled. There for a time he may be *praeceps et temerarius in prosperis;* but because sensuous pleasure does not finally correspond to his nature, which is derived from his rational soul, it palls, and he becomes *trepidus et pusillanimus in adversis.* And finally, through Grace, God's grace and the grace of nature that brings wisdom through suffering and maturity, he is restored to himself, *providus, et eruditis, et perfectus in regno caritatis,* or at least perfected in the order of virtue to which the poem has him aspire.

What I will be arguing, in the essays that follow, is that *The Castle of Perseverance, Wit and Science, Woodstock, Volpone,* and *King Lear* are all shaped with reference to that action. They are in my view representative plays, and before I turn to them I want to say something very briefly about why I have chosen to discuss them and not others.

The *Castle* and *King Lear* are really self-selecting because they mark the beginning and the end of dramatic imitations of the pilgrimage. The *Castle* is the earliest and most comprehensive morality play that we have in English. A case might be made that it is a prototype for many of the rest because it develops fully and at leisure the whole moral biography of Mankind, which later plays treat in more specialized and fragmented ways. So to characterize the moral myth of the *Castle* is to characterize in some measure the myth that underlies a substantial body of morality plays. As for *King Lear,* it is not chronologically the last play to be influenced by the morality tradition or even the last of Shakespeare's, but there is a sense in which *Lear* mounts so radical a challenge to the morality form, and through it a challenge to the notion that life can be understood as a pilgrimage, that one can never be entirely comfortable with either again. For Shakespeare developed the story that he found in the old play of *King Leir and His Three Daughters* in a dialectical fashion, fleshing out its implicit resemblances to the universal form of Mankind's pilgrimage so as to produce what O. J. Campbell would later call a "grandiose version of *Everyman*"[28] and, at the same time, setting over against that form the bristly and intractable elements in the experiences of the play's characters that no universal form could accommodate. The result is a play that calls into question a whole dramatic tradition, much as Shaw's parodies of nineteenth-century melodrama bring that form into question.

Between the *Castle* and *King Lear, Woodstock, Wit and Science,* and *Volpone* allow me to explore in detail something of the range of that tradition. *Woodstock,* which offers the special case of the pilgrim as king, allows us to examine the political implications of the pilgrimage metaphor, particularly the ways in which those implications are illuminated by the doctrine of the king's two bodies. *Wit and Science,* in contrast, is an elegant courtly comedy, seemingly fragile as a bubble but with the surprising tensile strength of a bubble, because Wit's erotic adventures in pursuit of Lady Science are steadily imagined as particular instances of the stages of the pilgrimage all men make toward their perfected identities. And in *Volpone* we have a mirror image of Redford's romance, a bleak satire of a world given over altogether to the false god of gold and so a parody of life's pilgrimage, whose end does not bring Volpone to regain the human form he had lost in the land of unlikeness but rather to assume forever the perverted image he had adopted there. Together these five plays allow me to follow, from stepping-stone to stepping-stone, the successively more complex engagements of the pilgrimage metaphor with the world of literal events.

O N E
The Pilgrim in the Castle

Stonde hereinne as stylle as ston;
Thanne schal no dedly synne the spylle.

[*The Castle of Perseverance,* 1697–98]

If, on the model of medieval cartographers of the heart, we were to make a map of the landscape of imaginative literature, the morality drama might be located on its outer perimeter, near the border of the moral essay and, more particularly, near its more ephemeral form, the sermon. That scheme is not intended to minimize the theatricality of morality plays or to pass lightly over the sheer playing demanded by every text, especially by the most solemn and apparently abstract among them. For of course morality plays are not abstract at all, nor are they merely verbal, as essays are and sermons may sometimes be. When such plays are set on stage, intellectual entities like Humanum Genus turn out to have blond hair or black, ruddy cheeks or pale, to have the solidity of living actors and all their vitality. Indeed, it was because they ignored the essential theatrical character of morality plays that earlier generations of readers found them dull, as is illustrated by E.K. Chambers' surprised acknowledgment that Poel's early production of *Everyman* was "quite unexpectedly impressive."[1] And we have only recently and fitfully begun to correct the imbalance between words and spectacle that occurred when the theater moved on to other dramatic forms and left the moralities to literary historians.[2]

On the contrary, to associate morality plays initially with sermons rather than with other forms of medieval drama or other forms of allegory has the advantage of highlighting the particular way in which they are theatrical. For morality plays and sermons respond to and are shaped by similar rhetorical situations, which neither biblical plays nor literary allegories share. Unlike literary allegories, morality plays and sermons are both modes of performance; consequently, both speak in complex languages, composed partly of words but partly, as well, of all the elements of inflection and gesture and costume and movement that make words more emphatic, qualify their meanings or contradict them, and in general transform words into elements in a larger vocabulary, peculiar to modes of performance. The vocabulary of a play may be richer and thus subtler, more complex, and capable of expressing a greater range of meaning than the vocabulary of a preacher; but it is not a different vocabulary from his, as it is different from the vocabulary of a literary text.

Other forms of medieval drama share this vocabulary, of course; but where they use it to imitate the actions of men, morality plays dramatize ideas. Like sermons, they do not seek to clarify literal incidents but rather to reveal moral probability itself, stripped of the accidents of individual experience that may obscure its outlines. They are shaped, as sermons are, to explicate and make persuasive a wide range of moral propositions, from the theological tenet that God is primarily merciful, upon which *The Castle of Perseverance* turns, to the brilliant theatrical exhortation to repentance that comes toward the end of *Enough Is as Good as a Feast,* when the Devil, standing over the dead body of Worldly Man, mockingly invites the audience to behave as Worldly Man behaved and so to come to the same end.

That is why the description of a morality play as an embodied sermon—not merely spoken but fully enacted—seems to me a useful critical proposition. By pursuing it, we can work through the particular homiletic address that *The Castle of Perseverance* makes to its audience to discover the underlying assumptions about the universal form of human experience that it imitates.

THE PREACHER IN THE CASTLE

The Castle of Perseverance is the richest of the sixty-odd morality plays that have survived. Some 3,700 lines long, it sets out the whole of the temporal and spiritual biography of Mankind,[3] from the state of fragile innocence, into which all men are born, to his eventual salvation by grace. The main body of the play seems to have been written around the end of the fourteenth century, perhaps in the area surrounding the cathedral city of Lincoln, although Mark Eccles has concluded that certain features of its language are more characteristic of Norfolk.[4] The play seems to have been designed, or perhaps later adapted, for touring, because the manuscript in which the text has survived includes directions for setting up the stage under different circumstances, and also because it includes some 150 lines of banns advertising a later performance of the play, with a space left blank so that the names of different towns might be inserted. It is the banns that suggest that the play may have been adapted for touring and not originally written for a touring company, because there is some reason to believe that they may have been written after the main body of the text. There is also some reason to believe that the debate among the Four Daughters of God about the disposition of Mankind's soul after his death may have been a later addition.[5]

The moral problem around which *The Castle of Perseverance* is organized is the problem of preserving mankind's connatural inclination toward virtue in a world hostile to it. Like Lydgate's Pilgrim or the Young Man in *Reason and Sensuality,* Mankind is born yearning for salvation: "Lord Jhesu, to you I bydde a bone," he prays in his very first speech, "That I may folwe... / the angel that cam fro hevene trone" (314–15). It is appropriate, then, that the key biblical text explicated by the play should be the promise given by the Gospel of Matthew that "qui perseveraverit usque in finem, hic saluus erit"(the one who endures until the end shall be saved). Those words are spoken by Meekness, the last of the Moral Virtues to welcome Mankind to refuge in the Castle of Perseverance after he has been recovered from the Seven Deadly Sins. They set a capstone on the moral instruction he has been given during the preceding 300 lines. And they are themselves underlined with theatrical ceremony as the Virtues lead Mankind into the Castle in formal procession, singing "eterne rex altissime." But as the play develops from that point, it is shaped so as to acknowledge the difficulty of perseverance in this world and to illuminate the surprising resources Mankind has through grace to practice it. Thus, as soon as Mankind has been installed in the Castle, his resolution is assailed by the forces of the World, the Flesh, and the Devil.

The besieged castle is a fertile image in medieval allegory. Owst derives it from meditations on the word *castellum* as it is used in the Vulgate, and he traces a great number of significations of the image, from the "castle" of the Virgin Mary in Bishop Grostête's *Chasteau d'Amour,* through the "castles" of the various monastic orders, such as those that appear in Lydgate's *Pilgrimage,* to the devil's "castles" that represent the temporal power of evil.[6] In *The Castle of Perseverance* the castle under siege clearly refers to the state of perseverance, in which Mankind is kept by his virtues from the assaults of the devil, the temptations of the world, and the sensuous urges of his own body.

The battle between these Virtues and the Vices that lay siege to the Castle can also be traced back, by way of the elaborately articulated

heroic combat between vice and virtue in Prudentius' *Psychomachia,*
to biblical sources.[7] But the conflict between vice and virtue is treated
in the *Castle* in a peculiar way, because the two sides are made to fight
on quite different imaginative planes. In the Prudentian tradition,
military conflict is a metaphor for the *bellum intestinum,* and both
vices and virtues are imagined to be warriors, armed and helmeted,
fighting on the metaphorical ground of man's soul for the right to
dominate it. It is clear that the Vices in *The Castle of Perseverance* are
also imagined to be warriors in military combat. Flesh directs his
forces on horseback, and he at least thinks that he cuts an imposing
figure:

> Whanne I syt in my sadyl it is a selkowth syt;
> I gape as a gogmagog whanne I gynne to gase.
> This worthy wylde werld I wagge with a wyt;
> Yone rappokys I ruble and al to-rase;
> Bothe wyth schot and wyth slyng I caste wyth a
>   sleyt
> Wyth care to yone castel to cracken and to crase
>   In flode.
>
> [1940–46]

Gluttony carries a burning faggot into the battle, Wrath a sling and a
crossbow. Envy also carries a bow. And Sloth, the engineer, has a
shovel with which to drain the moat around the castle. All of them,
with the exception of Lechery, who is armed with burning coals, are
men. The moral virtues, on the other hand, are all women, and they
seem neither to wear armor, as they often do in medieval art,[8] nor to
be themselves armed—except for the roses and banners they carry,
which turn out to be surprisingly powerful. When Pride challenges
Meekness, he threatens her in physical terms; but Meekness responds
merely by pointing to the model of Christ's humility:

> Whanne he cam fro the Trynyte
> Into a maydyn lytyd he,
> And al was for to dystroye the,
> Pride, this schalt thou knowe.
> . . . .
> Therefore thou schalt not comen us ny,
> And thou be nevere so sly,
> I schal felle al thi fare.
>
> [2091–2107]

Her defense against Pride's material weapons is simply the spiritual
proposition that, because Christ humbled himself to destroy pride,

Pride has no power over the man who trusts in Christ. And the other Virtues respond similarly to threats of stones, arrows, burning faggots, and hot coals by citing Christ's patience before his tormentors, his charity in dying for Mankind, his abstinence in the desert, and his chastity. Thus, while the Vices are endowed with forms of physical power and fight on thoroughly material, metaphorical grounds, the Virtues' defense of Mankind is of a different imaginative order, scarcely metaphorical at all. It is simply the expression of the Christian moral doctrines that will keep Mankind free from vice if he will embrace them. To be sure, the divine love that guarantees Mankind's safety is given symbolic form in the roses with which the Virtues pelt the Vices and drive them from the Castle, but that symbol speaks to and preserves, as it were, the mystery of the faith—the paradox of the irresistible power of love—while the slings and arrows of the Vices speak to the expectations of ordinary experience. What *The Castle of Perseverance* presents in the most vivid and theatrical of its sequences, then, is not the usual form of the *bellum intestinum*. It is rather a carefully worked-out illusion of a battle directed at an important spiritual problem in perseverance, the problem of hope.

To understand why that should be so, we must remember that moral virtues like humility and generosity and the moral habit of perseverance are simply capacities of what Aquinas has called the theological virtues: faith, hope, and charity. These three, the belief in God, the hope for future happiness with him, and the love of God, are called theological virtues because they incline man toward God, and they are sometimes called supernatural virtues because they cannot be acquired by man's own efforts but must be infused in him by God. In that respect they are the spiritual forms of grace, and, as such, they are the necessary spiritual preconditions for the exercise of any perfected moral virtue. Indeed, the theological virtues are the souls, as it were, of all other virtues, the spiritual states that inform and are made visible by moral acts. That is a point Saint Paul makes in the first of his letters to the Corinthians when, emphasizing the pre-eminence of charity among the gifts of the spirit, he describes the forms of behavior through which it appears: "Charity suffereth long and is kind; charity envieth not; charity vaunteth not itself, is not puffed up, doth not behave itself unseemly, seeketh not her own, is not easily provoked, thinketh no evil; rejoiceth not in iniquity, but rejoiceth in the truth; beareth all things, believeth all things, hopeth all things, endureth all things" (1 Cor. 13:4–7).[9] As they appear in the acts of men, the visible forms of charity are the moral virtues of patience, generosity, humility, circumspection, and so forth. We may misunderstand the picture of the moral life given in the *Castle,* then, and thus misunderstand the logic of the play's rhetoric, if we concentrate exclusively on the moral virtues themselves and so fail to remember that their exercise depends on the exercise of the theological virtues.

Ultimately, faith, hope, and charity are interrelated and interdependent parts of a single spiritual state. So, while Aquinas allows that in a certain limited sense faith and hope can exist without charity, he insists finally that without charity they "are not virtues properly speaking." And he goes on to explain that on its own part charity cannot exist without faith and hope because

> Charity signifies not only the love of God, but also a
> certain friendship with him; which implies, besides love, a
> certain mutual return of love.... Consequently, just as
> friendship with a person would not be possible were one
> to disbelieve in or despair of the possibility of any
> fellowship or intercourse with him, so too, friendship with
> God, which is charity, is impossible without faith, so as to
> believe in this companionship and life with God, or
> without hope of entering it.[10]

At the same time, however, while faith, hope, and charity are interrelated and interdependent, they are also, as individual theological virtues, associated with particular human capacities. Charity, of course, is the "mother and root of all virtue"; but faith is especially important as the ground of the intellectual virtues, which lead toward knowledge of God and belief in him, and hope is especially important as the ground of the moral virtues.[11]

The moral habit of perseverance, then, depends in a particular way upon the theological virtue of hope. In order to persevere until the end, Mankind must have hope for salvation—not a vague wish but a positive and joyful anticipation, a sense of confidence that the temporal pains of perseverance will produce an eternal reward.[12] Thus a play that aims at encouraging perseverance must attend as well to the problem of fostering hope and disarming its spiritual opposites, presumption and despair.

Despair is usually thought of as an exaggerated sense of one's own sinfulness that makes salvation seem impossible, but the term applies more broadly to the loss of hope for salvation for whatever reason, and more subtly and dramatically to the attenuation of hope by a feeling that the whole question of salvation is so remote that we may safely put it aside until later in our lives. And it is in that form that we first encounter the problem of hope in the play. The crucial argument that brings Mankind to set aside his connatural inclinations and devote himself to worldly pleasure is his Bad Angel's assurance that "wyth the Werld thou mayst be bold / Tyl thou be sexty wyntyr hold. / Wanne thi nose waxit cold / Thanne mayst thou drawe to goode" (416–19).

Almost everything about the play in its early stages conspires to encourage that sort of despair, for when Mankind first appears in the play he enters a playing area almost altogether possessed by the World, the Flesh, and the Devil. Its perimeters are defined by their scaffolds, the World to the west, the Flesh to the south, the Devil to the north. God's scaffold marks out the eastern boundary of the playing area; but, apart from whatever an audience might make of the symbology of its placement or its decorations, it is a theatically passive boundary. No one seems to appear on the scaffold itself, and nothing happens in relation to it until very much later in the play. And, if it has a curtain, it seems most likely that it is closed.[13] Questions of salvation, then, are literally remote on the stage on which Mankind is set to act. In contrast, the scaffolds of man's enemies are filled with noise and movement. Each of Mankind's enemies has a vaunting speech that gives him a chance to pomp, to establish his weight and mark out the reach of his power, so that, when Mankind enters, tottering into the middle of the place, he is literally surrounded by those who would draw him to hell. Where they are powerful and malevolent, elevated above him in the design of the stage, he is merely a child, just "born this nyth in blody ble," scarcely able to walk, and naked except for a "sely crysme myn hed hath cawth / That I tok at myn crystenynge" (294–95). That chrisom is important to the moral scheme of the play because it is the visible evidence that Mankind has received the sanctifying grace of baptism and thus has available to him the spiritual virtues of faith, hope, and charity. In that respect his chrisom is the visible corollary of his prayer that he may "folwe...the angyl that cam fro hevene trone." But the fact that he has only a chrisom and is otherwise naked is equally important to the theatrical scheme of the play, which seems calculated at this point to acknowledge all of the grounds on which Mankind might despair.

In keeping with the design of the stage, Mankind's Bad Angel is permitted to tempt him in specific and concrete terms. The pleasures of the senses are made theatrically real on the stage during the early part of the *Castle,* while the rewards of the spirit are made to seem merely hypothetical. When his Bad Angel promises Mankind a "fayre lady... / That in thi bowre thi bale schal bete" (366–67), we see her on the Flesh's scaffold in the person of Lady Lechery. We see that Flesh himself wears the "sylke sendel to syttyn in sete" that man's Bad Angel promises him he will wear if only he will come join the World. Flesh's "brod brustun gutte" testifies that the World's friends "fare wel at mete and mele." And Mankind has only to cross to the scaffold of the World, as we see in a moment, to be furnished with "riche rentys." All of the pleasures the Bad Angel dangles before Mankind can be instantly grasped and tasted. But what the Good Angel urges is literally remote. There is nothing he can tell Mankind to do except to "thynke on thyn endynge day / Whanne thou schalt be closyd undyr clay, / And if thou thenke of that aray, / Certys thou schalt not synne" (407–10). While Mankind desires connaturally to follow his Good Angel, then, the play itself, at least in its early stages, seems unwilling to tell him how to do it. Its image of virtuous action is, at its most concrete, an implicit acknowledgment that the pleasures of vice are closer and more vivid. And, appropriately enough, that image is secured only by the blank façade of the Deus scaffold. So, when Mankind goes off to serve the World, he follows a logic that seems to be invited by the play itself.

The question is why the play should invite that sort of logic, why it should construct Mankind's moral situation so as to embody a distinctly worldly view of it. The question might not arise if the *Castle* were a literal play, set in the material world. But it is not. It is a play of ideas, not bound to reflect a given point of view but, by definition, obliged to choose its own; and so it is a play whose construction of Mankind's moral situation is rhetorically significant. And that of course is the point. The perspective adopted by the play—material, vitiated by that form of despair that finds salvation a dim notion compared to the present pleasures of the world and the flesh—is precisely the perspective a homily of perseverance might seek to engage. To deny that this is how men in the audience might see their own moral situation would be rhetorically naïve, and the author of the *Castle,* whatever one may think of his moral theology, is never that. Instead, he invites despair out into the open, allows it to flourish within the boundaries of the play—not merely tacitly, in his construction of events, but also explicitly, in Mankind's changing opinions about values and proportions—in order to engage it

dramatically and disarm it. In that respect the dramatic rhetoric of
the *Castle* is like the rhetoric of certain visitation plays that, seeking
to disarm skepticism about the miracle of the Resurrection, allow it
free expression within the framework of the play.[14]

When Mankind follows his Bad Angel off to sample the World's
pleasures, the playwright contrives to make it clear that he has a
special rhetorical relationship with his audience, that they are
implicated in his point of view and that he in some sense speaks for
them. As the two actors cross the playing area toward the World's
scaffold, the World sends his messengers, Lust-liking and Folly, off
to stir up new followers for him. The stage direction calls for them to
"descend together," presumably from the World's scaffold onto the
playing area across which Mankind and his Bad Angel are now
making their way. And the form of Lust-liking's speech suggests that
the messengers make their appeal directly to the audience gathered at
the edges of the playing area:

> Pes, pepyl, of pes we you pray.
> Syth and sethe wel to my sawe.
> Whoso wyl be ryche and in gret aray
> Toward the Werld he schal drawe.
> Whoso wyl be fals al that he may,
> Of God hymself he hath non awe,
> And lyvyn in lustys nyth and day
> The Werld of hym wyl be ryth fawe,
> Do dwelle in his howse.
>
> [492–500]

When Mankind's Bad Angel leads him to Lust-liking, then, he is
made to come to him out of the audience itself (literally, if Southern's
model of the stage is accurate),[15] responding directly to Lust-liking's
appeal to them:

> Mary, felaw, gramercy!
> I wolde be ryche and of gret renoun.
> I yeve no tale trewly
> So that I be lord of toure and toun,
> Be buskys and bankys broun.
> Syn that thou wylt make me
> Both ryche of gold and fee,
> Goo forthe, for I wyl folowe the
> By dale and every towne.
>
> [566–74]

In this way the playwright dramatizes Mankind's role as the rhetorical surrogate for the audience. And at key moments thereafter, as Mankind abandons hope for salvation and embraces the Seven Deadly Sins, he is made to remind his audience that they are not mere onlookers at a show but are all implicated with him in the form of despair that values sensuous pleasures over the rewards of the spirit. So at the end of the sequence in which he is introduced to the Seven Deadly Sins, when Mankind sums up the course of his life—"In sowre swettnesse my syth I sende / Wyth sevene synnys sadde beset"—he switches suddenly from singular to plural pronouns so as to embrace the audience: "In dale of dole tyl we are downe, / We schal be clad in gay gowne." And then he turns to implicate them directly, evidently running his eyes over the audience as he speaks:

> I se no man but they use somme
> Of these seven dedly synnys.
> For commounly it is seldom seyne,
> Whoso now be lecherows
> Of other men he schal have dysdeyne
> And ben prowde or covetous.
> In synne iche man is founde.
> There is pore nor ryche, by londe ne lake,
> That alle these sevene wyl forsake,
> But wyth on or other he schal be take
> And in here bitter bondys bownde.
>   [1247–59]

A few moments later, prompted by Sloth to evade Shrift, he returns to his theme. "We have etyn garlek everychone. / Thou I schulde to helle go, / I wot wel I schal not gon alone" (1369–71).

Thus, as the play approaches the spectacular and noisy battle between the Vices and Virtues (I pass over the scene of Mankind's repentance because that needs to be discussed in another connection), it draws out and substantiates the spiritual state of moral irresolution, of wavering hopelessness, that a homily of perseverance might seek to engage—not merely in its development of Mankind's perception of his own moral situation but, more important, in its shaping the audience's perception of it. For the play has constructed the task of persevering as it might appear to someone in need of such a homily, acknowledging in both language and setting the apparent remoteness of God and his heaven and the correspondingly greater vividness and evidently greater power of vice.

The form of its action is in that respect similar to the form of a typical sermon on perseverance composed about the same time that the *Castle* was written. "Thou hast nede to rise now for-sothe," said the preacher, reminding his congregation of the persistent hostility of vice to virtue that the play dramatizes in the siege of the Castle, "for the iii stronge enmyes that have throwe the downe in synne, nyght and day thei strenght them to brynge the everlanger the lowere un-to the pitt of hell—that is thi flesche, the world, and the feend." And the play's denial of the expectations it has engendered in the serene power that the Virtues derive from the example of Christ provides just the sort of consolation the preacher seeks to provide:

> Awake from synne *and* rise owte of thi fowle lustis and loke abowt *and* be-hold thi mirrour in the Cros, *and* thou may see hym—is bake scourged, the hede sett with white thornes crowned, the side perched with a speyre, hondes *and* feete with nayles pershed and non hool parti in all is bodie but is tongue, with the which he preyed for synnefull men, that all men that beleved in hym shuld not perish but have ever lastynge liff. And therefore Crist seid thus on the Crosse, "O vos omnes qui transitis per viam, attendite et videte si est dolor, sicut dolor meus—all ye," he seith, "that goon by the wey of this world, abide ye in hope of mercy...." And therefore cri to hym that stedfastly woke for thi xl dais and xl nythes, and spred is harmes on the Cros to call the to hym. He is as plenteous of mercy as thou arte to aske itt.[16]

So Mankind, "ner mad" with fear as the Vices approach the Castle of Perseverance, calls on that "dynge Duke that deyed on rode / [to] this day my sowle kepe and safe!" (1995–96). And the Virtues repel the Vices, both by recalling, as the preacher would have his congregation recall, the examples of Christ's virtue, and by pelting them with roses, symbolic of his passion. The roses are of course images of the divine act of grace that secured hope and that makes perseverance possible, and they are translated by the play into surprisingly literal and perceptible forms of power. I may "syngyn weleawo," Wrath moans as he runs from the Castle, his sling and crossbow no match for Charity, "I am al betyn blak and blo / Wyth a rose that on rode was rent." A moment later Sloth abandons his shovel and cries, "I swone, I swete, I feynt, I drulle. / Yene qwene wyth hyr pytr-patyr / Hath al to-dayschyd my skallyd skulle" (2397–99).

The whole sequence brilliantly translates homiletics into the rhetoric of the theater. Through the peculiar way in which the assault on the Castle is developed, the distortions of time and space that make the attractions of the world and the flesh seem more compelling, more psychologically powerful than the hope of salvation, are acknowledged and corrected, and the secure though invisible grounds of hope are clarified. It seems to me that *The Castle of Perseverance* is here clearly an embodied sermon, marshaling all the resources of the theater to lead its audience to see through temporal illusions to the real form of Mankind's moral situation and, presumably, their own. It is thus more affecting than an ordinary sermon because it clothes the merely verbal formulas of the preacher in the bodies of living actors, whose illusions and discoveries are lively paradigms of our own. And it is more richly meaningful because it puts its audience in possession of the experience of a moral action.

The contrast in tone and rhythm that follows the spectacular and noisy battle is in its own way as dramatically sophisticated as the *catastasis* of Jonson's *Alchemist,* when Subtle and Face relax after the wild scene in which they have gotten rid of Surly and Ananias and Kastril and Drugger only to have Dol warn them that Lovewit is at the door and that the real *catastrophe* is at hand. For as the vices of the Flesh and the Devil run from the Castle, holding their broken heads, leaving the place strewn with roses, the lone figure of Covetous crosses toward it. He has no armor or weapons; he does not challenge his opposite, Largety, as the other vices had. There is none of the panoply of battle, no bluster, no obvious threats. What we saw during the siege, when Humility interposed herself between Mankind and Pride, or Patience between Mankind and Wrath, was a series of moral tautologies: the humble man is not proud, the patient man is not wrathful. But following the military assault, in the flush of moral success and lacking a clear-cut definition of the occasion, Mankind's defenses are slack. And when Largety attempts to step between Covetous and Mankind, Covetous simply brushes her aside—presumably because Mankind is insecurely generous—and speaks directly to Man himself, caressingly, with all the appearance of sweet reason: "How, Mankynde! cum speke wyth me, / Cum ley thi love here in my les. / Coveytyse is a frend ryth fre, / Thi sorwe, man, to slake and ses" (2470–73). Mankind resists him briefly, summoning up his newly recovered hope so as to persevere. Age and penance have made him suffer, he says, but "these ladys of goodnesse / Wyl not lete me fare amys, / And thou I be a whyle in dystresse, / Whanne I deye I

schal to blysse" (2505–8). But Covetous, by playing, as Man's Bad
Angel had at the beginning of his life, on Man's spiritual shortsighted-
ness, manages to fix his attention on the present moment and present
comforts:

> Ya, up and don thou take the wey
> Thorwe this werld to walkyn and wende
> And thou schalt fynde, soth to sey,
> Thi purs schal be thi best frende.
> Thou thou syt al-day and prey,
> No man schal com to the nor sende,
> But if thou have a peny to pey,
> Men schul to the thanne lystyn and lende
> And kelyn al thi care.
>
> [2518–26]

It is there, in the quiet insistence of worldly consolations, that
Mankind's spiritual battle is finally lost: "Covetyse, thou seyst a good
skyl" (2531).[17] And Mankind leaves the Castle of Perseverance to join
him on the green.

As he does so, the World, who has presumably returned to his own
scaffold, calls out across the green, "A, a, this game goth as I wolde."
Mankind's Bad Angel exults; and on the battlements of the Castle
itself the Moral Virtues each speak a stanza of resignation, pointing
out that Man's fall from perseverance is due not to a moral weakness
common to all men but rather to a peculiar failure in his own will.
There has been a gradual shift in the moral perspective of the play
and, with it, a redefinition of Mankind's relationship with the
audience. The stage that had earlier appeared to substantiate the
illusions of despair has now, with the successful defense of the Castle,
clarified the secure grounds of hope. So where the play may be
understood earlier to allow that there is a certain logic in Man's first
fall, it insists now that his second is merely perverse: "Syn he cam this
castel to," Humility complains,

> We did to hym that us befelle
> And now he hath us refusyd.
> As longe as he was wythinne this castel walle,
> We kept hym fro synne, ye sawe wel alle;
> And now he wyl ayeyn to synne falle,
> I preye you holde us excusyd.
>
> [2563–69]

And she is echoed by all of her sisters. "Resun," Patience says in summary, "wyl excusyn us alle. / He helde the ex by the helve. / Thou he wyl to foly falle, / It is to wytyn but hymselve" (2570–73).

The sequence that follows is handled with almost brutal irony. Mankind has scarcely a hundred lines to heap up treasure before Drery Death enters to strike him with his dart, catching him in full-blown despair: "If I myth alwey dwellyn in prosperyte, / Lord God, thane wel were me. / I wolde, the medys, forsake the / And nevere to comyn in hevene" (2774–77). Man's death agonies are unmitigated. His cry to the World for help is met simply with a shrug and a promise that there will be further pain: "Werldys good thou hast foregon, / And with tottys thou schalt be torne" (2878–79). Instead of help, the World sends a "lythyr ladde with a torne hod" to claim Mankind's treasure. And as this lad pokes at his body, intending to dump him into a lake as soon as he is dead, Mankind rouses himself for his last lesson. "Thou art not of my kyn," he says in some surprise, "Thou dedyst me nevere no maner good. / I hadde lever sum nyfte, or sum cosyn, / Or sum man hadde it of my blod" (2943–46). At the very least he would learn the name of his heir: "Loke that thou it not forgete," the boy tells him, "My name is I Wot Nevere Whoo" (2967–68). And on that bleak note Mankind dies, crying for mercy with his last breath.

There seems at this point to have been a debate between Mankind's body and his soul, but there is a hiatus in the text and we have only the first and last speeches of it. When the text resumes, the Bad Angel takes possession of the Soul, driving it around the *platea* (the unlocalized acting area) toward Belial's scaffold and then off with what is surely one of the most unintentionally charming exit lines in all of drama: "Have good day! / I goo to helle" (3128).

SERMON'S END

With the exit of Mankind and his Bad Angel for hell we may have come to the end of the portion of the *Castle* that was composed by its original author. Jacob Bennett has argued, on the basis of linguistic and stylistic differences among the parts of the text, that the banns were added by a second author and that the debate among the Four Daughters of God about the disposition of Mankind's soul after his death was a still later addition. While Bennett's argument for multiple authorship has not proved altogether persuasive,[18] it is certainly true that the terms of the debate strike out obliquely from the earlier part of the play. Neither the peculiar emphasis on God's mercy developed

during the course of the debate nor the fact that at its conclusion
Mankind is saved from hell could have been predicted from the
action of the play as it has developed to this point. For while the play
has stressed God's grace, it has done so with constant attention to the
limits of moral action, whose boundaries are life itself. Organized
around a homily of perseverance, the play echoes the preacher I
quoted earlier, who warned his congregation, as the Moral Virtues
warn Mankind: "now is the tyme of mercy, while that thou lyvest
here; for more tyme than we gett whils that we liff here shall we never
have aftur that we are passed hens, but oure owne werkes shall folowe
us where-ever that we goye." So Abstinence promises that when
Mankind is "dyth in dedys dole, / The ryth regystre I schal hym
rede; / He schal be tore wyth teneful tole; / Whanne he schal brenne
on glemys glede / He schall lere a new lawe" (2600–2604). But the
issue of the debate among Mercy, Peace, Justice, and Truth is
theological rather than moral.[19] Nothing that Mankind does has any
influence on its outcome. The only dramatic point it develops is
narrow, circumstantial, and never resolved. That is the question of
whether Mankind was sufficiently contrite when he died to qualify
for God's mercy. "Systyr, ye sey to me a good skyl," Justice says in
reply to Mercy's plea that Mankind be saved, "that Mercy pasyt
mannys mysdede. / But take mercy whoso wyl / He muste it aske
wyth love and drede" (3151–54). The debate touches that dramatic
point only in passing, however, and most of it concerns a fact that the
play has consistently assumed, the fact that God's nature is fundamentally merciful.

It is a statement about the nature of God, not the state of
Mankind's soul, that finally resolves the debate, when God himself
announces, "Misericordia Domini plena est in terra" (3574). Thus he
judges in favor of Mercy when his Four Daughters appeal their cases
to him. But after Mankind has been reclaimed from hell and installed
at his right hand, God turns to make precisely the distinctions among
men that Truth and Justice have urged:

> And thei that wel do in this werld, here welthe schal awake;
> In hevene thei schal be heynyd in bounte and blys;
> And thei that evyl do, thei schul to helle lake
> In byttyr balys to be brent: my jugement it is.
>
> [3637–40]

According to those terms, the Mankind of *The Castle of Perseverance*
ought to have been damned to hell, since he failed in perseverance.

But in the enlarged perspective of the debate his case is elevated to a question of theology and removed from moral consideration entirely.

It is necessary, then, that we understand the character of Mankind in two different ways. The cautionary homily of perseverance requires that we take him to represent merely the species of men who do not persevere until the end and whose sufferings may be instructive for all men. Unless we understand him in that limited way within the body of the play, the thesis from the gospel of Matthew is morally empty, for there is no point in saying that those who persevere to the end will be saved if the play intends to show, through the actions of Mankind, that *all* men fail to persevere. That is a fact we may lament, but, on its own showing, it is something we can do nothing about. At the same time, as the object of a debate between the claims of divine justice and divine mercy, Mankind must be understood quite literally as the genus of mankind, and we must understand that the moral failings that distinguish different sorts of men are irrelevant to God's favor toward him.

We need to recognize, then, that behind the homiletics of *The Castle of Perseverance* there lies a broader, more universal model of the stages of man's moral life, one that can accommodate the genus of mankind as well as particular moral species of men, and one that leads naturally to his salvation. I want to suggest that that is the model of life's pilgrimage as we have seen it developed in Saint Bernard's first parable and in Lydgate's *Pilgrimage of the Life of Man.*

THE PILGRIM IN THE CASTLE

In speaking of the *Castle of Perseverance* as an imitation of the action of life's pilgrimage, I am assuming what I take to be Aristotle's meaning of the phrase "imitation of action" in the *Poetics.* That is, I am assuming that the imitation of an action is the rendering, in the peculiar language of a particular narrative medium, whether music, poetry, or drama, of a synthesizing principle that draws together discrete episodes into a significant order with a beginning, a middle, and an end. It is this perception of the meaningful relationships between events, I assume, which lies behind a plot, informing its order and emphasis, and to which a plot in turn gives sensuous form. Aristotle defines the quality of this perception in the most neutral terms, characterizing the best plots as those held together by necessity or probability. Clearly, however, events appear to be related in necessary or probable ways only in some sort of defining context; and in fortunate times they may come together in intelligible patterns that are determined not solely by reason or literal experience but by a cultural unity that reveals itself in rituals or myths.[20] It is this sort of mythic pattern one finds in the literature of the pilgrimage, where events are organized to reveal the archetypal shape of man's developing moral life in conformity with Christian doctrine.

One difficulty in talking about the action of the pilgrimage, however, is that the term pilgrimage itself is ambiguous. It may refer either to the defining perception of the nature of man's life as a journey toward eternity through time and the spirit, or it may refer to the extended form of the pilgrimage metaphor, the narrative motif in which that perception may be imitated. These two meanings often work together, and thus in such poems as Lydgate's *Pilgrimage* and *Reason and Sensuality* narrative journeys give objective and consistent form to the belief that man in this world is "but in exile and wilderness, out of his kyndely contre,"[21] and that the process of "man's whole life is a pilgrimage, either from God, as Cain's, or from himself, as Abel's." But the fictional journey of a pilgrim through a symbolic landscape is itself only an imitation of the action of man's moral pilgrimage in terms appropriate to narrative poetry, and, theoretically at least, we might have analogous imitations of the soul's journey in music or drama, which would take different forms, using different languages.

Indeed, the nature of drama, enacted on a stage, militates against sustained use of the pilgrimage metaphor, which is peculiarly a part of the language of literary narrative. But the playing area for which the *Castle* was written—that great circle, with mansions set around its perimeter and the Castle in the center—provides in its own way a theatrical equivalent of the moral landscapes found in the literary pilgrimages and allows for similar metaphors of action. As the play develops and their inhabitants are characterized, the mansions become significant moral places. And throughout the play they serve, like the Valley of Despair or the Castle of Alma, as physical indices of Mankind's moral state. The *platea* itself, the neutral ground between the mansions, is the place of moral change, where the first stirrings of the spirit, toward God or toward the World, are given physical form in movements toward the symbolic scaffolds.

At his entrance, Mankind begins almost at once to speak of the processes of his life in images of travel, and throughout the scene of his temptation the language of travel persists as a way of manifesting the moral process at issue.[22] He alludes first in a telescoping metaphor to the temporal journey that has brought him to the moment of discretion, when he must choose his way:

> This nyth I was of my modyr born,
> Fro my modyr I walke, I wende,
> Ful feynt and febyl I fare you biforn.
>
> . . . .
>
> I not wedyr to gon ne to lende,
> To help myself myday nyn morn.
>
> [276–82]

Then he turns to define his moral situation. Like Lydgate's Pilgrim or the Young Man of *Reason and Sensuality,* he yearns connaturally for "heven trone," and there is real urgency in his prayer that he may follow his Good Angel: "Now Lord Jesu in hevene halle, / Here whane I make my mone. / Coryows Criste, to you I calle. / As a grysly gost I gruche and grone" (318–21). But the immediate delights offered by the Bad Angel intrigue him, and he quickly finds himself at a moral crossroads:

> Whom to folwe wetyn I ne may!
> I stond and stodye and gynne to rave.
> I wolde be ryche in gret aray,
> And fayn I wolde my sowle save.
> As wynde in watyr I wave.
> Thou woldyst to the Werld I me toke;
> And he wolde that I it forsoke.
>
> [375–81]

The issue is literally travel, in both the physical and moral senses. "Cum on, man," the Bad Angel cries, "Whereof hast thou care? / Go we to the Werld, I rede the, blyve" (384–85). And as Mankind turns to follow him, the Good Angel calls, "A, nay, man, for Cristys blod. / Cum agayn, be strete and style" (402–3). But just as Lydgate's Pilgrim is carried away from the path of Labour by his Youth, so Mankind is led off by the Bad Angel's temporizing argument that he is too young to be good:

> Ya, on thi sowle thou schalt thynke al betyme.
> Cum forth, man, and take non hede.
> Cum on, and thou schalt holdyn hym inne.
> Thi flesch thou schalt foster and fede
> Wyth lofly lyuys fode.

Wyth the Werld thou mayst be bold
Tyl thou be sexty wyntyr hold
Wanne thi nose waxit cold
Thanne mayst thou drawe to goode.

[411–19]

Thus the scene of Mankind's temptation turns on the same mode of travel with which it began. The weakness of his youth translates itself into the form of despair that values the moment over eternity. And for all his yearning for "heven trone," Mankind is revealed to be, like Filius Regis, "egens et insipiens." That point is underlined a moment later when Folly confesses that "Werldly wit was nevere nowt, / But with Foly it were frawt" (513–14).

Mankind's temptation is played entirely in the neutral space surrounding the Castle, which has not yet assumed its symbolic meaning. No governing journey to a particular place is postulated for Mankind; indeed, as we have seen, the Good Angel's offering is remarkably vague. But his situation in the opening scene is that of Lydgate's pilgrim at the beginning of his journey, and the action imitated in that brief scene is essentially the action of the first 12,000 lines of the *Pilgrimage,* stripped of the poem's compendium of doctrine and presented dramatically, in the temptation of Mankind, rather than obliquely, under the figure of a journey. Mankind has a spiritual "place" to which he naturally aspires, a place he cannot see but that is represented for the audience in the Deus scaffold, and the Bad Angel leads him away from that place toward the World and death. But while the sustained physical journey of the narrative poems does not appear as a motif in the fable of the *Castle,* the sense that life is a spiritual journey is sustained throughout the scene in verbal figures. And at the end of the scene, as at important moments throughout the play, the underlying action is manifested in physical movement, as Mankind and the Bad Angel set off for the Mundus scaffold, weaving a wandering path to symbolize a long journey.[23]

Throughout the middle section of the play the major stages of the action are marked by journies of this sort, and the playing area becomes a moral landscape as clear as that in the *Pilgrimage.* The scaffolds, as well as those who act upon them, objectify Mankind's moral state. As he leaves one or another behind in the course of his journey, we are made to see the successive stages of the moral life, just as we are made aware of similar stages through the articulated landscapes of the poems. The journey to the Mundus scaffold initiates Mankind's spiritual movement into the land of unlikeness.

He arrives with visions of pleasure, although he retains the comforting thought that he can repent when his nose grows cold. Thus at the base of the scaffold he is met by Folly, to whom he pledges his friendship. When he meets the World, however, he is ready to forgo heaven entirely for worldly pleasure: "Of my sowle I have non rewthe. / What schulde I recknen of domysday, / So that I be ryche and of gret a-ray?" (605–9). And to signal this advance, "ascendet Humanum Genus ad Mundum." Enlisted in the service of the World and symbolically dressed in "robes ryve / With ryche a-ray," Mankind is sent back across the *platea* in the company of Backbiter, symbolic of the way to get on in the world, to the scaffold of Covetous, who will henceforth be his chief guide. There his general self-indulgence sharpens to more aggressive, more particular sins, as he vows, under the influence of Covetous, that "I schal nevere begger bede / Mete nyn drynke, ne hevene blys, / Rather or I schulde hym clothe or fede, / He schulde sterve and stynke, iwys" (874–77).

Through Covetous, Mankind is introduced to the rest of the Seven Deadly Sins. But he does not travel to meet them as he might in a narrative poem, for the stage does not offer the infinite number of places an imagined landscape does. Theatrical economy reverses the journey. Covetous calls the Sins forth from their places on the other scaffolds, and they come in procession across the *platea* to be counselors of Mankind. Under their instruction, Mankind's spiritual journey continues step by step toward the pit. Like Filius Regis, he has become "praeceps et temerarius in prosperis," and with a glance at the preacher who lies behind every morality play he is careful to point out for the audience whence he has come and where he is going:

> Mankynde I am called by kynde,
> With curssydnesse in costys knet;
> In sowre swettenesse my syth I sende,
> With seven synnes sadde beset.
> Mekyl myrthe I move in mynde,
> With melody at my mowthis met.
> My prowde pouer schal I not pende
> Tyl I be put in peynys pyt,
> To helle hent fro hens.
>   [1238–46]

There is no way to tell precisely what Mankind looks like during this sequence, of course, but there is some reason to believe that he is made to appear steadily more grotesque as he becomes entangled in the Seven Deadly Sins. We see him first in his natural nakedness, and his Good Angel suggests that the appropriate covering for his body, the normative image of his yearning for "hevene trone," is poor and simple because "Criste in erthe and his meynye / All is povert here thei stode" (351–52). But the robes given to him by the World are twice said to be decorated with "besawntys bryth"—that is, presumably, hung all over with what appear to be gold coins. So when he enters the World's service, he apparently comes to look like wealth itself, shimmering and jingling as he moves and probably, with the weight and bulk of the costume, moving a good deal more pompously. The Sins who surround him on Covetous' scaffold (seven of them in a space seven by eight feet, if Southern's estimate is accurate,[24] so one's sense that he is entangled by them seems to have been borne out by the stage) are apparently not as grotesque as those represented in Lydgate's *Pilgrimage;* but, so far as one can tell from the language of the play, in their costumes and in the qualities of their movements they are made to seem like human caricatures of the motives they represent. Envy is ferret-like. He describes himself as "fleet as a fox," and he "folweth on faste" after the others because he is "loth to be the laste." Pride seems to be dressed in what the play regards as the more grotesque of the late fourteenth-century aristocratic fashions, since he urges Mankind to "use these new jettys; / Loke thou blowe mekyl bost / Wyth longe crakows on thi schos. / Jagge thi clothis in every cost, / And ell men schul lete the but a goos" (1059–61). Mankind is delighted with that advice, as he is with everything the sins tell him to do, and presumably he responds to each bit of instruction in some fashion, trying on Pride's plumes, perhaps, or miming the postures of Wrath. Certainly when Confession calls out to him to "cum doun and speke wyth Schryfte / And drawe the yerne to sum thryfte," Mankind answers with the indolent gestures of Sloth:

> A, Schryfte, thou art wel be note
> Here to Slawthe that syttyth here-inne.
> He seyth thou mytyst a com to mannys cote
> On Palme Sunday al betyme.
> Thou art com al to sone.
> Therfore, Schryfte, be thi fay,
> Goo forthe tyl on Good Fryday.
> Tente to the thanne wel I may;
> I have now ellys to done.
>
> [1346–54]

It seems reasonable to imagine, then, that as he becomes "with sevyn synnes sadde be-set" we see him lose his likeness to himself as he takes on all of the qualities that draw him from his natural inclinations.

There is no stage direction calling for Mankind to take off his golden gown and so regain his lost likeness, but it seems clear that he must do so at some point in the following scene, where Shrift guides him through the sacrament of penance. We should probably imagine him dressed now in the white robe of a penitent, to resemble the normative image of "Criste and his meynye."

In one respect, however, this whole sequence involving Mankind's recovery from the Seven Deadly Sins and the land of unlikeness is curious, because up to this point in the play the logic by which we have moved from scene to scene has been visible. Each scene has been explicitly linked to the one that follows it. Mankind enters with his Bad Angel, who sends him to the World. World sends him with Backbiter to the scaffold of Covetous, and Covetous calls the other sins from their scaffolds to join him. But no one calls for Shrift and Penance. They enter on their own and for reasons of their own. As part of the moral universe inhabited by fallen man, they are always theoretically present, as it were, always available as sacramental evidence of God's mercy. But the question the *Poetics* encourages me to ask is what sort of consecutive sense it makes to have them enter *The Castle of Perseverance* at this point in Mankind's moral career. The logic of the scene is clearly not dramatic in the ordinary sense of that term. And if it is probable in any sense that Penance would appear at this moment and cause Mankind to feel penitent, it can only be because, according to the model of human experience assumed by the play, penitence, the sorrow and anxiety Mankind feels when Penance touches him with his lance, is understood universally to follow the thoughtless arrogance of sin, as it does in Saint Bernard's formulation of the psychological rhythm of life's pilgrimage: "Primo enim est egens et insipiens: postea praeceps et temerarius in prosperis; deinde, trepidus et pusillanimus in adversis." So Mankind in "wepynge wo" (1407) cries, "Mercy, Schrifte, I wil no more" (1425). And just as Filius Regis, rescued from the land of unlikeness, is sent off to the Castle of Sapience, and the Pilgrim to the Castle of the Cistercians, so Mankind is sent by Shrift to the Castle of Perseverance, there to be instructed by the Seven Moral Virtues in "regno caritatis."

The lessons of the Virtues, like the instructions of the Vices, are thus not homiletic intrusions into the play. They are literally action, unclothed by fable. Each serves as a *remedium* for the lessons of the opposite vice, and together they bring Mankind step by step back from his deviant moral journey to a state in which he can receive God's grace—if he perseveres. Thus when Mankind enters the Castle, Humility observes that he is there to continue his spiritual journey in another form: "He hauntyth now hevene halle / That schal bryngyn hym to hevene" (1709–10). It is here, with Mankind at the midpoint of his temporal and spiritual lives, forty years old and restored to virtue, that Mercy sets out the thesis of perseverance: "Qui perseveraverit usque in finem, hic saluus erit." And hereafter, as we have seen, the action in the foreground of the play is shaped around the needs of a dramatic homily explicating that thesis. But we might note briefly how the general lines of this action are informed by the model of the pilgrimage and, in particular, how the siege of the Castle of Perseverance, which occupies the next thousand lines of the play, fits into that model.

Mankind has now passed through the major stages of life's pilgrimage. At the beginning he longed for heaven, but he was foolish, he was tempted, and he fell. For a time he wandered among the scaffolds of the World and Covetous, where he lost his likeness to himself, just as Filius Regis wandered through the vale of curiosity and the fields of licentiousness to the land of unlikeness. But now he has been recovered and installed in the Castle. When Filius Regis reaches a similar point in *Parabola I* and is taken to the Castle of Sapience, the Castle is attacked by the enemies of man. After Lydgate's Pilgrim reaches the Castle of the Cistercians, it is invaded by Fals Envye, Treason and Detraction, along with Scilla and her hounds. While it is the longest and most vivid of the play's sequences, then, the full-scale battle enacted at the center of *The Castle of Perseverance* does not identify the psychomachia as the basic metaphor of the play any more than the various battles enacted in the poems identify them as imitations of the action of Prudentius' poem.[25] The assaults of the Vices may dramatize different things for different poets—the interpersonal strains of monastic life for Deguile-ville, the dependence of moral theology on charity for Saint Bernard—but an assault of some sort is a common feature of the pilgrimage allegory, revealing, as it does in the *Castle,* the implacable hostility of vice to virtue and thus the danger of the spiritual life even after the pilgrim has reached a moral haven. The siege of the Castle of Perseverance by the forces of the World, the Flesh, and the Devil is thus simply an incident in the pilgrimage of the life of Mankind and one whose particular form is dictated by the homiletic concern of the play with the moral habit of perseverance and the spiritual virtue of hope.

The successful defense of the Castle takes place, we learn, during Mankind's vigorous middle years. But after the battle, when Mankind has become "a-party wele in age" and his moral resolution has been colored by the fears attendant on the weakness of age, he is easy prey for the temptations of Covetous. The self-indulgent youth, who had remained securely in the Castle of Perseverance during his manhood, now becomes an aged miser, heaping up treasure against the blowing of the wind. And this moral change is signaled, as we might expect, by a journey back to Covetous' "castel cage."

During this second movement of the action, several stock motifs of medieval literature appear, as Mankind is summoned by Death, his Body and Soul engage in a truncated debate, and the Four Daughters of God debate whether he should be granted mercy or held to the strict rigors of justice. Like the siege of the Castle, these allegories, as they have been called, imitate stages in Mankind's moral journey. The homiletic thesis of the play demands that he be saved at the last moment, as it were, so that his failure in perseverance may be instructively harrowing for the audience. Thus he persists in avarice until Death strikes. And then, "trepidus et pusillanimus in adversis" once more, he cries for mercy. His dying cry initiates the debate between Justice and Mercy, and it is only in consequence of that debate, through rhetorical shifts we have already examined, that Mankind reaches the goal he had prayed for at the beginning of his life and comes to "hevene trone." That last alteration in perspective bridges, again rather undramatically perhaps, the gap between the predicament of Mankind in a homily of perseverance and his destiny as life's pilgrim. But like all the other variations in perspective and motif, it too serves to realize the form of the pilgrimage that shapes the play.

For all the apparent simplicity of its address to its audience, then, the *Castle* has a complex structure, at once homiletic and mimetic. The thesis of perseverance that it argues is a particular and limited form of the universal model of life's pilgrimage that it imitates. Indeed, as we have seen, it is only when we understand that the *Castle* is an imitation of that model that we can hold together the various parts of the play. While the nature of the stage militates against imitating the action of the pilgrimage through a fable about a journey, it provides equally effective modes of its own. The isolated mansions of the *Castle* reflect the process of spiritual growth as effectively as the continuous space of Lydgate's *Pilgrimage,* and the physical and psychological representations of an actor reveal it as clearly as and more vividly than symbolic traveling.

It is for that reason that the motif of the journey is progressively submerged and finally drops out altogether in the three versions of Wit's education that Spivack sees as the only moralities to imitate the figure of the pilgrimage.[26] Together the plays provide a classic example of the stage's adaptation of a useful but awkward metaphor. The allegorical journey is an oblique literary device that the stage finds not only physically difficult but also unnecessarily indirect. Hence *Wit and Science,* the play in which the motif is clearest, merely suggests the journey of Wit to Mount Parnassus and concentrates instead on the direct encounters between Wit and the humanistic vices and virtues that hinder and aid his development. And in the relatively more literal, more urban settings of *The Marriage of Wit and Science* (1568-70) and *The Marriage between Wit and Wisdom* (1579), the motif of the journey is absorbed into verbal metaphors, just as it is in the *Castle.* The mode of the imitation of action in the *Castle* suggests that the stage—or at least the popular stage—prefers direct and concrete representation.

Scio Ergo Sumus: The Marriage of Wit and Science

The *Castle of Perseverance* deals solely with ideas and is almost wholly indifferent to the translation of those ideas into the concrete substance of a particular world. The peculiarities of its dialect aside, the *Castle* might have been written in any time or place for all the account it takes of the world of late fourteenth-century England. There is a reference to the gallows of Canwick, which helps to locate the play geographically, and there are from time to time fleeting references to fashions of dress or behavior, such as Pride's advice to Mankind to "use these new jettys. / Look thou blowe mekyl bost, / With longe crakows on thi shos, / Jagge thi clothis in every cost, / And ell men schul lete the but a goos" (1057–61). But for the most part its language is timelessly abstract, befitting a play that takes its rhetorical stance somewhere between discourse and mathematics.

From that position the *Castle* dips down from time to time to find metaphors for the ideas with which it is concerned. The Castle itself is the most evident of these. And the servant-and-master relationship among the Vices, the language of travel, even the division of roles according to sex, are further examples of the willingness of the play to characterize its hypotheses at least one step beyond the stage of personification itself. But no more than one. Such metaphors as the play employs depend from the ideas they illustrate at a single point. Thus we are told that to persevere in this world is like being in a castle under siege, that lechery is a feminine vice, and that Lechery, Sloth, and Gluttony are like servants of the master temptations of the Flesh; but none of these metaphorical vehicles is developed to characterize further the tenor of thought. Gluttony does not care for his own interests to the detriment of his master's, as he might reasonably be imagined to do; Lechery has none of the supposed characteristics of women; and those in the Castle do not concern themselves with their supplies of food and water or the good repair of their battlements—any or all of which would be consistent with the moral significance of those metaphors. The mode of *The Castle of Perseverance* is the mode of the preacher, and its metaphors, like his, are diverse and discrete, caught up in passing but not held long enough or tightly enough to compose a continuous hypothetical world. Thus there is in the *Castle* no corpus of fictional logic to complicate the structure of thesis and myth.

That is generally true of fifteenth-century morality plays, which may from time to time be minutely realistic but which make their sallies into the concrete from a structure whose only continuous principle is the exposition of moral doctrine. Such plays as *Mankind* and *Wisdom, Who Is Christ* are literally embodied sermons, and we may understand their design only by understanding that the episodes of which they are composed are merely the visible forms of continuous moral arguments. The vice episodes in the play of *Mankind,* for example, apparently emerge *ex vacuo,* neither developed from nor developing a consecutive fable that can provide motivation for the entrances and exits of the Vices. Properly understood, they are *exempla* for the sermon that Mercy begins to preach as the play opens, *exempla* directed first at Mercy's audience and only gradually brought to bear upon the figure of Mankind, who comes to stand within the play as surrogate for the audience addressed by the play.

As Mankind begins, Mercy is preaching about true and false felicity, warning his audience to "dyverte not yowrsylffe in tyme of temtacyon / That ye may be acceptable to Gode at yowr goyng hence."[1] His sermon is interrupted by Mischief and then by New Guise, Now-a-Days, and Nought, whose scatalogical mockery provides an illustration of the corrupt felicity of "thyngys transytorye." Having displayed their qualities, the Vices abruptly leave the stage, and Mercy resumes his sermon, drawing on the examples they have provided to "dyscomende the bycyouse gyse" of now-a-days. At this point Mankind enters, complaining about the division between his soul and his body and seeking "gostly solace." That slender thread draws Mercy's audience onto the stage, and with hardly a break Mercy addresses his sermon now to the character Mankind. He warns him against undue attention to things of this world and, "in specyall," against New Guise, Now-a-Days, and Nought. As Mercy speaks, the trio of Vices mock him from offstage, with Now-a-Days tapping what he at least imagines to be a fund of resentment in the audience against Mercy's interminable preaching. "If ye would go hens," he shouts,

> we xall cum everychon,
> Mo then a goode sorte,

> Ye have leve, I dare well say.
> When ye wyll, go forth yowr way.
> Men have lytyll deynte of yowr pley
> Because ye make no sporte.
>
> [263–68]

When Mercy leaves the stage, making way for their sport and for the exemplary temptation of Mankind, the play briefly takes up a dramatic image through which to develop Mankind's perseverance and around which to organize his temptation. Mankind, we are to understand, is a farmer. But even as that image is introduced, we see that its function, like the function of the Castle of Perseverance, is merely to provide a local metaphor for one of the invisible processes of Mankind's soul. "Thys erth wyth my spade I xall assay to delffe," Mankind tells us, reminding us of Adam and fallen man, and then goes on to explain that his digging is simply a moral strategy, adopted so as "to eschew ydullnes." After it has served its purpose, the notion that Mankind is a farmer is simply dropped and never touched on again. Having been told in a dream, stage-managed by Titivillus, that Mercy is dead, Mankind sets off to explore the delights of "thyngys transytorye," and the play moves into an extended comic episode, loosely shaped around the image of Mischief's court *"sub forma jurys."* As the Vices are gleefully transforming Mankind, however, Mercy enters again, the Vices scatter, and the play returns to the expository mode of its beginning, as together Mercy and Mankind draw out the implications of his fall in a sermon *de contemptu mundi.*

Thus, although Mercy is offstage during the middle part of the play, the episodes then dramatized are given form only by the moral propositions laid down in his sermon. They are the *exempla* on which he draws, and together they pose and explore these hypothetical questions: What if we ignore Mercy's lesson? What if we assume that there is no mercy? The answer, given by Mischief's court, is disorder and despair. Even the strain of mocking contempt for Mercy's sermon is part of the logic of its rhetoric. For the mockery is designed to clarify the rebellions of the flesh and the fancy against his ascetic doctrines and to reveal the ends to which the flesh and the fancy lead when man does not regard each moment *sub specie aeternitatis.*

The history of the morality drama in the sixteenth century is, in part, the history of the moderation of Mercy's theme and the transformation of *Mankind*'s method. The eschatological vision of the fifteenth-century moralities, which informs their otherworldly teaching, was not abandoned entirely in the sixteenth century, but, displaced by the humanistic redirection of energy that marked the Renaissance, it moderated to an interest in the rewards and penalties of this world, which were seen, not always perfunctorily, as emblems of the rewards and penalties to come. In that respect the moralities of the early humanists, such as Henry Medwall's *Nature* (derived in part from *Reason and Sensuality*),[2] led the morality drama to fulfill a promise made for it two centuries earlier, when it originated in the efforts of the Church to educate its flock in the implications for men's lives of Christian theology. Questions of all sorts were opened up in the sixteenth-century moralities: child-rearing in *Nice Wanton* (1547–53), education in *The Nature of the Four Elements* (1517–18), the achievement of wealth in *Impatient Poverty* (1547–53), the right uses of wealth in *Magnificence* (1513–16), and a host of political and sectarian quarrels in *Respublica* (1553) and other plays. Because these were limited themes, the universal figure of Mankind gave way to limited personifications and types representing stages of life (such as Youth), attributes of men (such as Wit), and the social conditions in which men live (such as Abundance and Poverty). And these in turn grew more substantial until the question of whether Youth should be understood as a personification of that time of life or as a young man became moot. Gradually literal characters made their way into morality plays out of historical chronicles (Bale's *King Johann,* 1530–36), out of the Bible (*King Darius,* 1559–65), and even out of romance (*Patient and Meek Grissil,* 1561–65, and *Appius and Virginia,* 1575).[3] The transformation of the morality drama was not, however, brought about by the secularizing of its themes, by the narrowing and thickening of its characters, or by the adoption of a substantial locality for its action. Each of these contributed to the change, but the change itself—by which I mean the transformation of the expository mode we have seen in *Mankind* and *The Castle*—awaited the adoption by a morality play of a continuous fable, a self-contained hypothetical world, that could make demands on the conduct of the action. The play I want to discuss in this chapter, John Redford's *Wit and Science,* stands on the very edge of that transformation.

THE MORAL PLAY OF WIT AND SCIENCE

Wit and Science was the first of three plays that dramatize the process of education under the figure of a marriage between Wit and the Lady Science. The other two, *The Marriage of Wit and Science* and *The Contract of a Marriage between Wit and Wisdom,* appeared during the 1570s, or about thirty-five years later than Redford's play. Both derive more or less distinctly from *Wit and Science,* the *Marriage* reworking Redford's fable with act and scene divisions, the *Contract* taking over the general thesis and situation to hold together a chaotic farce. Together they offer an interesting example of the progress of a dramatic trope, rather like the progress of *King Lear* in the Restoration, first elevated to brittle classical "respectability," then theatrically debased. But neither the *Marriage* nor the *Contract* will concern us here, except insofar as the similarities and differences between the *Marriage* and *Wit and Science* may help us to see what Redford is doing.

Because of those similarities, we can guess that *Wit and Science* was fairly well known during the sixteenth century, although we have no records of either its performance or publication. The play was written with a good deal of theatrical care, however, and it seems clearly to have been intended for performance, perhaps by the children of St. Paul's during Redford's tenure as choirmaster. Its text, lacking a few sheets at the beginning, has survived only in a notebook, along with some fragments of other interludes and some songs. For that, at least, we can be grateful, because *Wit and Science* is in its own way a remarkable play, welding together thesis, myth, and fable into a clear and resonant dramatic sermon.

As in *The Castle,* the mainspring of that sermon is a sequential thesis, here concerned not with the way to achieve salvation but with one of its secular corollaries, knowledge. In place of "Qui perseveraverit usque in finem, hic saluus erit," we have essentially this: The mind that seeks knowledge can achieve it if its quest is informed by reason and guided by instruction. Unlike *The Castle,* however, *Wit and Science* clothes its thesis in a romantic fable. The untutored mind is imagined to be a young man in love with Lady Science. The match is favored by her father, Reason, who recognizes in Wit those "gifts of graces...which Science doth axe" (16–20).[4] But there is an impediment in the form of the giant, Tediousness, who guards the approach to Science's mountain, Parnassus. To win his lady, Wit must get by Tediousness and climb Parnassus, for "who attaineth once to sleep on that mount, / Lady Science his own he may count" (961–62). Reason provides Wit with a trio of guides to help him on his journey, Instruction, Study, and Diligence, and secures the services of Honest Recreation to refresh him along the way. At the end of this first, truncated scene, Wit sets out on his secular pilgrimage.

I will return to Wit's "pilgrimage" in a moment. But first let me examine the way in which Redford's thesis controls the linear development of the play so that we may see more clearly the elements in the structure of the play that lie outside its thesis.

THE EDUCATION OF WIT

The first movement of the play is organized to demonstrate what happens to Wit when he lacks the guidance of Reason and Instruction, just as the first movement of *The Castle* is organized to demonstrate what happens when Mankind neglects his Good Angel and tries to live for the present moment. Accordingly, when first we see Wit on his journey, he is already in the process of shaking off all authority. Having outrun his mentor, Instruction, he comes onstage alone, closely followed by Study and Diligence, the only powers of his mind that he can command without aid. For all Wit cares, he has lost Instruction; but he has also, logically enough, lost himself. And as he and Study and Diligence try to puzzle out which way to go, Diligence suggesting the best-traveled path and Study complaining of a headache, Instruction comes panting onstage to tell Wit that he really must go back and take an easier route. This way is dangerous, he explains, because it will bring Wit within range of the giant, Tediousness, before Wit is ready to fight with him. He must wait until he has received a token from the Lady Science, the Sword of Comfort, "which is the weapon, doubtless / That must serve you against Tediousness" (95–96). Redford's point, of course, is that the student must proceed at a measured pace, letting more difficult studies wait until he has mastered preliminary materials so that they have become easy for him. But Wit will have none of it. If he lacks Comfort, he has at least enthusiasm, a species of false confidence, and he plunges ahead with Study and Diligence. Study's headache provides a foretaste of what is to come. And as they go off, Instruction, the quintessential schoolteacher, underlines the pedagogical moral:

> When wits stand so in their own conceit,
> Best let them go, till pride in his height
> Turn and cast them down headlong again.
> As ye shall see proved by this Wit plain.
>   [133–36]

Instruction's prophecy is immediately confirmed. Wit encounters Tediousness and is battered to the ground. According to the stage direction, he *"falleth down and dieth"* (210), thereby providing a theatrical image of the mind deadened to the pursuit of knowledge by its difficulty. But Reason has foreseen that problem, and he has sent

Honest Recreation after Wit. She arrives at this point, and through charm-like song and dance she revives him. Reason, who has come along with her, tells Wit that he must start off on his journey again. But Wit, a little unsteady after his "hard chance," has found Honest Recreation attractive. "I shall," he tells Reason, "to your daughter all at leisure." At that, Reason stalks off, angered by Wit's disobedience, and Wit is left, reasonless, to his own baser inclinations.

Lacking Reason, Wit is no longer a student. He turns abruptly to Honest Recreation: "Come now, a basse!" (291). When Honest Recreation replies that she will kiss him only "in gage of marriage," Wit agrees, disclaiming all interest in Lady Science: "Shall I tell you truth? / I never loved her." Honest Recreation is not so easily won, however. Wit must prove his skill even in her domain. Can he dance? she asks him. Wit takes off his "garment cumbering," his scholar's gown, and they do a galliard. At its end, Wit sinks down exhausted into the lap of Idleness, who has slipped onstage during the dance. Honest Recreation is shocked: "It is an harlot! May ye not see?" (340). The point, of course, is that he cannot. Lacking Reason, Wit is unable to distinguish between Honest Recreation and Idleness. And now, as Wit turns his attention to Idleness, Redford modulates him into a sort of sneering lout. "Lo, now for the best game," he says, settling his head on Idleness' lap, "While I take my ease, your tongues now frame" (344–45). But Wit is prevented from hearing their debate by the logic of Redford's thesis. For having settled upon Idleness, he promptly falls asleep. *"Neque vox, neque sensus,"* she observes, "a meet man for Idleness" (431–32). While Wit sleeps, Idleness completes the process begun when Wit abandoned the guidance of Reason. She dresses him in Ingnorancy's (*sic*) gown, puts a fool's cap on his head, and blackens his face: "Now are ye weel, / By virtue of Idleness' blessing tool, / Conjured from Wit into a stark fool" (604–6).

This summary of the first 600 lines of *Wit and Science* omits only one scene, Idleness' abortive attempt to teach Ingnorancy his name, and I think it preserves Redford's emphases. Apart from the omitted scene, which needs to be discussed in another connection, Redford closely and economically models the events of the story around his thesis that knowledge must be pursued within the bounds of reason and under the guidance of instruction. Having shown what happens when these two are lacking, he turns around to show how they bring Wit to his goal.

The pivotal scene is one in which Wit is brought to recognize what he has become without Reason and Instruction. While Wit is sleeping, Lady Science enters with her mother, Experience, looking for Wit, who has not kept his promise to come to her. As she talks with Experience, Wit wakes up and, still lacking Reason, rudely demands a kiss. Because of his fool's costume, Science does not recognize him or at least claims that she does not. He does not look at all like his picture; she takes him rather for a fool,

> no natural fool
> Brought up among the innocents' school,
> But for a naughty, vicious fool,
> Brought up with Idleness, in her school.
> Of all arrogant fools, thou art one.
>
> [798–802]

And she stalks out. Wit is furious and bewildered. There is no point, he thinks, in taking pains to win a woman who lacks the simplest points of courtesy. He takes out the glass of self-examination Reason had earlier given him, intending to confirm for himself that he is not the fool Science would have him be:

> Ha! Gog's soul! What have we here, a devil?
> This glass, I see well, hath been kept evil.
> Gog's soul! A fool! A fool, by the mass!
> What a very vengeance aileth this glass?
> Other this glass is shamefully spotted,
> Or else I am too shamefully blotted.
> Nay, by Gog's arms, I am so no doubt.
>
> [815–21]

With that recognition, Shame enters with his whip, with Reason close behind. While Shame whips him, Wit begs Reason's forgiveness. Because Wit has submitted himself to punishment, Reason grants it and turns Wit over to Instruction to be prepared to try his journey once more. As they go out, Reason draws for the audience the moral of Wit's first failure: "Who list to mark now this chance here done, / May see what Wit is without Reason" (893–94).

The remainder of this speech, along with a few lines from Confidence, explaining that he has brought the Sword of Comfort to Wit and is returning to Science with a token of Wit's love, gives Wit time to wash his face and change his costume offstage. When he returns, evidently dressed in the scholar's gown he wore at the beginning of the play, we are to understand that he is at the base of Parnassus, prepared once more to fight with Tediousness. Redford is not especially concerned with how he got there, nor is he especially concerned with *how* Wit comes to be united with Lady Science. His thesis is limited to showing the need for Reason and Instruction; he does not discuss the function they serve when they are present. Thus the last sequence of the play is quite brief. Wit listens docilely to Instruction's advice about how to fight the battle (none of it translatable into the language of learning), which then takes place offstage. At its conclusion, "Wit cometh in and bringeth in the head upon his sword" (974). As he does so, "Confidence cometh running in" to tell Wit that Lady Science has watched the battle "from yonder mountain high." "Ye have won her," Confidence announces, "body and all" (983). While everyone sings "Welcome, Mine Own," Science enters with her company, and she and Wit are joined together. All that remains is to warn Wit that he must use Science well, "unto God's honor, and profit both / Of you and your neighbor" (1077–78). The play ends with a glance back toward the eschatalogical concern that had animated *The Castle of Perseverance:*

> Among our wedding matters here rendering,
> Th' end of our lives would be in remembering;
> Which remembrance, Wit, shall sure defend ye
> From the misuse of Science, and send ye
> The gain my mother to mind did call,
> Joy without end.....
>
> [1109–14]

As the embodiment of its thesis, *Wit and Science* is simple and straightforward, just the sort of pedagogue's plea for obedient students we might expect from a man charged with the education of the Children of Paul's. But there is more to the play than that. I have tried to keep out of my summary of Redford's thesis most of the coloration it takes on from the fable of chivalric romance in which it is cast. But I have not been able to keep it wholly free of its romantic colors because the play takes its rhetorical stance halfway between its thesis and its fable, and it pays more or less equal attention to both. Dramatic imagery in plays like *The Castle* and *Mankind* is used to illustrate a single point in the moral thesis being developed, and it thus tends to function as a single term in an explicit moral simile. But in *Wit and Science* the case is rather different, for Redford's imagery often functions in a truly metaphorical way. At such moments Wit is not merely a representation of intellectual capacity striving for knowledge; he is in fact a lover whose aspirations toward his lady imply intellectual aspirations. Similarly, Science is at moments not *scientia* but rather a lady whose changing relationship with her lover implies the changing relationship of knowledge to the mind. Such moments are sufficiently frequent in *Wit and Science* to compose a world of continuous metaphor, although it is now more, now less, substantial as the needs of Redford's thesis dictate. For example, when Wit rushes into battle with Tediousness against the advice of Instruction, Redford provides him with a motive that is linked in both form and content with Wit's role as lover. He will not take an easier way around, he tells Instruction, "ere my sweetheart / Shall hear that Wit from that wretch shall start / One foot, this body and all shall crack" (108-9). The general point is clear enough, of course: Wit is foolhardy. But the form his temerity takes is not translatable into expository terms, as Instruction's advice to take an easier path is, because it requires a set of assumptions about Science that are not applicable to *scientia.* That is equally true of the fable at large, which requires that we imagine *scientia* as having the characteristics of a young woman who shows herself delighted, sad, and angry in turn.

Redford's fable, then, has a density and consistency new to the morality drama, and because of it *Wit and Science* has a structure quite different from the structure of *The Castle* or *Mankind.* I think it is a mistake, however, to rest too much too quickly on the metaphorical surface of the play or indeed to consider its romantic fable apart from the thesis that informs it. It seems to me that Spivack, for example, sets out in precisely the wrong direction when he observes of the metaphors of *Wit and Science* that "through them Eros becomes dignified into a symbol of the moral Good, the love between man and woman spiritualized into a type of salvation," and then goes on to say that "the theme almost sums up the last four centuries of our literature."[5] For in pulling Redford's metaphors loose from the imaginative web of the play and merging them into a literature that truly values Eros, he obscures their function and blurs them beyond recognition. Rather than consider how Redford's figures reflect the predominant interests of our literature, I want to ask why he has chosen to dramatize his pedagogical argument through those figures.

THE ROMANCE OF WIT AND SCIENCE

Why did Redford cast Wit's education in the form of a chivalric romance? And does he realize in the play the implications of having done so? Those are questions to which we are not likely to get definitive answers, but they do provide a way to consider the relationship between Redford's thesis and his romantic fable. There is a certain rhetorical advantage, of course, in a teacher's suggesting that learning might be a heroic enterprise, that a student slogging his way through Latin grammar might be like a knight battling giants to win his lady. And there was historical precedent. Medieval romances tended to concern themselves with the education of their heroes in chivalric virtues, and, some thirty years before *Wit and Science,* Stephen Hawes turned romantic formulas to the service of educational allegories in his *Example of Vertue* (1504) and *The Pastime of Pleasure* (1505). But there are indications in *Wit and Science* that Redford may have chosen his fable a bit less limply, with a sharper eye toward its implications, than mere precedent or rhetorical advantage suggest. Let me develop these implications by way of a specific question.

When Lady Science comes onstage, looking for Wit, after he has been lulled asleep by Idleness, she finds the personifications of Fame, Worship, Riches, and Favor waiting for her. They greet her with a song, "Exceeding Measure," the expression of an "unfortunate wretch" doomed "ever to serve where I may not attain." The song has no particular allegorical point, although it is emotionally appropriate to the situations of Wit and Science, whose love seems in jeopardy at this moment, and it expresses loosely and hyperbolically the intentions of Fame and his companions. They have been sent by the World, they explain, to serve Lady Science. As we might expect, Science refuses their offer of service. "I thank the World," she says politely,

> But chiefly god be praised
> That in the World such love to Science hath raised.
> But yet, to tell you plain, ye four are such
> As Science looketh for little nor much;
> For, being as I am, a lone woman,
> Need of your service I neither have nor can.
>
> [669–74]

Nothing disturbs the even flow of expected sentiment until those last two lines. Until then the scene looks a good deal like a decorative pageant, defining, a bit too elaborately perhaps, Science's independence from worldly muck, but not really part of the developing action of the play. But those last two lines are a puzzle. They form the ground of Science's rejection of worldly treasures. And if I read them accurately, Science's speech is not a high-minded distinction between knowledge and things of the world; it is simply a conditional refusal of worldly favors because of her situation at the moment.[6] Because she is a "lone woman" she neither needs, nor can she need, Fame and his companions. The implication that she might otherwise accept them is strengthened when Experience notes that Science is unusually sad (655) and when Science herself explains that she has "small cause to care for the World's favoring, / Seeing the wits of the world be so wavering" (683–84). What, precisely, does Science mean, and what is Redford getting at?

It is tempting to suggest that he is here drawing on both thesis and fable, resting his characterization of the independence of knowledge on the situation of his forlorn heroine. But that simply does not make sense. For, while a lone woman might not need Fame, she could surely use, precisely because she is lone, Riches and Favor. And if she has rejected them because of their relationship to a suitor with whom she is angry, then, in pursuing his fable, Redford has trivialized the chief virtue of the play.

Moreover, while Science here claims that she does not need worldly treasures, her suitor expects that she will have them and indeed loves her in part because they are her dowry. After Science has rebuffed Wit, he reviles himself at some length, ending with these lines:

> And those four gifts which the World gave her
> I had won, too, had I kept her favor:
> Where now, instead of that lady bright,
> With all those gallants seen in my sight—
> Favor, Riches, yea Worship, and Fame—
> I have won Hatred, Beggary, and Open Shame.
>
> [847–52]

Wit's regard for what Spivack has called the "renaissance beatitudes" offers no difficulty in itself. Fame, Worship, Favor, even Riches, are classical virtues, accommodated by the less ascetic Christian poets long before *Wit and Science.* Indeed, in the later play, *The Marriage of Wit and Science,* Nature rather flat-footedly argues that God has made the pursuit of Science difficult precisely so that poor men who are able to manage it can achieve riches and favor. If it were not difficult, she explains,

> The meaner sort that now excell in virtues of the mind
> Should not be once accepted there, where now they
>   succour find.

> For great men should be sped of all, and would have
>   need of none;
> And he that were not born to land should lack to
>   live upon.[7]

We might simply note that the "wit" plays have a more worldly ethos than *The Castle of Perseverance* if it were not for the fact that Science herself has earlier rejected these gifts. Because she has, we have at least the appearance of an unresolved contradiction between the lady and her lover. If we are to understand from the earlier scene that science is to be purely regarded as an end in itself, independent of the worldly treasures it might bring, then Wit has an imperfect love for his lady, which ought at some time to be rectified. The fact that it is not, that Wit is never disabused of his prudential regard for Science, suggests that the play does not understand learning in quite so idealistic a way. And that in turn sends us back to wonder again why Science refuses Fame and his companions.

This is a minor question, to be sure, involving two lines that have no consequence in a play of almost 1,200 lines. But it strikes at a point where Redford reveals assumptions about the nature of Science that he is not concerned to develop explicitly in the play, and thus it provides us with an opening on the sort of logic that shapes his characters. What is there about being a lone woman that causes Science to reject the World's gifts? Why does she say not merely that she does not need them but that she cannot need them? And what would enable her to accept them if she were no longer a lone woman? The answers to these questions turn, I think, on the fact that *scientia* alone does not exist. Things exist whether they are known or not. Millions of flowers blush unseen, and the oceans of the world are presumably full of unrecorded species of fish. But knowledge comes into being only when things are grasped by the mind. Knowledge can *be* only in a mind that knows. Until Science is possessed by Wit, to adopt the metaphors of the play, her existence in and for the World is merely potential.[8] It is for that reason I suggest that she refuses the World's gifts but implies that under other circumstances she could accept them. For at the time the World sends them, she is as yet unpossessed, "unknown" to Wit. In that state she cannot use or need them because she literally *is* not. Why, then, does the World send them? Because, according to the time scheme of the fable, Science was to have been joined to Wit before the gifts arrived. They are in the nature of a wedding present that arrives just after the happy couple has decided to call it off.

If I am right about Science's reasons, her rejection of the World's gifts provides us with an opening onto a substratum of action that nourishes Redford's pedagogical thesis, one that he does not develop explicitly in the play but that informs his development of the play. At this level the ground of action is not the schoolroom, figured in chivalric romance; it is rather the loosely platonic ground of being itself, upon which we are invited to watch, through Science's disappointment at what seems to be the inconstancy of Wit, the yearning of an ideal form to come into being in the world. Wit, too, strikes roots down to that ground, for by definition he represents merely the set of mental abilities that can achieve knowledge. Thus, like Science, he too is unrealized before their marriage. Wit's love for Science, which, in the thesis, figures the schoolboy's desire for knowledge, figures at this deeper level the intuitive yearning of the mind to realize its potentiality—in effect, to come into being. That point is immanent but not explicit in *Wit and Science,* perhaps because the manuscript is defective at the beginning and we lack the initial discussion between Wit and Reason about the nature of Wit's feeling for Science. But the implication is sufficiently clear that we can draw on the first scene of *The Marriage of Wit and Science* to flesh it out.

In this later play the feeling described as Wit's love for Science is at first a sense of dissatisfaction, a longing to be settled somewhere. "So run I to a fro with hap such as I find," Wit complains to his mother, Nature;[9] "Now fast, now loose: now hot, now cold: inconstant as that wind." He feels himself in love, he says, but weakly so. What he chiefly wants is for nature to "settle this unsettled head in some assured place: / To lead me through the thick, to guide me all the way, / To point me where I may achieve my most desired prey" (p. 326). But that is beyond her power, Nature explains. Wit must achieve his desires on his own. Her role is limited to implanting desire, and in that role she serves as the agent of God,

> That hath received unto his disposition
> The soul of man, which he of special love
> To gifts of grace and learning eke doth move.
> . . . .
> He makes the frame, and I receive it so,
> No jot therein altered for my head;
> And as I receive it, I let it go,
> Causing therein such sparkles to be bred
> As he commits to me, by whom I must be led.
>   [P. 329]

Wit's love for Science is one of those "sparkles," a desire implanted by Nature in the service of God. It is an intuitive glimpse of a role to which he is called by God through Nature. Thus, in pursuing Science, Wit pursues as well the completed form of his own being.

Only when he possesses Science can Wit be Wit, and only when she is possessed by Wit can Science be Science. The sexual connotations of that verb or any other we might choose to express their normative relationsip are inescapable; for Wit and Science, in fact as well as in the fable, are male and female, each the enabling complement of the other. Recognizing that, we can recognize the precise and traditional logic in Redford's use of the figure of marriage to represent the accomplishment of education, the union of intellectual capacity and knowledge. It is not at first a romantic figure, although, once adopted, it naturally attracts romantic colors. It comes rather from an unforced analogy between the realizations of intellectual and sexual identity. It is thus a product of the same order, if not degree, of imagination that we find in the myths of Adam and Eve or Cupid and Psyche. We ought not, then, to seek the roots of Redford's erotic metaphors in the literature of *amoure courtoise,* where those of the *Pastime of Pleasure* are to be found, nor should we accept too easily their absorption into what we ordinarily think of as erotic literature.

Perhaps more to the point, we need to recognize that the logic behind this part of Redford's fable is not the logic of his thesis. Images of love and marriage are, at best, appropriate vehicles for Redford's insistence that the quest for knowledge must be informed by reason and guided by instruction, just as they are appropriate vehicles for Hawes' allegory; however, they are not produced by it. The figures arise rather from the groundwork of assumptions Redford makes about the nature of the mind and knowledge and of their complementary relationship. While he does not explicitly pursue these assumptions in developing the fable, the lines along which he does develop it are clearly informed by them. And at one point at least, when Science rejects the World's gifts, we can understand the fable only by striking down to those assumptions. Our consideration of Science's motives has thus given us a purchase on what we might call the mythic structure of the play, the network of basic hypotheses that are articulated in Redford's thesis and embodied in the metaphors of his fable. We can strengthen that purchase if we take up again the question of Wit's normative role.

If what I have said thus far is accurate, Redford imagines Wit in just the way that such poems as *Reason and Sensuality, The*

Pilgrimage of the Life of Man, and *Parabola I* imagine the pilgrim, and with just the same consequences. Insofar as Wit's love for Science figures the natural yearning of the mind to realize its potentiality in the possession of knowledge, it is of a piece both with the prenatal vision Deguileville's pilgrim has of the New Jerusalem, where he may return to himself in God,[10] and with Nature's prodding of the indolent pilgrim at the beginning of *Reason and Sensuality.* Each represents man's intuitive perception of the state in which he may be most fully realized, and, in the metaphors of the poems, each results in a journey toward that state. When Nature appears to the pilgrim in *Reason and Sensuality,* he is lying in bed, luxuriating in the warmth of the springtime. His sensuous indulgence angers her because she has provided an ideal pattern of behavior for men, a normative form in which their humanity consists and toward which they must aspire if they are to be fully human. Alone among creation, she explains, man possesses "understandyng and reson, / By whiche of ryght, with-oute shame, / Of a man he beareth the name" (724–26). That "clere intelligence" distinguishes him from beasts, "and of nature ys resemblable / To goddys that be pardurable" (729–30). In order to realize the nature of his own being, she warns him, he must embrace the powers that are peculiarly his against the "sensitive intelligence" he shares with beasts; only thus can he pursue the opening onto the divine provided by the fact that he was made in the image of God. According to Nature, then, man's very identity as a man depends on his fulfilling the divine potentialities of his reason, to which he is called by God through Nature. Those who do not do so "falsly wirke ageynes kynde" (860).

The consequence for those who work against nature is, of course, the loss of their human identity, which is figured in the poem by the loss of their human image. So Diana warns the Young Man that those who have strayed from the path of reason and entered Venus' Garden have there been fed drinks through which they "ytourned weren to lyknesse / Of bestys and, maked bestial, / Lost hir reson natural. / Thynke wel thereon," she warns him, "this was the fyn, / Some wer asses, somme swyn, / To foxes fals and engynous, / And to wolves ravynouse, / And yet wel wors peraventure" (3424–31).

Venus' Garden, in its capacity to metamorphose those who enter it from their natural human forms into forms that represent their true spiritual conditions, is merely one place in that figural country Saint Bernard calls the "land of unlikeness," the state of mind in which man substitutes his own sensuous interests for the interests of God and so loses the likeness of his will to the will of God. In consequence, man becomes a parody of himself; he retains, as a parody does, the skeletal configurations of the model in whose image he was made, but its form becomes blurred and distorted by his perverse inclinations. For Saint Bernard, the terrible and logical end of this process of self-caricature is the absolute loss of man's likeness to God, a perversion of the will so complete that God is unable to recognize himself in the creature he has made and, consequently, is unable to love that creature.[11]

Wit and Science does not, of course, bear the awful weight of Bernardine moral theology, nor does it really involve, except by implication and extension, matters of the ultimate state of the soul. Nevertheless, Redford does imagine Wit's educational pilgrimage within a set of coordinates similar to those that frame representations of the pilgrimage to the New Jerusalem; and with the same sort of logical astringency as Saint Bernard, he manipulates the relationship between Wit's appearance and his natural form in order to manifest Wit's progress toward the realization of himself in the possession of Science. Let me illustrate that by looking again at the middle section of the play.

THE METAMORPHOSIS OF WIT IN THE LAND OF UNLIKENESS

When Reason leaves the stage at line 288, angry because Wit would rather stay with Honest Recreation than set off again on his difficult journey, Wit enters the second stage of his pilgrimage, becoming, in Saint Bernard's phrase, "praeceps et temerarius in prosperis." His rescue by Honest Recreation, whom he finds attractive, was a piece of good fortune, and he looks back on his encounter with Tediousness only to shudder. We need to imagine a psychological state of that sort, mingling fear, relief, and delight, in order to understand why Wit decides to remain, against the advice of Reason. But perhaps it is a mistake to try; for Redford, in one of the few allegorically obscure moments in the play, provides us only with the fact that Wit does remain, and his aim is not to explain Wit's choice but simply to characterize it as unreasonable. In any event, having chosen to put off his journey, Wit has nothing to do but play, and he enters into it thoughtlessly and wholeheartedly. "He is angry," Honest Recreation says in reference to the departed Reason. "Yea, let him be," Wit replies, "I do not pass. / Come now, a basse" (289–91). Having been a devoted suitor of Lady Science, he becomes now an indiscriminate lover, floating from woman to woman. A "burlesque lover," Werner Habicht calls him, "a parody of his better self."[12] Will Honest

Recreation kiss him only "in gage of marriage"? "Marry, even so!" Wit shouts, "A bargain, lo!" (296–97). As for Lady Science, "Shall I tell you truth? / I never loved her" (300–301). A moment later, his head settled in Idleness' lap, he is delighted to find two women quarreling over him. And when he wakes, to find Lady Science onstage, after Idleness and Honest Recreation have left, he rudely demands a kiss from her, insisting, when she refuses, that "by the mass, / I will have a basse ere I hence pass!" (756–57).

This transformation in Wit's character as a lover is matched, stage for stage, by transformations in his appeareance. Before he dances with Honest Recreation, to show that he is skilled in playing, he takes off his scholar's gown and drops it on the stage. He is then no longer visibly Science's man (we can only guess at what he wears under his gown; probably it is something appropriate to a Tudor playboy but muted in color so that the fool's motley he later puts on will contrast dramatically with his scholar's black). Following the dance, he sinks into Idleness' lap, taking unawares the same supine position into which Tediousness had battered him. And there he drifts slowly into sleep, tired from his dance and lulled and rocked by Idleness. Because we see so clearly here how Idleness renders Wit insensible, more pleasantly but no less surely than Tediousness, it seems a bit superfluous for Redford to have Idleness blacken Wit's face if his point is merely to show that Wit has been "darkened" by Idleness. Wit is, after all, sound asleep. We probably would, and should, think of the dimness of Wit's wit as Idleness lovingly paints his face, for in the folk plays the dim-witted traditionally appeared with blackened faces.[13] But while Idleness' painting of Wit's face serves to characterize him at this moment, it also contributes the visible sign of this moment to the process Wit is undergoing, and thus it prepares for Wit's meeting with Science and her failure to recognize him.

Before that meeting, however, Redford has placed a scene that has puzzled critics of the play. It is the scene in which Idleness attempts to teach Ingnorancy his name, and it is puzzling because the attempt is irrelevant both to Redford's thesis and to his fable.[14] It has no consequences whatever for Wit, who is asleep throughout, and Idleness and Ingnorancy never appear again. But I think we can understand why Redford has included the scene if we remember that his dramatization of this part of the play is informed by the image of Wit's passage into the land of unlikeness.

After Idleness has blackened Wit's face, she whistles her "boy" onto the stage so that she can "play the schoolmistress" and reveal

"what doctrine by Idleness comes" (51–52). The theme of her lesson
is, as we might expect, the realization of her student's identity, and
through it Redford brings into the foreground of the action the
assumptions we have seen shaping so much of the play. Idleness will
teach Ingnorancy his name, doggedly sounding it out on his fingers,
syllable by maddening syllable, but she is defeated at every stage by
Ingnorancy's invincible self:

> IDLE: And what's half Ingland? Here's "Ing" and here's
> "land". What's this?
> ING: What's this?
> IDLE: What's this, whoreson? What's this? Here's "Ing"
> and here's "land". What's this?
> ING: 'Tis my thumb.
>
> [457–61]

The scene is staged, of course, as a parody of the major themes of the
play, much as the intercut comic scenes in a play like *Doctor Faustus*
are staged in parody of the more serious action. In its form Idleness'
lesson parodies the forms of pedagogy: memorization and recitation.
But the content of her lesson goes further to mock Wit's attempt to
realize his identity in the absence of Reason, and together the form
and content of the lesson combine to set the schoolroom, to which all
of the action ultimately refers, in the land of unlikeness, with Idleness
as Instruction and the pure and perfect blank of Ingnorancy
portraying Wit. Ingnorancy's very name indicates a void, an emptiness that, like sin, has merely nominal existence. And lacking in that
void even the consciousness of his name (so that when Idleness asks
him what he has learned, he replies "Ich cannot tell"), Ingnorancy
embodies the nonexistence toward which Wit has been traveling.
Through the peculiarly theatrical forms of the transformations in
Wit's appearance, Redford has been showing us that Wit is "traveling"
toward Ingnorancy by losing his likeness to himself and assuming a
likeness to the fool. His blackened face mirrors Ingnorancy's;
the garment of Science lies discarded on the stage; he is even, if
only momentarily, unconscious. It requires simply that he put on
Ingnorancy's motley to complete the process, and that is a step
Idleness takes for him at the end of the scene, when she puts the fool's
coat on the sleeping Wit and dresses Ingnorancy in the scholar's gown.

But Wit is merely in transit, as it were—a learned, not a natural,
fool. While he has lost his likeness to himself, he still retains, in Saint
Bernard's convenient paradox, his image, the skeletal configuration

from which his outward form has departed. Redford uses the difference in physical stature between his actors to make that point. For Wit's gown is much too big for Ingnorancy. "'Twool not bide on," the fool complains (584). And thus we may assume that Ingnorancy's motley is too small for Wit and that Idleness' protests that it fits perfectly are directed at emphasizing ironically that his new gown does not quite cover Wit.

It is at this piont, when Wit has traveled furthest from Science into the land of unlikeness and their mutual realization seems most in doubt, that Redford brings Science onstage to refuse the World's gifts because she is "a lone woman." Throughout the scene Wit lies sleeping in full view of the audience, at once present in body and absent in form. And then, when the World's messengers depart, he wakes, to be brought gradually to see that he has lost his likeness to himself. Science, of course, does not recognize him. "Who is this?" she asks when Wit approaches her. "Ingnorancy or his likeness," her mother replies, "It is much like him." Science notices a difference from Ingnorancy, however: "his tongue serveth him now trim" (733–35). And by the end of the scene she seems to have discerned the image of Wit through the likeness to Ingnorancy, for she calls him "no natural fool...but a naughty, vicious fool, / Brought up with Idleness, in her school" (798–801). Still, throughout the scene, Science and her mother profess to take Wit for Ingnorancy, though he angrily protests that he is Wit, tries to force himself upon her, and finally asks in pathetic bewilderment (as Saint Bernard's pilgrim might ask under far more urgent circumstances), "Know ye not me?" "No," Science answers, "How should I know ye?" (774). He is certainly not Wit, she says, for she has the true image of Wit, the picture he had sent her, and he is nothing like that image. Where the Wit she loves is "fair, pleasant and goodly," the fool before her is "foul, displeasant and ugly" (787–88), and she holds up Wit's picture to measure the difference between the two.

That difference functions during this section of *Wit and Science* in a way analogous to the function of distance in the pilgrimage fable. Both are visible indices of spiritual progress or regress. As we know where the pilgrim stands spiritually by where he stands in the landscape of the poem, so we know where Wit stands by what he looks like or unlike. And just as the pilgrim's wandering in the land of unlikeness is at once a measure and a cause of his exile from God and himself in God, so Wit's loss of his likeness is at once a measure of his estrangement from himself and a cause of his estrangement from

Science, in whom he must be realized. That is what Wit recognizes when he looks into the glass of Reason:

> the stark fool I play
> Before all people. Now see it I may.
> Every man I see laugh me to scorn.
> Alas, alas, that ever I was born!
> It was not for nought, now well I see,
> That those two ladies disdained me.
> [835-40]

Wit's acknowledgment of the audience's laughter comes at a fortunate point, because it reminds us that we ought not to insist too solemnly or too literally on the trope of the land of unlikeness as the informing figure of the play. *Wit and Science* is an elegant courtly comedy. But when we allow for its comic and practical accents, I think we can catch, in Wit's lament for the loss of that "lady bright, / With all those gallants seen in my sight— / Favor, Riches, yea Worship and Fame," and in his fear that now he will have only "Hatred, Beggary and Open Shame," a peculiarly humanist echo of the terrible cry of Deguileville's pilgrim when he perches, lost and frightened, on a rock in the sea of the world, where he fears he must stay forever, exiled from the New Jerusalem.

The comparison is not altogether flattering to *Wit and Science,* which looks a bit like a decadent miniature when set beside the medieval allegory. But recalling the tropes that inform Redford's fable is instructive, for in their light we can understand why he should set Wit to regain his likeness in a scene shaped around the sacrament of penance, complete with contrition, confession, and satisfaction. Like Saint Bernard's prodigal pilgrim, Wit is now "trepidus et pusillanimus in adversis." As Shame whips him, Wit kneels before Reason in the classic position of the penitent, abasing himself in language almost sacramental. "Oh, sir, forgive me, I beseech you," he cries, "Oh, sir, I am not worthy to carry / The dust out where your daughter should sit" (874, 878-79). And largely because of the charged formality of the language, when Wit is sent out at the end of the scene to be dressed in new apparel, the episode seems to draw into balance all the dimensions of the action. In the pedagogical thesis, the mind, again informed by Reason, again submits itself to instruction; in the romantic fable, the fouled suitor goes to dress before paying court to his lady once again; Wit goes to regain his likeness; the penitent pilgrim goes to put on the new robe, the outward sign that he has been made clean. And perhaps behind all of these dimensions we might see the biblical type of the penitent pilgrim, the prodigal son—upon whom Saint Bernard drew in developing his image of the land of unlikeness—welcomed home with a new robe.

The remainder of Wit's pilgrimage is simply and easily traced, for, now that Wit is back under the control of Reason and Instruction, Redford takes scarcely a hundred lines to bring him together with Science. The length of this section of the play is controlled by Redford's thesis, which is directed, as I have noted, to the conditions necessary for learning, not to the stages by which knowledge is gained. Thus Redford telescopes the process of Wit's reformation. When next we see him, Wit has almost reached his goal. He stands at the base of Parnassus, having washed his face and put on his scholar's gown and apparently having received all the instruction he is going to get—all of it offstage during forty lines of speeches by Reason and Confidence. But, brief as it is, this sequence traces Wit's progress through each of the terms in the last stage of Saint Bernard's formula. Where Wit had been "egens et insipiens" in his first encounter with Tediousness, he is now "providus." Instruction has contrived a plan that requires him to marshal his forces carefully against Tediousness, biding his time in ambush while Study and Diligence lure the giant into a trap. And Wit follows it out to the letter. The battle itself takes place offstage, its progress made evident to the audience by the descriptive shouts of the combatants. When Wit reenters with Tediousness' head upon his sword, Confidence runs in to announce that he has won Science, "body and all," and to give him, from Science, a new "Gown of Knowledge," perhaps a master's gown, which he is to put on for his marriage. That gown signifies, as it does in graduation ceremonies, that Wit is now "eruditus." And when Wit and Science are at last joined in marriage, we are to understand that Wit is, in the final term of Saint Bernard's formula, "perfectus," although his perfection lies in the domain of knowledge rather than charity and signals the assumption of his human existence rather than spiritual salvation.

The Romantic Tale of Wit and Science

The song Wit and Science sing as they come together onstage, "Welcome, My Own," is peculiarly appropriate to what I have called the mythic structure of the play, for in that structure each requires the other in order to realize himself, and thus each is precisely the creature of the other. It is also true, however, that, word by word and stanza by stanza, "Welcome, My Own" is simply a love song, not sharply confined in its application to Wit and Science, to whom it makes no reference, and certainly containing no acknowledgment of the thematic burden it may be understood to bear. That fact is worth noting, for it leads us back to something I touched on earlier and directs us to a difference between the structures of *Wit and Science* and *The Castle of Perseverance* that must now be emphasized. The difference is this: While the fable of *Wit and Science* is informed by the myth of the pilgrimage, as the thesis of the *Castle* is contained by it, that fable has sufficient density and consistency to compose a hypothetical world of its own. I said earlier that I thought Spivack was wrong in relating the erotic images of the play to erotic literature generally because these images are firmly grounded in the play's imaginative structure. But I now have to admit that in a certain sense he is right, just as Richard Southern is right in emphasizing the "very delicate, very sensitive and wholly intriguing love-affair" the play dramatizes, its "first-rate entertainment," and the "shrewd psychology of character" that Redford displays.[15] For in a certain sense the play invites us to take its metaphors almost literally. If it is true that we can understand Ingnorancy's lesson only in light of the trope of unlikeness, it is equally true that we can understand other elements of the play only with reference to the key metaphors of its fable.

Where *Wit and Science* differs from *The Castle of Perseverance,* and from earlier morality plays in general, is in its construction of dramatic images out of the logic of its fable, with only a glancing reference toward thesis or myth. We have already noted several elements in the play, both brief moments and extended sequences, that refer chiefly to the focal metaphor of courtship and marriage. In addition to "Welcome, My Own," there is also the song "Exceeding Measure," with which the World's messengers greet Lady Science at her first entrance. Unlike "When Travail Great in Matters Thick," which Honest Recreation sings to revive Wit, neither of the other songs has a distinct place in the thesis of the play. Both are intellectually detachable from the moments at which they are sung;[16] their presence is supported merely by the romantic atmosphere the fable generates around the Lady Science.

Wit's motive for rushing into battle with Tediousness, I have noted, is comprehensible only if we imagine him in his role as lover, since it requires assumptions about the Lady Science that cannot be applied to *scientia.* But Redford himself consistently makes these assumptions, for he develops his heroine with a good deal more attention to the lady than to science. If the songs I mentioned have any dramatic point, it is to serve as marks of romantic punctuation for the entrances of Lady Science, who never appears onstage without a song. And, when she does appear, it is to exhibit the complex variety of emotions of a young woman in love. At her first entrance, she is distantly polite to the World's messengers, and her mother notices an undercurrent of sadness in her address to them, a sadness that flashes momentarily into resentment when, as Favor and his companions leave the stage, Science bitterly exclaims, "Indeed small cause given to care for the World's favoring, / Seeing the wits of the world be so wavering." She is both puzzled and saddened, we learn, by Wit's failure to meet her, as Confidence had promised he would. And, at the end of the exchange with her mother, during which she has received merely the skeptical advice of an old wife about the intentions of young men, she is ready to agree that Wit is just a hasty lover, "soon hot and soon cold" (711). Thus, when Wit approaches dressed as a fool, she seizes at what seems to be a distraction. Throughout the scene that follows, as Wit tries to force himself upon her, she is by turns delighted at his oddness and bewildered by his familiarity. And when at last she begins to recognize him—"So, lo! Now I perceive ye more and more" (791)—she grows angry, shouting, as she leaves, the classic line of lovers quarrels: "Of all arrogant fools, thou art one!" (802).

This characterization of the lady, if not of science, prepares us for Reason's fears that his daughter will now have nothing to do with Wit no matter how hard he sets about to redeem himself—fears that otherwise we would not understand. For it makes no sense to imagine that *scientia* will not yield to anyone of sufficient capacity who sets about to acquire it, but it makes a good deal of sense for Reason to imagine that his daughter will resist Wit simply out of feminine whim. "His misbehavior perchance even striking / Her heart against him," Reason says, as Wit goes off to try Parnassus once more, "She now misliking— / As women oftimes will be hard-hearted— / Will be the stranger to be reverted" (917–20). These fears in turn motivate Reason's exit at line 927, where he goes off to talk with Science about Wit, thus clearing the stage for Wit's second battle with Tediousness and preparing for Reason's formal reentrance later as a member of Science's company. As it bears upon Science and Reason, this whole sequence of action is significant only within the premises of the fable.

Even with the few examples I have given here, it is clear that no single category—neither thesis, myth, nor fable—is adequate to explain even the linear development of *Wit and Science,* let alone all of the dimensions of its structure. The play takes its form from all three sets of premises, all three of them at work simultaneously, although now one and now another is most prominent as we move from scene to scene. During the middle section of the play, when Redford sets out the second stage of his thesis, his development of the transformation of Wit without Reason is distinctly informed by the image of the land of unlikeness, and in many ways the mythic substructure of the play seems here quite close to its surface. But following Wit's encounter with Science and his reclamation of his lost likeness, the premises of the fable seem to be most prominent, although the relative brevity of this section of the play is a consequence of the emphases of Redford's thesis, and in developing it he continues to shape the union of Wit and Science so as to reveal the complementary relationship between knowledge and the mind.

Clearly, then, the notion that a morality play is a *sermo corporeus,* accessible only to rhetorical analyses, begins to break down in *Wit and Science,* chiefly because in *Wit and Science* the metaphorical *exempla* of the sermon come together in a continuous fable that makes demands of its own on the conduct of the action. Certainly the moral interlude is a limited and limiting form. But within that form *Wit and Science* is an extraordinary play, far more complex, more dense, more imaginatively precise than the term "humanist morality" might suggest. What is perhaps most extraordinary about it, however, is the fact that the considerable imaginative energy it embodies was expended, so far as we know, for the sake of a single performance, and its author took it so lightly that he left the text only in a copybook. In its own way, that, too, is a minor triumph of courtly style.

T H R E E
Richard II and the *Imago Regis*

As we are his body's counterfeit,
So will we be the image of his mind.

[*Woodstock,* 2. 1. 93–94]

MORALITIES AND HISTORIES

Even the earliest moralities imply the themes and arguments of
Elizabethan history plays; for in setting out to induce their audiences
to have contempt for the pleasures of this world, morality playwrights
naturally constructed arguments that the things of this world cannot
be trusted, especially at their best. Their touchstone is the biblical
question "What does it profit a man if he gain the whole world and
lose his soul?" To show that it is no profit at all, the author of *The
Castle of Perseverance* arranges to give Mankind all of the delights of
worldly favor before he is cut down by Death's dart and made to
realize that his happiness requires more than this world's blessing. In
that respect even the most remote and formulaic morality plays touch
on the problems involved in the uses and limits of temporal power.
Youth's boast that he is "the heir of all my father's land. / It is come
into my hand: / I care for no more" (*The Interlude of Youth,* 56–58) is
everyman's moral expression of the beginning of a process of thought
and feeling whose inevitable and disillusioned end is expressed by a
host of naïve rulers, among them Shakespeare's King Lear:

> They flattered me like a dog, and told me I had white
> hairs in my beard ere the black ones were there. To say
> "ay" and "no" to everything I said! When the rain came to
> wet me once and the wind to make me chatter; when the
> thunder would not peace at my bidding, there I found 'em,
> there I smelt 'em out. Go to, they are not men o' their
> words: They told me I was everything: 'tis a lie, I am
> not ague-proof.

[4. 6. 97–109]

Thus it was natural for those who first put history and politics on the stage (Skelton, Lyndsay, Bale) to do so in forms provided by the morality drama, since the problems of kings in managing power are merely local instances of the universal problems of Mankind in managing his worldly life. The story of Magnificence or the historical example of King John are illustrations *a fortiori* of the story of Mankind. That is why almost all serious history plays are tragic, at least in implication. For in a Christian view worldly pomp and power must betray their possessors, yet kings are, by virtue of their roles, committed to their possession. Only those kings, like Henry V, who can accept the tragic limits of power can escape the contradictions encircled by the crown and avoid the failure they usually ensure. Hall reports that to Henry the crown was not an honor but an "onorarious charge and daily burden" under which he suffered.[1] Otherwise the kings of dramatic history err on the side of the *naïf,* to whom the endurance of crowns implies the immortality of kings (Tamburlaine, Richard II, King Lear); or they try to abandon the role in which they have been cast in favor of a vision of private sanctity (Henry VI) or private pleasure (Edward II), and, in the process, they betray their communities to the suffering that comes from having a ruler who will not rule and lose their own identities as well.

In either case, whether they involve monarchs who would be private men or those who do not understand that they are private men, the tragedies of dramatic kings ultimately involve questions of identity. For their almost insoluble problem is to combine the public and the private—to be neither Richard, nor Edward, nor Henry, nor king but to be, rather, King Richard, King Edward, King Henry—and the tragic feeling proper to such a king is the feeling of identity lost, of namelessness. "What are kings when regiment is gone," asks Marlowe's Edward II, "But perfect shadows on a sunshine day?"

But there is another reason why the earliest historical playwrights found the forms of the morality drama congenial, and it helps to explain why the Renaissance history play is rarely as amply tragic as the foregoing suggests it might have been. This is the fact that the morality provided a ready-made argumentative vocabulary to play-wrights whose ends were polemical rather than theatrical. It was not really until Marlowe that kings were dispassionately represented. Bale's target was the Counter-Reformation, not the paradoxical nature of power, and Sackville's and Norton's was the question of succession. In their theater the Renaissance history play was shaped into a polemical form in which the narrow rhetorical habits of the moralities, their ability to express concepts directly and unequivocally, were exploited while their tragic insights on power were left largely untouched. In their place we have detailed analyses of the intellectual, moral, and political errors of kings and their courtiers—errors that prudence could have led them to avoid. Bale, for example, setting out in *Kyng Johan* to argue that Henry VIII's Reformation was the glorious conclusion of a long-fought battle for independence, waged by England against the Roman church, can dramatize the significance of historical events by having his characters shift between historical names and the labels of personifications. The papal legate to King John is impersonated by Sedition; this clarifies Bale's polemical thesis that the power of the church is universally exercised through civil strife and that the historical Stephen Langton was simply an embodiment of the spirit of sedition itself.

To this extent, the story of the moral history play in the middle of the sixteenth century belongs as much to the history of partisan rhetoric as to the history of drama, and Skelton and Bale and Udall perhaps deserve to be treated more often in the company of More and Cranmer and Hooker than as forerunners of Marlowe and Shakespeare. Nevertheless, the combination of historical incident and morality form made by Skelton and the others did bear fruit in the professional theater of the 1590s in a rich and supple drama in which the ironic relationships between everyman and the king, implied as early as *The Castle of Perseverance,* were fully explored, and the mere facts of history were given a significant, if often unhistorical, form. The play I want to examine in this chapter is one of the earliest, one of the clearest, and one of the best of the secular and unpolemical moral history plays, *Thomas of Woodstock.*

Historical Fact and Morality Form
Thomas of Woodstock deals with the reign of Richard II from about the time of Richard's marriage to Anne of Bohemia in 1382 until the arrest and murder of Richard's uncle Thomas of Woodstock, the duke of Gloucester, in 1397. Like *Wit and Science, Woodstock* has survived only in a single and defective manuscript (some pages at the end are lacking). We have no evidence that it was ever printed, but the evidence that it was performed is a good bit more substantial than that for the earlier play. For while *Woodstock* is itself clearly dependent on the second part of Shakespeare's *Henry VI,* Shakespeare's *Richard II* is in turn clearly dependent on *Woodstock,* and in ways

that suggest that Shakespeare assumed that his audience was familiar with it. For example, a rumor reported by Holinshed that Richard had farmed out the realm to his flatterers is taken in *Woodstock* to be a fact and is elaborately dramatized. That translation of historical rumor into dramatic fact is then assumed in *Richard II*, and the farming of the realm is included in the catalogue of Richard's political sins. As A. P. Rossiter has pointed out, the complaints of Gaunt and York about that and Richard's other abuses are "barely graspable... unless we know *Woodstock* or are edified from without in some other way."[2] And that is true as well of the character of Thomas of Woodstock himself, for it was chiefly in *Woodstock* that the baron whom Holinshed describes as "fierce of nature, hastie, wilfull, and given more to war than to peace"[3] was transformed into the man Shakespeare's Gaunt later calls a "plain, well-meaning soul." The duke of Gloucester everyone remembers at the beginning of *Richard II* was a dramatic rather than a historical character. And if his transformation was accomplished, as Wolfgang Keller first suggested,[4] by modeling Woodstock on the plain and well-meaning Duke Humphrey of Gloucester in *2 Henry VI*, we can assume that *Woodstock* was written sometime between 1591 and 1594.

The history of *Woodstock* itself is a good bit simpler than the history of the period it dramatizes, and the author of *Woodstock* has so freely reduced the events of that period to an order they never had that in one respect at least it may not seem to be a history play at all. For many of the events in *Woodstock* either never happened or happened quite differently, and many of the characters have been as radically transformed from their historical counterparts as Thomas of Woodstock himself. In giving dramatic form to the pivotal years of Richard's reign, the author of *Woodstock* has collapsed into one action two historically distinct but essentially similar episodes in which the older aristocrats rose against unworthy favorites at Richard's court. Robert Tresilian, Richard's lord chief justice in 1388, who, along with other early favorites of Richard, was driven from the court by a group of nobles headed by the duke of Gloucester, is made contemporary with Richard's later favorites of 1399, Sir William Scroope, Sir John Bushy, Sir William Bagot, and Sir Henry Greene. It was of them that the "common brute ran that the king had set to farm the realm of England,"[5] and the author of *Woodstock* makes Tresilian the inventor of the scheme, though it was hatched, if at all, ten years after his death. In the same fashion, the historical Tresilian is given dramatic revenge on his old enemy. For Tresilian is made responsible for the device in the play by which Woodstock is kidnapped and murdered by a group of masquers, though in fact, nine years before his own arrest, Woodstock had "caused [Tresilian] forthwith to be had to the tower, and from thence drawne to Tiburne, and there hanged."[6]

But while the facts of *Woodstock* are only nominally historical, the form of *Woodstock* is essentially historical; that is, it at least embodies a reasonable interpretation of history, to which it reduces facts in order to clarify their logic. That interpretation derives from Holinshed's summary of the tragedy of Richard II, which probably seemed less simple to the author of *Woodstock* than it may to us, for we have had the advantage of Shakespeare's later and more ample formulation. As Holinshed understood Richard's career, he was "deprived of all kinglie honour and princelie dignitie, by reason he was so given to follow evill counsell, and used such inconvenient waies and meanes, through insolent misgovernance, and youthfull outrage, though otherwise a right noble and woorthie prince."[7] The play stops short of Richard's deposition and death, unless a good many more pages are missing from the end than its editors believe; but it otherwise chooses characters and incidents from Richard's reign and shapes them to clarify the pattern of his career set forth by Holinshed. The clearest example of its methods is the transformation of Thomas of Woodstock from historical person to dramatic character.

In *Woodstock* Richard's favorites are opposed by a party made up of the duke of Lancaster, the duke of York, and the earl of Arundell, the lord admiral, but their chief opponent is Thomas of Woodstock. Woodstock's preeminence in that group is attested by history; he was in fact the leader of the baronial party that forced Richard's favorite ministers from the court in 1388, and for a dozen years he was Richard's chief political enemy. But his dramatic character owes little to history. What one gathers from Holinshed is that the historical Woodstock was a proud, vengeful, and, at last, fatally reckless man. Richard ordered him arrested and put to death, Holinshed reports, when he learned that Woodstock had conspired with a group of barons "to take king Richard, the dukes of Lancaster & Yorke, and commit them to prison, and all other lords of the king's counsell they determined shuld be drawne and hanged."[8] In the play, however, Woodstock is absolutely blameless. Richard agrees to Tresilian's plan to have him kidnapped and murdered because "Plain Thomas" has refused to lend his moral authority to the use of blank charters for extorting money from the commons. Woodstock's office in the play, that of lord protector, given to him by the playwright though he never held it in life, is emblematic of the role in which the playwright casts him: as conservator of the crown, even against Richard, and conservator of the best interests of the nation against Richard's friends. In the course of the play, the coat of "simple frieze" he customarily wears acquires the status of a theatrical symbol of the simplicity and plain dealing that mark his character and qualify him for that role. "Plain Thomas," York says of him just before his entrance in act 1, "by th' rood so all men call him / For his plain dealing, and his simple clothing: / Let others jet in silk and gold, says he, / A coat of English frieze, best pleaseth me." (1. 1. 99–102). And, just before he is murdered in act 5, we are given a last glimpse of his selfless plain dealing. While the murderers are preparing to enter his cell, Woodstock sits writing to Richard,

> Not to entreat, but to admonish him
> That he forsake his foolish ways in time
> And learn to govern like a virtuous prince:
> Call home his wise and reverend councillors,
> Thrust from his court those cursed flatterers
> That hourly work the realm's confusion.
> This counsel if he follow may in time
> Pull down those mischiefs that so fast do climb.
>   [5. 1. 185–92]

In short, the playwright has transformed Woodstock into a character whose most prominent and consistent traits are precisely opposite to those that led to Richard's fall. Where Richard was disposed to "follow evill counsell," to "insolent misgovernance, and youthful outrage," Woodstock is good counsel itself, with the wisdom and responsible prudence suited to someone a generation older than Richard. Incidental details may have been modeled on Duke Humphry in *2 Henry VI,* but in the fundamental design of his character Woodstock is the product of a dialectical dramatic method rooted in the morality drama, a method that seeks to throw moral qualities into high relief by measuring them at every stage against their opposites. Insofar as he embodies the spiritual and political qualities that Richard ought to embrace if he is to be a successful king, Woodstock was created by the same sort of dramatic thought that created Humility and Charity in *The Interlude of Youth* as *remedia* for Youth's attraction to Riot.

Bushy and Bagot and Greene might be understood in much the same way and with even less violence to the facts of history. Except for Sir John Bushy, who was speaker in the Parliament of 1397 that tried Woodstock's coconspirators and who is described by Holinshed as "an exceeding cruell man, ambitious and covetous beyond measure,"[9] they are all shadowy figures in Holinshed's *Chronicles,* mere names in the lists of names of those who had wrongfully influenced the king. But the author of *Woodstock* has shaped those names into dramatic characters who clarify in relatively unmixed forms the insolent misgovernance and youthful outrage toward which Richard was drawn. "Embrace us, gentlemen," Richard cries at the beginning of act 2, just after he has turned from his uncles to Bushy, Bagot, and Greene. "Your youths are fitting to our tender years / And such shall beautify our princely throne" (2. 1. 2–5). They are all carefully individuated, just as the members of Woodstock's baronial party are; but corporately, as a dramatic group, Bushy, Bagot, and Greene are set to play Riot to Woodstock's Charity. And between them, the object of their constant attention, Richard Plantagenet is cast as Youth.

I do not intend to collapse *Woodstock* into a morality play or to suggest that it is in any precise way indebted to *The Interlude of Youth* or any other morality. Indeed, I will argue in a moment that if we allow the notion of the morality play to figure too prominently in our final conception of *Woodstock,* we not only impoverish the play but may also find ourselves in the curious position of maintaining that the ends of virtue are vicious. That may be true enough for a character like Malvolio in a play like *Twelfth Night,* but it is altogether too delicately ironic for *Woodstock,* which aims at the less epigrammatic point that good men may sometimes be disastrously shortsighted precisely as a result of their most conspicuous virtues. The fact is that the author of *Woodstock* understands his history in a way richer and more variegated than the dramatic thought of a play like *The Interlude of Youth* would allow. He is not a morality playwright giving theatrical substance to doctrine. He is engaged in the poetic task of discovering the universal patterns that hold particular events together, of giving intelligible dramatic form to history. But it is true, nonetheless, that he has built his dramatization of history on a morality scaffold, modeling Richard's political career and those who took part in it on the forms of Mankind's spiritual biography.

The most significant relationships between *Woodstock* and the morality drama are not so much matters of technique as they are matters of thought, of the logic of action, the construction of characters, and the conception of the relationship between the way in

which a king is related to the political community in a history play
and the way in which Mankind is related to the theatrical "country"
he inhabits in a morality play. In each case the ground on which the
action takes place is in important ways the soul of the central
character himself. That is clear enough in the indefinite space of a
morality play, where the will of man simply chooses between the
different promptings of his own heart, clearly labeled as such. When
Youth abandons Riot for Humility, that is an action taken within his
own soul, externalized and given the theatrical form of the stage
itself. When Richard II abandons his uncles for Bushy, Bagot, and
Greene, however, he may seem to do so in the realistic theatrical space
of a royal court, populated by discrete characters. But there is a sense
in which that court is as much the ground of Richard's soul as the
indefinite space of the moralities is the ground of Youth's soul.

Ernst Kantorowicz has pointed out that in Elizabethan political
and legal theory kings were regularly imagined to have two bodies:
one, in the language of an Elizabethan lawyer, is his "body
natural...subject to all the infirmities that come by Nature or
Accident, to the imbecility of Infancy or Old Age, and to the like
Defects that happen to the natural Bodies of other People"; the
second is a "body Politic...that cannot be seen or handled, consisting
of Policy and Government, and constituted for the Direction of the
People, and the management of the Public Weal."[10] The king's
second body is thus the form of the political community itself. Its
institutions and offices are his limbs, articulating his political spirit as
the limbs of the natural body articulate the soul. And *in propria
persona* he is its will, just as Youth is the will of the moral body that
constitutes the world of *The Interlude of Youth*. According to this
model, the king is a twin person, at once individual and corporate,
mortal and immortal, king and King; the king's natural body inhabits
for a time the King's Body Politic.

It is this model of the king's two bodies, one individual the other
corporate, that Woodstock has in mind in act 1 when he identifies
those who flatter the king's natural body as wanton humors infecting
his Body Politic; and he and York go on to speak of eliminating
individuals from the government in terms of purging the King's Body.
"Good brother," Woodstock tells York,

> WOOD.:   I have found out the disease:
> When the head aches, the body is not healthful.
> King Richard's wounded with a wanton humour,

Lulled and secured by flattering sycophants;
But 'tis not deadly yet, it may be cured:
Some vein let blood—where the corruption lies,
And all shall heal again.
YORK: Then lose no time, lest it grow ulcerous.
The false Tresilian, Greene, and Bagot
Run naught but poison, brother, spill them all.
[1. 1. 142–51]

Just as the action of a morality play is set within the soul of Mankind, the action of *Woodstock* is set within the extended body of the King. As the lines just quoted indicate, the principal concern of the play is the political health of that body. And that health depends on the state of its will, the king *in propria persona*.

At the beginning of the play Richard hangs "as yet in ballaunce," undecided between the promptings of his political motives. Like all the pilgrims we have considered, he is naturally inclined toward the fulfillment of his own identity. That inclination is tacitly imaged from the first in quite traditional ways, for Richard is said to look like the Black Prince, his father, the model of chivalric virtue. And later on, when he hears the story of his father's heroism, he vows to perfect in himself his father's image by acquiring his father's virtues. "As we are his body's counterfeit," he assures Bushy, "So will we be the image of his mind" (2. 1. 93–94). His love for Anne à Beame reveals in another way the direction of his natural inclinations and their form, for Anne is steadily conceived by the playwright as the embodied voice of political responsibility. Their marriage—between a king newly come into his inheritance and a princess who embodies the proper valuation of it—thus has something of the emblematic quality of the marriage of Wit and Science. And Richard's subsequent neglect of Anne and what she values provides a continuing image of the paradoxical blend of right nobility and youthful outrage in which Holinshed located his tragedy. Still, in act 1, Woodstock has good reason to believe that "this so noble and religious princess / Will mildly calm his headstrong youth to see / And shun those stains that blur his majesty" (1. 1. 185–87). But Richard's affection for Anne is made to compete with his boyish delight in all the immediate sensuous pleasures in which Bushy, Bagot, and Greene entangle him, and under their influence his intention to perfect in action the image of his father in which he was made is turned to vainglorious displays.

Richard is thus set by the playwright in a place worn smooth by generations of pilgrims. He is, in Saint Bernard's phrase "egens et insipiens," drawn contrarily by responsibility and indulgence, charity and cupidity, the realization of himself as a king in the rule of his kingdom and the loss of his identity through self-deposition. And in spite of Woodstock's confidence that he will mature into "a king loving and kind," we are led to understand in the opening scene that Richard has already gone some distance along the path to the land of unlikeness. For Bushy, Bagot, and Greene, who will "alter the kingdom" when Richard finally gives himself to their direction, are already sure enough of his favor that they have tried to poison Lancaster, York, and Arundell. The incident, which has some historical basis in an aborted plot to poison Woodstock in 1386, reveals the vulnerability and relative powerlessness of the traditional institutions of Richard's Body Politic. For Woodstock warns his brothers that they may not act directly against Richard's minions, however certain they may be of their guilt, because "Fruit that grows high is not securely plucked, / We must use ladders and by steps ascend / Till by degrees we reach the altitude" (173–75). Thus, even as Woodstock goes on to assure them that Richard's marriage will bring him back to his senses, we can see in his image of climbing cautiously up to the precarious heights of Richard's lowborn flatterers the emerging outlines of that "topsy-turvy turned" world to be created at the end of act 1, when Richard confirms his affection for Bushy, Bagot, and Greene by giving over to them the direction of his corporate body.

The occasion for that gift is the celebration of Richard's marriage to Anne, during the course of which Woodstock lectures him on the waste of his resources until Richard can finally take it no longer: "We shall ere long be past protectorship," he warns Woodstock, and, until then,

> Young Henry Greene shall be Lord Chancellor,
> Bagot, Lord Keeper of our privy seal,
> Tresilian, learned in our kingdom's laws,
> Shall be Chief Justice: by them and their directions
> King Richard will uphold his government.
> [1. 3. 184–88]

As Richard angrily leaves the stage with his new counselors, we learn immediately that "the men of Kent and Essex do rebel" (233)—"the fruit," Woodstock explains, "thy lewd licentious willfulness hath sown" (239). What the playwright seems to have had in mind was the Peasants' Revolt of 1381, which did break out in Kent and Essex over the issue of a tax to finance adventures in France.[11] But while it has some historical foundation, the rebellion that follows Richard's investiture of his friends really occurs in the conceptual kingdom of his Body Politic, where space and time no more intervene between cause and event than they do in *The Castle of Perseverance*.

Richard's new chief justice, Robert Tresilian, has a special place among Richard's counselors, and the author of *Woodstock* has done some juggling with historical fact to give it to him. In the play, Bushy, Bagot, and Greene seem to have introduced Tresilian to Richard, and it is they who have urged that he be made chief justice. But in fact Robert Tresilian's tenure in that office long predated their influence. His name is woven through Holinshed's account of the early years of Richard's reign as a loyal member of the king's party and a severe judge, harsh in his treatment of the commons but pliant in bending the law to Richard's interests. The different faces he presented to the king and the commons may indeed have been what commended him to the playwright, for there is a certain essential accuracy in the portrait of him given in *Woodstock*. His role in the events of the play may be historically false, but the man who promises Greene that he will "screw and wind the subtle law / To any fashion that shall like you best," and then sends his man Nimble off to search out privy whisperers among the commons and to arrest those who even whistle dissent, is faithful to the form of Tresilian's career.[12] At the same time, the role he is given in the events of the play clarifies the form of Richard's career. Tresilian was not in fact introduced to Richard by Bushy, Bagot, and Greene or urged by them as chief justice. But as the author of *Woodstock* understands Richard's career, it was his youth, his fondness for easy sensuous indulgence over harsh responsibility, that led him to the perversions of the law for which Tresilian is here made responsible. So in that sense Tresilian was virtually introduced to Richard by Greene, just as Pride was introduced to Youth by Riot, or Courtly Abusion was introduced to Skelton's Magnificence by Fancy.

Richard's uncles lump Tresilian together with Bushy, Bagot, and Greene, but the author of *Woodstock,* like a morality playwright, is careful to keep them visually distinct. Only Tresilian wears a beard, and, though Greene insists that being clean-shaven is the badge of the king's party, the playwright will not let him shave it off. Of course Robert Tresilian hardly belonged to the Party of Youth, having been a Fellow of Exeter College, Oxford, some thirteen years before Richard was born; but his visual distinction, like everything else about him, clarifies a conceptual rather than a factual point. He is the head of the legal corruption of Richard's Body Politic, as Bushy, Bagot, and Greene are corporately the head of its spiritual corruption. He is in one sense their minion, since he depends for his office on their influence; but once he is in place as chief justice, he embodies a separate branch of Richard's degeneration, and one not dismissible as youthful folly.

In his definition of characters and their relationships, then, the author of *Woodstock* worked steadily and in detail to rearrange historical facts to provide dramatic and theatrical substance for what he took from Holinshed to be the significant form of Richard's political career. In spite of the counsel of his uncles, Richard transforms himself in vanity and luxury through Bushy, Bagot, and Greene, and through Tresilian he transforms his Body Politic by perverting its laws. That word *transform* is not merely a figure of speech, for the author of *Woodstock* imagined Richard's fall as the loss of his likeness to himself, and the dramatic images in which he gives that action substance are "realistic" counterparts of the purely symbolic images of *Wit and Science*.

RICHARD II AND THE *Imago Regis*

In its verbally most explicit form the theme of Richard's transformation turns on his resemblance to his father. Lancaster brings up the subject at the beginning of the play, just after he and York have learned from Woodstock of the plot to poison them, and he dwells at some length on the *differences* between Richard and the Black Prince. Woodstock has a "heavy charge," Lancaster says,

> To be protector to so wild a prince
> So far degenerate from his noble father,[13]
> . . . .
> But heaven forestalled his diadem on earth
> To place him with a royal crown in heaven.
> Rise may his dust to glory! Ere he'd 'a done
> A deed so base unto his enemy
> Much less unto the brothers of his father
> He'd first have lost his royal blood in drops,
> Dissolved the strings of his humanity,
> And lost that livelihood that was preserved
> To make his (unlike) son a wanton king.
> [1. 1. 27–45]

The parentheses around that word "unlike" in the manuscript indicate that it is to be pronounced with special rhetorical emphasis—

in a saddened tone of voice, Rossiter suggests.[14] And throughout the play Richard's uncles continue to underline and to regret the differences between Richard and his father.

Richard himself, however, is struck more by their similarities. At the beginning of act 2, as he sits listening to Bushy read from the chronicles of his father's exploits at the Battle of Poitiers—how with an army of only 7,750 men he encountered a French force of 68,000 "and in one hour got the victory"(2. 1. 78)—Richard's imagination is stirred by his extravagant heroism. He resolves to be like his father in more than just appearance, although, characteristically, he seems to believe that his father's military skill and success were largely matters of luck. Indeed, the substance of chivalric virtue escapes him entirely, and he sees only the personal advantage to be gained from reputation. He has been fuming over his quarrel with his uncles at the end of act 1, and when he hears of his father's heroism he thinks first of how his uncles would not dare frustrate him if only he were a hero:

> O princely Edward, had thy son such hap,
> Such fortune and success to follow him,
> His daring uncles and rebellious peers
> Durst not control and govern as they do.

It is then that he makes his vow:

> But these bright shining trophies shall awake me,
> And as we are his body's counterfeit,
> So will we be the image of his mind,
> And die but we'll attain his virtuous deeds.
> [88–95]

And, almost immediately, Richard gets a chance to put his new resolution into practice.

As Bushy goes on reading in the chronicle, he finds what he seems to have been looking for all along, the account of Richard's birth on the third of April, 1365.[15] When Richard hears the date, he realizes that he is twenty-one years old, already "past protectorship"—as Bushy intended that he should. "Shut up thy book, good Bushy," he says immediately, "Bagot, Greene, / King Richard in his throne will now be seen. / This day I'll claim my right, my kingdom's due. / Our uncles well shall know they but intrude: / For which we'll smite their base ingratitude" (115–19).

In the scene following, while Richard toys with his uncles, preparatory to dismissing them from their offices and banishing them from the court, the playwright in turn toys with Richard's intention to mark out his own place in the chronicles. His uncles have come to get him to confirm a parliament called to deal with the uprisings in Essex and Kent—uprisings we heard about at the end of act 1. But before Richard will answer them, he insists that they first resolve an appeal from an heir who has been cheated out of his inheritance of three crowns by a rich man. The story he tells them has been trumped up out of self-pity—Richard is the heir, and the crowns are those of England, Ireland, and France—and throughout the charade Richard hugs to himself the secret of his joke. But York is eager to take seriously any evidence of Richard's responsibleness, however slight, and he seizes on the little story in order to promise Richard fame greater than his father's, or his father's father's, in return for his compassion: "Such deeds as *this* will make King Richard shine / Above his famous predecessor Kings / If thus he labour to establish right" (2. 2. 78–80). Thus when Richard, smirking with the air of a child who has made fools of his elders and is about to turn them out, reveals that he is himself the hero of his story, his triumph has already been diminished and set within a critical framework by York's pathetic wish that he were a hero indeed. And it is further diminished by Woodstock's puzzled sadness that Richard should "thus have doubled with his friends": "Was this the trick, sweet prince! Alack the day... / The right I hold, even with my heart I render / And wish your grace had claimed it long ago: / Thou 'dst rid my age of mickle care and woe" (93–97).

We have much the same image of Richard, standing small on what he imagines to be a pinnacle rivaling his father's, when he finally does stake out his place in the chronicles at the beginning of act 3. He has now assumed his throne, banished his uncles, and deliberated with his new council about altering the kingdom, and he turns to show off his new glories to Anne, imagining how grand it will all look to history:

> My royal tables richly furnished
> Where every day I feast ten thousand men:
> To furnish out which feast I daily spend
> Thirty fat oxen and three hundred sheep,
> With fish and fowl in numbers numberless.
> Not all our chronicles shall point a king
> To match our bounty, state, and royalty.
> Or let *all* our successors yet to come
> Strive to exceed me...and if they forbid it,
> Let records say, Only King Richard did it.
>   [3. 1. 84–93]

That conversion of the Battle of Poitiers into the Feast of Westminster is the ironic fulfillment of Richard's vow to be the image of his father's mind.

The progressive loss of the heroic image of the Black Prince in Richard's vain luxury—all the while that Richard imagines he is perfecting the image—is, however, only the most obvious part of a broad and deep network of figures concerned with changes in the appearance of Richard's natural body and his Body Politic. Indeed, in the course of the play, as Richard follows the promptings of Bushy, Bagot, and Greene on the one side and Tresilian on the other, he himself gradually disappears, much as Wit disappears under the influence of Idleness, but with this difference: the rhetoric of *Woodstock* is obliquely "realistic" where that of *Wit and Science* is directly symbolic.

Richard's disappearance begins in the middle of act 2, when he throws off the protectorship, dismisses his uncles from their offices, and turns the guidance of his Body Politic over to his minions, whose "youths are fitting to our tender years." For Woodstock, Richard's action in establishing a government of the young is precisely unnatural, the equivalent, in the political community, of overturning nature's most fundamental orders:

> Shall England, that so long was governed
> By grave experience, of white-headed age,
> Be subject *now* to rash, unskilful boys?
> Then force the sun run backward to the east,
> Lay Atlas' burden on a pygmy's back,
> Appoint the sea his times to ebb and flow;
> All that as easily may be done as this....
> [2. 2. 146–52]

We need not appeal to Tudor political metaphysics to see what he means, for the play makes visible the perversion of basic natural processes in Richard himself. As soon as Woodstock, Lancaster, and York leave the stage, Richard and his minions bubble with schemes for transforming the kingdom. Most of them are schoolboy jokes, inspired by the bravado that comes from releasing the tension of Richard's confrontation with Woodstock. It is at this point that Greene suggests they make wearing a beard an act of treason, and, when that gets a laugh, he pushes the joke a bit further: "Pox on't, we'll not have a beard amongst us; we'll shave the country and the city too, shall we not, Richard?" (178–79). There is no one on stage to protest, as Shakespeare's York later does, the omission of King Richard's title. And perhaps it does not matter. Richard's answer is virtually an abdication, yielding, as it does, the will of his Body Politic wholly to their whims: "Do what ye will, we'll sword and buckler ye" (180).

The graver implications in Richard's licensing of vanity, suggested in Greene's joke about shaving the country and Richard's reply, wait while Richard and his minions tend to what seems to them first things first. "Shaving the country" is Tresilian's business, and he is not onstage during this scene because injustice in the Body Politic logically follows vanity at court. "We must have money to buy new suits, my lord," says Scroope; "The fashions that we wear are gross and stale. / We'll go sit in council to devise some new" (205-7). And, with mature judgment banished from the council, that is what they do.

In the scene immediately following, the new business of Richard's Body Politic is measured against its old and neglected business. Queen Anne, the duchess of Gloucester, and "other maids with shirts and bands and other linen" (stage direction) sit sewing clothing for the poor and lamenting Richard's neglect of "the types of honour and nobility" in the disgrace of his uncles. Perhaps even more than Woodstock, Queen Anne seems to embody rather than express attitudes that the play would endorse. One can drop Richard's title but not hers. In ways that I will discuss in a moment, the play insists that we make careful distinctions between Woodstock and his political opinions, so that we will recognize that the responsibility for Richard's tragedy and his own is a bit more complex than he makes it out to be. But there is virtually no Anne to distinguish from the attitudes and values she expresses. They seem to have been generated by a simpler form of the dialectical dramaturgy that created Richard's minions and his uncles out of their historical counterparts, and Queen Anne simply provides them a gracious voice. She is in effect an animated part of *Woodstock's* conceptual structure, embodying Richard's formal allegiance to right government in her marriage, measuring his departure from it in Richard's neglect of her, and expressing from time to time its obligations, both public and private. If she sounds a bit like the Princess Pompiona at her marriage, insisting on the superiority of all things English, she sounds here like Respublica itself, the sensible and compassionate spirit of the Body Politic, numbering, as no mortal queen could, the precise figure of the poor and hungry within that body and suffering in herself its corporate pains:

Alack the day! though I am England's queen
I meet sad hours and wake when others sleep.
He meets content, but care with me must keep.
Distressed poverty o'erspreads the kingdom:
In Essex, Surrey, Kent, and Middlesex
Are seventeen thousand poor and indigent
Which I have numbered; and to help their wants
My jewels and plate are turned to coin
And shared amongst them. O riotous Richard,
A heavy blame is thine for this distress,
That dost allow thy polling flatterers
To gild themselves with others' miseries.

[2. 3. 15–26]

It is against this background—the queen and her ladies sewing, clothing strewn about the stage, maids bundling it up for the poor— that we first hear about the sorts of new fashions it has been the business of the king's council to devise. And largely because of that setting, we are invited to understand the grotesquerie of Richard's costume as the visible form of his grotesque political behavior, cut and sewn out of the suffering of his Body Politic. We have come less than two hundred lines, scarcely ten minutes' playing time, from Woodstock's complaint that to turn the kingdom over to boys is to overturn nature, when Richard and his minions enter, dressed in

wild and antic habits
Such as this kingdom never yet beheld:
French hose, Italian cloaks, and Spanish hats,
Polonian shoes with peaks a hand full long,
Tied to their knees with chains of pearl and gold.
Their plumèd tops fly waving in the air
A cubit high above their wanton heads.

[2. 3. 89–95]

That is how Richard is dressed when he describes the Feast of Westminster and marks out his claim on history.

With him now is Tresilian ("We must have money to buy new suits, my lord"), who, as lord chief justice, has sat with Richard's council "devising taxes, and strange shifts for money / To build again the hall at Westminster / To feast and revel in" (2. 3. 97–99). The first of these "strange shifts for money" are the infamous blank charters, intro- duced at the beginning of act 3. They are the legal forms, the equivalents in the law that shapes the Body Politic, of Richard's outlandish dress. And they are introduced with the same giggling exuberance with which Richard and his friends put together their costumes. They, too, are a joke of sorts:

> TRES.: See here, my lord: only with parchment: innocent
> sheepskins. Ye see, here's no fraud: no clause, no
> deceit in the writing.
> ALL: Why there's nothing writ!
> TRES.: There's the trick on't.
> These blank charters shall be forthwith sent
> To every shrieve through all the shires of England
> . . . .
> All landed men....
> Then in your highness' name they shall be charged
> To set their names, and forthwith seal these blanks;
> That done, these shall return to court again,
> But cartloads of money soon shall follow them.
> [3. 1. 11–24]

Greene recognizes in Tresilian's "wit" the realization of his earlier joke about shaving the country, and it is then that he thinks Tresilian, too, should be shaved: "Thou send'st our barbers there to poll the whole country, / Sfoot, let some shave thee" (29–30).

Like Richard's new fashions, the blank charters are outlandish. They distort the traditional forms of the political community and pervert its customary practices, just as Richard's new dress distorts his appearance. "Strange, unheard-of vile taxation" (3. 2. 67) Lancaster calls it, just after Woodstock has observed that "never was English king so habited" (38). And Woodstock goes on to nail the point home:

> This is a thing was never spoke nor done.
> Blank charters, call ye them? If any age
> Keep but a record of this policy
> (I phrase it too, too well!) — flat villainy —
> Let me be chronicled Apostata,
> Rebellious to my king and country both!
> [73–78]

The fact that such a thing has never been heard of before is particularly important if one thinks of the weight given in English political thought to custom and common law. Traditional prerogatives and traditional freedoms were especially important, Kantorowicz has observed, "in an England which relied predominantly on unwritten laws and customs."[16] In abrogating them, Richard has virtually unkinged himself.[17] That is why Woodstock, as soon as he hears that Richard has made his right to tax into a right to expropriate, concludes that rebellion will follow:

> Can they be rebels called, that now turn head?
> I speak but what I fear: not what I wish.
> This foul oppression will withdraw all duty,
> And in the Commons hearts hot rancours breed,
> To make our country's bosom shortly bleed.
>
> [85–89]

Lancaster, York, and Woodstock set out immediately to prevent the rebellion Woodstock fears by preaching submission even to tyranny. But what the playwright dramatizes is neither that orthodox Tudor doctrine nor the crude revolutionary justice it seeks to avert. Instead he shows us, in peculiarly theatrical terms, that the loss of Richard's identity as a king is rooted in the very composition of his acts and is not to be prevented by doctrines of the divine right of kings or advanced by insurrection. It is this interpretation of Richard's fall that informs the playwright's treatment of Woodstock's arrest in act 4 and his development there of the rumor that Richard had farmed his kingdom to Bushy, Bagot, and Greene.

By sanctioning Tresilian's perversion of the law, Richard has initiated the loss of his own identity. That loss is figured theatrically in his adopting the extravagant fashions his minions have devised; and the relationship between the lost identity and the new costumes is sustained and developed when we discover that Tresilian's man Nimble, who actually serves the blank charters on the commons, has himself "crept into the court fashion" (3. 1. 117). We can of course only guess at what Nimble wears; but because his role is so clearly indebted to the role of the mocking, comical vice of the moralities, it seems reasonable to assume that whatever grotesque dignity Richard is able to preserve in his own dress collapses in Nimble's costume into frank burlesque. If Richard's plume stands as high as a plume can stand, Nimble's may stretch out a bit higher and topple over. If Richard's chain sets forth "a kind coherence twixt the toe and knee" (55), Nimble's seems to sag and jangle ludicrously when he walks. Nimble suggests as much when, comparing himself to a morris dancer with his bells on, he asks Tresilian, "How do you like the rattling of my chains, my lord?" (115).

It is difficult to believe that the folly of Richard's dress really requires a clarifying burlesque, although some Elizabethan fashions were scarcely less extravagant. But Nimble's adoption of Richard's fashion does sustain Richard's image while Richard himself is offstage, particularly in act 3, scene 3, when Nimble and Bailey Ignorance tyrannize over the citizens of Dunstable "like so many St. Georges over the poor dragons," ferreting out privy whisperers and grumblers and even discovering a man who "whistles treason" because he whistles the tune of a ballad to which some words mocking Tresilian had been set. Through Nimble's costume, then, the playwright is able to keep onstage a degenerated image of Richard himself and so to locate visually the source of Nimble's whimsical and mindless tyranny, at once comic and horrifying, in Richard's disposition to vanity. The means and the effect are uniquely theatrical.

But before the scene at Dunstable we are at Woodstock's estate, where a messenger arrives from Richard to summon Woodstock back to court. What Richard wants is Woodstock's moral authority, "should the commons grow mutinous about these blanks" (3. 1. 104). Woodstock, of course, refuses to give it to him. The scene is far longer than this simple exchange requires, however, and through most of its length we simply contemplate the foolish dress and behavior of Richard's messenger, who, like Nimble, has also "crept into the court fashion."

By now, with all of Richard's courtiers and agents dressed alike, it might be fair to say that the court fashion is worn not merely by a number of individuals but rather by the Body Politic itself. It might be fair to say that what we see in Bushy, Bagot, Greene, Scroope, Nimble, Richard, and here the exquisite fool, his messenger, all dressed in "French hose, Italian cloaks and Spanish hats," is the visible form of the extended corporate Body of the King[18]— "Consisting of Policy and Government, and constituted for the Direction of the People, and the management of the Public Weal"— made over into a tyrannical fool and disappearing before our eyes in successively more degenerate images. It is true at least that Woodstock's response to both public policy and courtly fashions is the same. "O strange metamorphosis!" he says when he sees Richard's messenger, "Is't possible that this fellow that's all made of fashions should be an Englishman?" (3. 2. 155–56). And the playwright calls our attention to the degeneration of Richard into his messenger, or perhaps "flowering" is a better word, by giving each of them a speech in which he describes his costume and explains the significance of the chain that links the knee with the curled toe of the shoe. Richard's vanity ("This kind coherence twixt the toe and knee / To have them chained together lovingly") sounds in retrospect almost sober once we have heard his messenger expound on the coherence of toe and knee:

> For these two parts, being in operation and quality
> different, as for example: the toe a disdainer, or spurner:
> the knee a dutiful and most humble orator; this chain
> doth, as it were, so toeify the knee and so kneeify the toe,
> that between both it makes a most methodical coherence,
> or coherent method.
>
> [3. 2. 216–21]

Woodstock confines himself to saying that the English court has grown altogether "too fine" in its fashions and its policy for his "English plainness."

The messenger's exposition of the logic of vanity occupies only the second half of his scene with Woodstock. The first half concerns a point touched on earlier, in the scene between Nimble and Tresilian at the beginning of act 3, and suggested later by Lancaster. This is the fact that, with court fashion spreading to servant and fool, distinctions of rank have collapsed and, with them, the bases of order. Tresilian calls comic attention to the leveling of the court through fashion when he remarks, on Nimble's capering in plumes and chains, "O villain, thou wilt hang in chains for this!" (3. 1. 116). And Richard's fine messenger provides a more sustained comic image of the same point when he takes the duke of Gloucester for a groom because of his plain dress and sets him to walk his horse. With a fool lording it over a duke because of his dress, and the king dressed like the fool, what is in store for the Body Politic? Lancaster points to the end of the process when he observes, just before the entrance of Richard's messenger, that the leveling of the court in fashion merely figures a deeper sort of leveling. "We could allow Richard's clothing...," he says, "But we have four kings more are equalled with him: / There's Bagot, Bushy, wanton Greene, and Scroope / In state and fashion without difference" (3. 2. 39–42). The implications of these remarks are realized in act 4.

Holinshed reports that there was a rumor current in 1399 that the king "had set to farm the realm of England." But the rumor was apparently without foundation, because there is no reference to such an act in the thirty-three articles of deposition drawn against Richard later that year. Nevertheless, the rumor seems to have struck the author of *Woodstock* as essentially true, for he translates it into a dramatic fact and develops it with solemn and special emphasis in the first scene of act 4. We have heard nothing earlier in the play about such a plan, although in act 1 Greene confesses that Richard's minions hope to rule "the realm and him" (1. 2. 19). The logic behind the placement and development of Richard's decision to farm the realm to Bushy, Bagot, Greene, and Scroope for £7,000 a month, making them in effect tributary kings, each with absolute power over a part of England, is not, however, the logic of the fable nor obviously the logic of chronicle history. It is instead a dramatization of a principle of political philosophy involving the relationship of kings to the law, which is in its form a good deal like the model of Mankind's relationship to God.

Whatever the prerogatives claimed by individual kings, most political philosophies of the Middle Ages and Renaissance understood the king to be a creature of the law, put in place originally by a compact among the people to yield authority in exchange for order. Once set on the throne and anointed, as the medieval English jurist Henry Bracton argued, the king might well be God's vicar before his subjects, but the king came to the throne as the *vicarius* of those subjects. He was created by the *lex regia,* the fundamental grant "by which the people transferred to him and on him all its power and authority."[19] Properly speaking, he was thereafter the agent of the law, dependent on it for his very identity "because the law makes the king.... For there is no king where arbitrary will dominates and not the Law."[20] That principle had the force of nature itself for Aquinas, who argued that for kings to seek their own interests rather than the common good was to pervert the natural end for which governments were created and so to exchange the name of king for the name of tyrant.[21] Some three hundred years later one of Elizabeth's privy counselors, Sir Thomas Smith, was making essentially the same distinction: a king, he wrote, "doth administer the Common-wealth by the lawes of the same," while a tyrant "breaketh the Lawes alreadie made, at his pleasure, maketh other without the advice and consent of his people, and regardeth not the wealth of his Commons, but the advancement of himself, his faction, his kindred."[22]

According to this principle, Richard virtually unkings himself— that is, loses the name of king—by sanctioning Tresilian's plan to subvert the law through the use of blank charters, since his identity as king derives from and depends on his adherence to the law. That is obviously not a realistic or a historical premise. A king who has become a tyrant might continue to reign in his natural body for the rest of his natural life, as history demonstrates. But it is this premise that seems to have informed the playwright's understanding of history and his translation of it into drama, for he has made the farming of the realm, which he treats as virtually an act of abdication, literally a consequence of Richard's use of the blank charters. Their logical relationship is clear in the temporal order of the play, because the scene in which Richard signs the articles follows immediately upon the scene in which Nimble serves the blank charter on the commons. And it is equally clear as a proposition about motives, because farming the realm is suggested to Richard as an even easier stratagem for raising money.

In a passage later marked for cutting, the playwright originally had Richard act as his own chorus, pronouncing judgment himself on the farming of the realm and recalling his father's selfless heroism in order to throw into sharper relief his own waste of his patrimony:

> We shall be censured strangely, when they tell
> How our great father toiled his royal person
> Spending his blood to purchase towns in France;
> And we his son, to ease our wanton youth
> Become a landlord to this warlike realm,
> Rent out our kingdom like a pelting farm
> That erst was held, as fair as Babylon,
> The maiden conqueress to all the world.
> [4. 1. 142–49]

Rossiter has suggested that the passage was to be cut because Richard's hesitation was irrelevant to the action of the scene and contradictory to his already stated intention to cede Calais to the king of France.[23] Whatever the reason for its cutting, the author has preserved Richard's painful self-consciousness in the solemn deliberation with which he is made to attend to every detail of the agreement. While Richard tries to put the best face on it, insisting, with what I take to be awkwardly pretended severity, that he will be a punctilious and demanding landlord, punishing the least infringement against the terms of the lease, the playwright insists that we hear, and that we watch Richard assent to, every one of the shameful conditions by which he transfers his royal prerogatives and responsibilities to his friends:

> ...by these writings, surrenders to their hands: all your
> crown lands, lordships: manors, rents: taxes, subsidies,

fifteens, imposts; foreign customs, staples for wool, tin,
lead and cloth: all forfeitures of goods or lands confiscate;
and all other duties that *do,* shall, or may appertain to the
king or crown's revenues....

[4. 1. 185–90]

In sum, Greene explains, "your grace...farming out the kingdom to
us four, shall not need to trouble yourself with any business—this old
turkeycock Tresilian shall look to the law, and we'll govern the land
most rarely" (134–37). And when Richard has agreed to those terms,
we must then hear and watch him give over to his minions, bit by bit,
every particle of the land, calling for a map to mark out the divisions,
naming each of the thirty-nine counties of England, and assenting to
the transfer of each to the authority of Bushy, Bagot, Greene, and
Scroope. Listening to his recitation of "London, Middlesex, / Essex,
Suffolk, Norfolk, Cambridgeshire, / Hertfordshire, Bedfordshire,
Buckinghamshire..." (252–54), it is difficult to imagine a more
painstakingly or more thoroughly dramatized abdication or one
more sharply calculated in its insistence on the legal minutiae of an
unenforceable contract to illuminate its roots in the perversion of law.

It is at this point, having discarded mature counsel, sacrificed the
integrity of the law to his vanity, and signed away his royal
prerogatives and responsibilities, that Richard plans his most egregious violation of the law. And in the course of it he disappears—not in
a puff of smoke, of course, but behind a mask as precisely revealing in
its own way as Wit's black face and motley cloak. The act is the
kidnapping and murder of his uncle, Woodstock.

When Richard enters in act 4, scene 1, he has not yet formally
agreed to the farming of the kingdom. He is disposed toward it, and
the "smooth faced, flattering Greene" has been urging him on, but
Richard has been distracted by word of Woodstock's refusal to come
to court. This has made him so angry "that nothing can remove the
gall thereof / Till with his blood mine eyes be satisfied" (76–77).
Richard cannot act openly against Woodstock, however, because
"he's so well beloved / As all the realm will rise in arms with him"
(81–82). The historical Richard had much the same problem of
enticing Woodstock from his estate, where he was well protected, so
that he might be arrested more easily, and the historical Richard
solved that problem with the same sort of straightforward duplicity
with which he put down the Peasants' revolt: he rode in person to
Woodstock's estate, told him that his presence was required in
council, and then, when Woodstock had set out for London, had him

seized on the road and shipped to Calais.[24] But the playwright has given his dramatic character a much more complicated strategy, and one that develops into a very telling image of the last stage of Richard's progress into vanity: he has Richard adopt a plan devised by his chief justice to send a troupe of masquers to Woodstock's estate,

> and in the name of some near adjoining friends, offer their
> sports to make him merry, which he no doubt will
> thankfully accept. Then in the mask we'll have it so
> devised (the dance being done and the room voided) then
> upon some occasion single the duke alone, clap a vizard
> on his face, and so convey him out o' the house at pleasure.
> [91–97]

Indeed, Richard is so taken with the plan that he decides to go along as a masquer to see Woodstock's discomfort in person—thereby serving at once his own narrow purposes and the playwright's larger ones.

It is not stated what sort of mask Richard wears in act 4, scene 2, the scene of Woodstock's kidnapping. It is probably a hunter's costume, since the story of the masque is organized around a hunt for a wild boar. If so, the image is appropriate to Richard's intentions in the scene. But the fact that he is disguised matters as much as the particular disguise he wears.

In the act of kidnapping Woodstock, the king becomes a masquer. That is a dramatic image so delicately poised that I hesitate to translate it in flat-footed exposition, but there are several things that need to be said about it. The most obvious point is that Richard has found it necessary to hide himself and his purposes. In kidnapping Woodstock, he is not the vicar of England, wielding the corporate "power and authority" of the people. Indeed the "realm [would] rise in arms" if it knew what he was doing. And Richard has already made provision to protect himself from the judgment of his own people by appealing to a foreign king:

> Lest the commons should rebel against us,
> We'll send unto the King of France for aid,
> And in requital we'll surrender up
> Our forts of Guisnes and Calais to the French.
> Let crown and kingdom waste, yea, life and all,
> Before King Richard see his true friends fall.
> [4. 1. 120–26][25]

In thus divorcing his own interests from those of the kingdom, Richard has become merely a player king, exercising tyrannically an authority no longer rightfully his own.

Certainly it is clear in another sense that Richard has been merely a player king if one thinks of his devotion to vanity—to feasts, fashions, and flatterers—and his willingness to sacrifice the kingdom and its laws to his own pleasures. In that sense King Richard as a masquer is the perfected form of the Richard we have seen earlier choose flattery over counsel, deliberate about fashions while his kingdom starved, serve as the glass of form and fashion for court fools, and finally rent out the kingdom, leaving himself merely "the name of king."

But, of course, as a masquer Richard does not literally play a king; instead he hides one. In adopting his mask, Richard obscures both the *imago regis* and his own natural image, the "counterfeit" of his father, who is in heaven. And in that respect, Richard as masquer, his face now hidden, is the completed form of other tendencies we have seen developed earlier in the play, just as the obscuring of Wit's image under the costume of Ingnorancy is the completed form of Wit's disregard of Reason. The progressive loss of the heroic image of the Black Prince in Richard's vanity, the subversion of the Body Politic in lawlessness, and the corresponding degeneration of the *imago regis,* all of them tendencies toward the unkinging of King Richard, are illuminated and perfected when Richard hides his face behind a mask. Richard Plantagenet may be present at the kidnapping of Woodstock, but the king is not. The king has literally disappeared in the composition of the act itself. The playwright calls our attention to this sense of the image of King Richard as a masquer through the repetition of Woodstock's cries for the king and the repeated denials that he is present:

> WOOD.: Speak, is King Richard here?
> ALL: No, no, my lord.
> . . . .
> WOOD.:   I know that voice full well.
>   Afore my God, False men, King Richard's here.
> . . . .
> BAG.: You're still deceived, my lord, the king's not here.
>   [4. 2. 179–92]

Indeed, he is not.

MORALITY FORM AND DRAMATIC FACT

I have treated Woodstock's kidnapping as climactic because it marks the furthest point in Richard's progress into the land of unlikeness. In act 4, Richard virtually unkings himself, although he is still literally king, and act 5 deals with the consequences of his acts, which are chiefly the actual murder of Woodstock and the rebellion of Lancaster and York, who rise to protect themselves and to avenge Woodstock's death. At a point in the morality drama similar to the point Richard has reached in kidnapping Woodstock—when Mankind, for example, has thoroughly explored the Seven Deadly Sins, or when Wit has been transformed into a fool—the central character is touched in some fashion by Providence and brought to his senses. In *The Castle of Perseverance* Providence appears in the forms of Shrift and Penance, the perceptible evidences of God's mercy, who plant a "seed of sorrow" in Mankind; in *Wit and Science* it is the contemptuous anger of Science that leads Wit to recognize his folly and return to Reason. In *Woodstock* it is the death of Queen Anne that performs a similar function for Richard.

Even in her death Anne of Bohemia is scarcely differentiated from the conceptual structure of the play. We first hear of her sickness in act 4, scene 2, just after Richard has farmed out the kingdom and just before the masquers seize Woodstock, and the progress of her disease runs parallel with the progress of Richard's self-destruction. She has been the only redeeming grace in Richard's Body Politic, says Woodstock; "Her charity hath stayed the commons' rage / That would ere this have shaken Richard's chair / Or set all England on a burning fire. / And—fore my God—I fear, when she is gone, / This woeful land will all to ruin run" (4. 2. 58–62). After Woodstock has been kidnapped and sent to Calais to be murdered, we hear that Queen Anne has died. In fact, Anne of Bohemia died some three years before the arrest of Woodstock, but it is clear that the playwright has advanced the date so that the death of this woman, who has been consistently associated with right government and royal compassion, would coincide with Richard's most egregious tyranny. He has also made Richard sensitive to the meaning of her death. Bushy reports that in his own grief Richard found the model of the grief of "Woodstock's hapless wife,"

> And would have there revealed her husband's fall
> Amidst his passions, had not Scroope and Greene

By violence borne him to an inward room;
Where still he cries to get a messenger
To send to Calais to reprieve his uncle.
[4. 3. 125–29]

When Richard enters, it is clear that what he has discovered in Anne's death is not merely compassion for others but also some sense of his errors:

Anne à Beame is dead, for ever gone!
She was too virtuous to remain with me,
And heaven hath given her higher dignity.
O God, I fear, even here begins our woe:
Her death's but chorus to some tragic scene
That shortly will confound our state and realm.
Such sad events black mischiefs still attend,
And bloody acts, I fear, must crown the end.
[144–51]

A moment later, "trepidus et pusillanimus in adversis," he tries again to recall his order for Woodstock's death: "For heaven's love, go, prevent the tragedy. / We have too much provoked the powers divine / And here repent thy wrongs, good uncle Woodstock" (172–74). But he fails—historical fact and the playwright's conception of the logic of history being against him—and the "bloody acts" follow. Greene is killed in act 5, scene 4, Bushy and Scroope are captured by Richard's uncles in scene 6, and, when the text breaks off a moment later, it is clear that Tresilian is about to be hanged.

It is unlikely that Richard himself was either deposed or killed at the end of *Woodstock*. The well-known facts of his deposition by Henry Bolingbroke and subsequent death argue against that. And while there is some ambiguity about the intentions of Lancaster and York (it is not clear how far they mean to go to avenge Woodstock's murder), on the whole their aims seem to be as limited as they were in act 1. What they seem to seek is the restoration of the proper form of the king's body politic: the purgation of its wanton humors and the return of mature wisdom to its council.[26] Those, at least, are the demands they make on Richard when they confront him just before the battle in act 5, scene 3. It seems likely, then, that the play ended as generations of morality plays had ended, with Richard passing back under the control of his uncles, who have expelled from the Body Politic those who urged him toward vanity. If it did, the playwright deftly negotiated a passage between the claims of historical truth and the political dangers of seeming to advocate the deposition even of a tyrant; for he has dramatized the logic by which Richard historically deposed himself without ever showing him deposed.

But if Richard did come to rest under the guidance of his uncles at the end of the play, it is difficult to believe that he did so willingly. He is more likely to have been a prisoner than a penitent. For while Richard may regret his part in Woodstock's death and recognize that providential justice follows from it, he is far from willing to submit himself to Lancaster and York or to give up his flatterers. The reason is that both Richard and the playwright, for different purposes, make a distinction between virtue itself and characters who speak for virtuous actions—a distinction that was not made in the morality drama. The playwright has generally aligned Richard's uncles with political virtue in the design of the play, but he clearly does not regard them as Virtues. Lancaster, in particular, exhibits the arrogant vindictiveness of his historical namesake, and, when he accuses Richard of procuring the murder of Woodstock, the playwright has Richard accuse him in turn of a particularly hideous murder:

> You have forgotten, uncle Lancaster
> How you in prison murdered cruelly
> A friar carmelite, because he was
> To bring in evidence against your grace
> Of most ungracious deeds and practices.
> [5. 3. 75–79]

To this accusation, Lancaster makes no reply.[27]

It is true that *Woodstock* follows the model of the morality drama in its larger movements, reshaping the facts of history to embody political responsibility in Richard's uncles and vanity in Bushy, Bagot, and Greene in order to illustrate the essential form of Richard's career; but it is also true that, within that general pattern, the author of *Woodstock* insists upon the particularity and complexity of the action to an extent far greater than any morality playwright. If *Woodstck* opens up on one side toward the pure and transparent conceptualism of the morality drama, it narrows down on the other toward the mixed, almost opaque facticity of history itself. On that side, too, what the playwright was after is an essentially accurate dramatization of the form of history. I want now to consider briefly that side of the play.

In act 2, scene 1, when Bushy tries to stir Richard to defy his uncles by reading to him from the accounts of his father's battles, he begins with an incident out of the reign of Richard's grandfather, Edward III, who, "although young and under government, / Took the Protector then, proud Mortimer, / And on a gallows fifty foot in height / He hung him for his treachery" (2. 1. 62–65). Richard of course sees himself and Woodstock in his grandfather and Mortimer, as Bushy hoped he would. But the playwright has had Bushy choose this particular passage because its historical context reflects ironically on Richard's present situation, just as the referencess to the Black Prince later serve as an ironic measure of Richard's aspirations to fame. The ironies were not restricted to those who had read the chronicles. Any theatergoer who had seen Marlowe's *Edward II,* or heard of it, would have known that though the rise and fall of proud Mortimer did not really offer an instructive precedent for Richard's relationship with Woodstock it did provide a very striking precedent for Richard's relationships with his minions. For Mortimer rose as Edward II fell, and Edward fell—was deposed and killed—because he came under the influence of flatterers much like Bushy, Bagot, and Greene. The passage is particularly interesting because, in showing how Bushy selectively distorts the chronicles to make history serve his ends, the author of *Woodstock* implicitly claims that his own handling of the chronicle has been different. He implicitly claims that he has been true to history, accurate in presenting its qualifications and complexities, where Bushy has been false.

As we have seen, that is certainly not true at the level of historical facts, for the incidents of *Woodstock* are almost entirely false, either in themselves or in the order in which they occur. But it is true, or at least arguable, at the level of historical form, for the playwright has invented some facts and has rearranged others to clarify the process, half-discernible through the thicket of mere incidents in the chronicles, by which Richard's disposition to vanity led him to violate the law and ultimately to bring about his own deposition. That is the action to which Holinshed points at the end of his account of Richard's deposition, and he underlines it in the most solemn of preacherly accents, with references to the "wrath of God whetted against the fowle enormities wherewith his life was deformed." But then Holinshed turns, rather surprisingly, to say that that is the formal and public view of Richard's fall but that, in his own opinion, the responsibility for Richard's fall was more complex. Richard "was a prince the most unthankfullie used of his subjects," Holinshed writes,

> For although (through the frailtie of youth) he demeaned
> himselfe more dissolutelie than seemed convenient for his

roiall estate, & made choise of such councellors as were
not favoured of the people, whereby he was the lesse
favoured himselfe: yet in no kings daies were the commons
in greater wealth, if they could have perceived their happie
state: neither in any other time were the nobles and
gentlemen more cherished, nor churchmen lesse wronged.
But such was their ingratitude towards their bountifull
and loving sovereigne, that those whom he had cheeflie
advanced, were readiest to controll him; for that they
might not rule all things at their will, and remoove from
him such as they misliked, and place in their roomes
whom they thought good, and that rather by strong hand
than by gentle and courteous meanes, which stirred such
malice betwixt him and them, till at length it could not be
asswaged without perill of destruction to them both.

What Holinshed has in mind are the running battles between Richard
and the baronial party over such royal favorites as Robert Vere, the
duke of Ireland. And the "cheefe instrument of this mischeefe,"
Holinshed says, was Thomas of Woodstock.[28] Just as the author of
Woodstock adopted and dramatized Holinshed's interpretation of
the main lines along which Richard fell, so he also adopted and
dramatized Holinshed's qualification that Richard was not solely
responsible for his fall, that it was due partly to the quality of
Woodstock's opposition.

The problem is that he has reinvented the "fierce, hastie and
willful" duke of Gloucester as Plain Thomas, the soul of political
virtue and the voice of patient submission to the crown, in order to set
in high relief Richard's vain willfulness; and so he has had to reinvent
the substance of Woodstock's own measure of responsibility for
Richard's fall in terms suited to his new character and to his place in
the design of the play. The historical duke of Gloucester could simply
gather a small army and ambush Richard's friends, as he did in 1388,
but Plain Thomas cannot. Essentially, what the playwright has done,
in carefully measured ways, is to show that Woodstock's good
intentions expressed themselves in ways that encouraged Richard's
folly.

For example, we are kept aware that Woodstock is imprudently
simple and disingenuous, that not only is he free from duplicity
himself but he does not suspect it in others. Just after he has evaded
the poisoning plot in act 1, scene 1, York asks Cheyney whether
Woodstock suspects a plot against his own life, and Cheyney replies
that he does not: "His mind suits with his habit / Homely and plain:

both free from pride and envy, / And therein will admit distrust to none" (106–8). Such simplicity may be admirable under ordinary circumstances, but in the Protector of a young and "wild" king, at a court inhabited by cynical opportunists who have already suborned a Carmelite friar to poison the king's uncles, it is almost perverse. And references to Woodstock's imprudence run as a leitmotif throughout the play: from his own rather proud claim that his "English plainness" does not suit the court; through Tresilian's easy assumption that Woodstock will "of course" admit the masquers who come to seize him, and York's answering complaint that "it was an easy task to work on him. / His plainness was too open to their view; / He feared no wrong because his heart was true" (5. 3. 6–8); to the otherwise rather strange plea by the ghost of the Black Prince, which appears to Woodstock just before he is murdered to urge him to "wake! prevent thy doom! / Thy blood upon my son will surely come: / For which, dear brother Woodstock, haste and fly, / Prevent his ruin and thy tragedy" (5. 1. 73–76). At that point there is nothing much that Woodstock can do about it, as the ghost surely knows, for he is a prisoner and the murderers are at the door. But the theme of Woodstock's culpable imprudence never comes to a dramatic point; it is simply woven through the play to make available another moral perspective on the action. What the play does bring into dramatic focus, however, is the place of Woodstock's good-natured tactlessness in Richard's decision to put his Body Politic under the guidance of Bushy, Bagot, and Greene.

When Woodstock enters in act 1, scene 1, he speaks himself for the need to deal with Richard by "gentle and courteous meanes." While the plot against the lives of Lancaster and York originated with Richard's friends, he says, Richard had no part in it. The king is young and high-spirited, but he is fundamentally good. And Richard's uncles may hope that the "happy marriage / Of this so noble and religious princess / Will mildly calm his headstrong youth to see / And shun those stains that blur his majesty." If that fails, there will be time enough to act more harshly to "remove those hinderers of his health." Indeed, Woodstock is so convinced that Richard's uncles must accommodate themselves to the young king and allow time and nature to mature him that he allows himself to be persuaded to exchange his life-long dress of simple frieze for a more elegant costume in celebration of Richard's wedding.

Since that costume is the visible expression of Woodstock's policy of patience and generosity toward Richard, I think we may assume that it sits rather awkwardly on him in act 1, scene 3—that it is too small or too large, that its cut is wrong or its color. For the scene turns from the celebration of Richard's marriage to the overturning of his state in part because Woodstock is unable to carry out his own policy. And the playwright deftly underlines his failure. If *Woodstock* were a morality play, Woodstock himself would be its Virtue and the point of view of the play would be centered in Woodstock, just as the point of view of *Wit and Science* is centered in Reason. But the point of view is in fact relatively objective, and from the beginning of act 1, scene 3, Woodstock is the object of gentle but distinctly analytical comedy. A certain quality of obtuse officiousness, inherent in the morality Virtue but not charged against him in morality plays, is neatly mocked early in the scene, when Woodstock cuts off Lancaster's greeting to Queen Anne after only seven lines on the grounds that, if everyone spoke so fulsomely, the ceremony would last for a week and then proceeds to make his own greeting three times as long. In the course of it he marches stubbornly onto ground that seems all too familiar to Richard, perhaps even embarrassing, in exactly the way that what seems to us our relatives' gaucheness can embarrass us before strangers we wish to impress. The playwright indicates that Richard can guess what is coming and that he protests with some gesture. But, like a grandfather hauling out baby pictures, Woodstock rides over Richard's protests to lecture Anne on Richard's faults:

> Nay, Nay, King Richard, 'fore God I'll speak the truth!
> Sweet queen, you've found a young and wanton choice,
> A wild head...yet a kingly gentleman...
> A youth unsettled; yet he's princely bred
> Descended from the royal'st bloods in Europe,
> The kingly stock of England and of France.
> Yet he's a harebrain, a very wag i'faith,
> And you must bear, madam; 'las, he's but a blossom;
> But his maturity I hope you'll find
> True English bred, a king loving and kind.
>   [1. 3. 23–32]

Richard may cringe a bit during that speech, but he takes it with ironical good grace. When he turns to do as much for Woodstock, however, and teasingly "lay his faults all open to the world" (69–70), Plain Thomas will not allow it. He makes an effort. When Richard teases him about his "golden metamorphosis / From homespun houswifery" (75–76), Woodstock claims that he is "no stoic...To make my plainness seem canonical, / But to allow myself such ornaments / As might be fitting for your nuptial day / And coronation of your virtuous queen." But lest he be thought soft, he is careful to add that he does not like it, that he really is a stoic, "and were the eye of day once closed again / Upon this back they never more should come" (78–84). As Richard continues to tease Woodstock, gently, about his plain dress and old-fashioned speech, Woodstock's stoicism, that strain of moral tenacity, comes more and more into the open and finally bursts out in a full-blown sermon against the luxury of dress:

> Ay, ay, mock on. My tother hose, say ye?
> There's honest plain dealing in my tother hose.
> Should this fashion last I must raise my rents,
> Undo my tenants, turn away my servants,
> And guard myself with lace; nay, sell more land
> And lordships too, by the rood. Hear me, King Richard:
> If thus I jet in pride, I still shall lose;
> But I'll build castles in my tother hose.
>
> [102–9]

What Woodstock says is morally impeccable, but the playwright uses Queen Anne to point out that he ought not to say it now, that his moral earnestness is in excess of the situation: "The king but jests, my lord, and you grow angry" (110). And as Woodstock thunders on, Lancaster and York make sure that we understand that he has lost sight of the generous patience he called for: "S'foot, he forewarned us, and will break out himself" (113).

The point is important and deserves underlining, because the quarrel developing here will culminate in Richard's impulsive transfer of his Body Politic to Bushy, Bagot, and Greene as a way of slapping back at Woodstock: "So sir. We'll soothe your vexed spleen, good uncle, / And mend what is amiss. To those slight gifts / Not worth acceptance, thus much more we add: / Young Henry Greene shall be Lord Chancellor,..." (181–84). Once he has done that and left the stage, Richard's uncles and their supporters will speak as if Richard were a morality hero and his act simply revealed his ingrained moral perversity:

> WOOD.:   what's the cause
> Of this remiss and inconsiderate dealing
> Urged by the king and his confederates,
> But hate to virtue — and a mind corrupt
> With all preposterous and rude misgovernment?
> . . . .

SURREY: It is his custom to be prodigal
        To any but to those do best deserve.
ARUND.: Because he knew you would bestow them well,
        He gave it such as for their private gain
        Neglect both honour and their country's good.
                         [216–227]

Our view of the scene has been different from theirs, however. For while they have watched what seemed to them a morality play, what we have seen is a historical event—almost an accident in some respects—produced by the combination of Richard's unfortunate weakness and Woodstock's unfortunate moral tenacity. While all of the moral advantages in the scene may lie with Richard's uncles, the dramatic initiatives that lead to Richard's crucial act also belong to his uncles. The salient moral fact about act 1, scene 3 is that Richard chooses vanity over mature counsel, and from that choice the general events of the play logically follow: he wastes his patrimony in luxury, perverts the law to support his pleasures, and in doing so unkings himself. But the precise dramatic fact is that Richard does not choose vanity and break with wisdom solely because he prefers one over the other; he does so in part, at least, in response to Woodstock's tactlessness and moral inflexibility.

It is those qualities in Woodstock that Richard anticipates in act 2, scene 1, just before he assumes the throne and banishes his uncles from the court. And it is those qualities that still rankle in act 4, scene 1, when Richard decides on the kidnapping and murder of Woodstock: "I tell thee, Bagot, in my heart remains / Such deep impression of his churlish taunts / As nothing can remove the gall thereof / Till with his blood mine eyes be satisfied" (74–77). Thus we can see in the fabricated events of *Woodstock,* as Holinshed saw in the events of history itself, that Richard's tragedy was not a simple moral event. Its main roots lay in his "youthful outrage and insolent misgovernance," to be sure, but those moral faults were compounded by the tactlessness of those who sought to "remove from him such as they misliked, and place in their rooms whom they thought good, and that rather by strong hand than by gentle and courteous meanes, which stirred such malice betwixt him and them, till at length it could not be asswaged without perill of destruction to them both."

While the author of *Woodstock* thinks like a morality playwright, then, reshaping with a free hand the characters and events of history into a pattern very like the pattern of everyman's moral pilgrimage, *Woodstock* is not a morality play. It is a history play. For what we discover, as Richard retraces the steps of generations of morality heroes, disfiguring himself in vanity, is not a confirmation of moral law, or not that alone; it is instead the form of a discrete historical fact. Richard fell, partly because he violated certain fundamental moral principles in his political career, and partly simply because his uncles nagged at him in the wrong ways and at the wrong times. In that combination of universal law and historical accident, the generalizing and illuminating capacity of morality forms is brought to focus on a discrete historical fact. We are enabled to understand it without distorting its essential shape. And for the moment, at least, morality forms and the bristly, opaque complications of experience are set in balance.

F O U R

Volpone in the Land of Unlikeness

> Where we may, so, trans-fuse our wandring soules,
> Out at our lippes, and score up summes of pleasures...
>
> [*Volpone*, 3.7. 234–35]

In his prologue to *Volpone,* Ben Jonson seems to invite a reading of the play along lines that later came to be called neoclassical. Brushing aside the practices of less artistically self-conscious playwrights, who provide "such a deale of monstrous and forc'd action / As might make *Bet'lem* a faction," he offers *Volpone* as a model of comic structure, informed by its fable, contained by the unities, and shaped according to the best theories. Others might write mere collections of jokes and pass them off as comedies, he implies, but he has not

> made his play, for jests, stolne from each table,
> But makes his jests, to fit his fable.
> And, so presents quick *comoedie,* refined,
> As best Criticks have designed,
> The lawes of time, place, persons be observeth,
> From no needfull rule he swerveth.[1]

It is ironic that Jonson should call particular attention to his management of the fable, resting on it his claim that *Volpone* is a proper comedy, for that is the point at which his classically inclined critics have most often balked. Indeed, the foremost of them, and surely the most appreciative, Dryden, relegated *Volpone* to the second rank of Jonson's comedies precisely on the grounds that its fable was not managed as well as it might have been. But in recent years Dryden's stature as a critic of Jonson has declined. We have been taught that criticism of Jonson that begins with classical or neoclassical assumptions misses the fundamental principles of Jonson's dramaturgy and that when such criticism finds what it takes to be errors in the plays it has merely convicted "by the laws of one literary country a man who wrote by those of quite another."[2]

113

In the main I think that sentiment is just. I have no intention of trying to reconstitute here the image of Jonson as a formal classicist, doggedly assembling his plays on the models of Plautus and Terence. Indeed, in the course of this essay I want to go in just the other direction, to lay bare still more of the medieval and popular roots of *Volpone* and to consider, in particular, the ways in which its structure is informed by the Bernardine figure of the soul's passage into the land of unlikeness. Still, I think there is some point in beginning an examination of the structure of *Volpone* by discussing the objections laid against it by Jonson's neoclassical critics, not only because Jonson seems to invite such a perspective, but also because Dryden and others have raised questions about the structure of the play that have not, I think, been satisfactorily answered.

There have been two major objections: first, that the main plot of *Volpone* is not unified and that its resolution is arbitrarily managed; second, that the play includes characters and episodes irrelevant to the main plot. That latter point can be disposed of relatively easily, since it turns on the assumption that Elizabethan standards of coherence were, or ought to have been, like those of the eighteenth century. "The play has two characters which have nothing to do with the design of it," John Dennis wrote in a letter to Congreve, and "which are to be look'd upon as Excrescencies."[3] The two are Peregrine and Sir Politic Would be, whose activities are linked to those in the main story only when they witness Volpone's performance as a mountebank and when Lady Would Be later mistakes Peregrine for the courtesan with whom Mosca had claimed to have seen Sir Politic. Otherwise the two men carry out their designs outside the main fable. Assuming that they should not, those who set about, in the eighteenth century, to improve *Volpone* by revising Jonson's text excised Peregrine and Sir Politic so as to give the play a single plot. But, as Jonas Barish has shown us, the play is designed to include the two independent fables within a larger unified structure.[4] Sir Pol is the parrot in Jonson's animal satire, modeling himself on the Fox and reducing his politic machinations to folly. Thus, while their stories are separate, Volpone and Sir Pol are bound within a single plot in just the same sense in which Lear and Gloucester are bound within a single plot in *King Lear*.

While objections to Peregrine and Sir Pol are relatively trivial, the complaints that Jonson forces the development of the main fable are a bit hardier, more difficult to put aside. Essentially they come to this: Jonson manages the resolution of *Volpone* only at the cost of the unity of action and only by having his characters behave in ways they would not naturally behave. The first point is Dryden's, and, since I want to return to it from time to time, I will quote the relevant passage here in its entirety. It comes from the *Essay of Dramatic Poesy,* where Neander, the spokesman for Dryden's own views, hesitates about including *Volpone* among his examples of the ability of English playwrights to knit together complex yet whole plots, various and regular. "I was going to have named *The Fox,*" he says, having already named *The Alchemist,*

> but that the unity of design seems not exactly observed in it, for there appear to be two actions in the play, the first naturally ending with the fourth Act, the second forced from it in the fifth; which yet is the less to be condemned in him because the disguise of Volpone, though it suited not with his character as a crafty or covetous person, agreed well enough with that of a voluptuary; and by it the poet gained the end at which he aimed, the punishment of vice and the reward of virtue. So that to judge equally of it, it was an excellent fifth act, but not so naturally proceeding from the former.[5]

That seems to me a remarkable piece of criticism, accurate and suggestive, economically drawing together matters of character, fable, plot, and moral design into a judicious estimate that act 5 works but that it rattles a bit. For the next few pages I want to trail in its wake, examining *Volpone* along the lines Dryden suggests.

COMIC ACTION: THE DEVELOPMENT OF THE FABLE

In assuming that *Volpone* ought to have a single action, Dryden assumes no more than Jonson himself; but in assuming that the unity of action ought to be found in a single intrigue, pursued over five acts, and thus that the play ought to be accessible to the usual terms of mimetic analyses, he is assuming more than the evidence of act 1 warrants. Certainly the first act of *Volpone* does not look very much like the sort of play Dryden is talking about because it does not develop any lines along which it may go forward until just before the act comes to an end. Until Mosca mentions Corvino's beautiful wife and Volpone forms his intention to see her, act 1 seems to be organized to demonstrate certain propositions, laid down in scene 1, concerning the cleverness with which Volpone and Mosca manipulate the hopes of Voltore, Corbaccio, and Corvino each to be

Volpone's heir. "Now, now, my clients / Beginne their visitation!" Volpone shouts, as we hear a knock on the door and he scurries to get into his costume; "Vulture, kite, / Raven and gor-crow, all my birds of prey / That thinke me turning carcasse, now they come" (1. 2. 87–90). If we add that each of them comes alone, each brings a gift, and that the gor-crow, if Volpone intends that bird for Lady Would Be, is put off until later, we will have outlined the fable of act 1.

Only two salients appear during the visits of the *captatores*, neither of them distinct enough to allow us to build expectations for the future course of the action. A good deal is made of Corbaccio's will later on in the play, but in act 1 we learn simply that he has agreed to name Volpone as his heir, disinheriting his son, and that at some unspecified future time he will send the revised will to Mosca. And there the subject is dropped until Mosca meets Bonario at the beginning of act 3, after the Celia episode has gotten fully under way. If we are able to form any expectations on the subject of Corbaccio's will, they are merely of the fact of its revision, since act 1 does not describe Corbaccio's son in such a way as to lead us to expect complications. The other salient, the postponed visit of Lady Would Be, is even less distinct. It is settled in the space of six rather neutral lines, which lead us to expect that a somewhat pretentious person will come at some future time, but no more. Otherwise, the first 700-odd lines of act 1 merely circle round a fixed point, and, if it were to end some twenty lines earlier, it would do so without having touched the strand of action around which the fable is thereafter organized.

The movement of act 1 is thus the sort of movement characteristic of satire rather than comedy. It develops and perfects an angle of vision upon human folly by peopling and vivifying the world, informed by the lust for gold, that is defined in Volpone's first speech.

Then, almost out of the blue, Mosca mentions Corvino's wife, and the satiric situation is translated into comic action. Here we enter Dryden's sort of play, one shaped around a single dominant intrigue, which carries along "underplots, or by-concernments of less considerable persons and intrigues... with the motion of the main plot."[6] The animating intention from which that action develops is formed at the end of act 1, and almost every stage in its development thereafter follows logically and naturally from the one preceding. Volpone's curiosity is piqued by Mosca's description of the "blazing starre of Italie" (1. 5. 108), and he determines to see her. Since she is "kept as warily as is your gold" (118), and since he cannot in any event be seen outside his house, he hits on the charade of the mountebank, which he plays out in the first scene of act 2. When, at the end of that scene, Celia throws down her handkerchief, Volpone's first intention is fulfilled and another one arises from it. This new intention is defined in the next scene, where, as Mosca helps him out of his mountebank costume, Volpone plays the conventional lover of romantic comedy, shot by Cupid's bolt, burning with passion, unable to live "without the hope / Of some soft air from her refreshing breath" (2. 4. 9–10). From this point on the comic fable is organized around Volpone's intention to seduce Celia.

Through this part of the play the fable is similar to the typical fable of romantic comedy, particularly to the sort of erotic *fabliau* upon which Machiavelli constructed *La Mandragola*—although in the transformed world of *Volpone* it is played with all its romantic values upside down.[7] The yearning lover is neither young nor tender; the coyness of the lady is not an obstacle to comically approved passion; and the comic resolution is not the bedding of the lady but her salvation from rape and the salvation of her lover from justice. But, allowing for the inversion of its values, the skeleton of the conventional comic fable is clear. Like Machiavelli's Callimacho, Volpone suffers with love for the chaste wife of a jealous man. And, like Ligurio, Mosca gives his master some hope of possessing the lady by inventing a scheme to enlist her husband's aid in cuckolding himself. The development of that scheme is the business of the third scene of act 2, where Corvino's towering jealousy is displayed—only to be turned on the fulcrum of his greed to an equally towering passion to be cuckolded. The lever is Mosca's carefully placed lie that doctors procured by Voltore and Corbaccio have advised that Volpone should sleep with a young woman. Anxious to preserve his own advantage with his *captatio,* Corvino goes off to force his wife into Volpone's bed. By means of that scheme Jonson begins to draw the satiric and thus far static situation of act 1 into the service of the developing comic action, for Corvino is made to offer his wife to Volpone in act 2 in consequence of the same desire that had led him in act 1 to offer Volpone a pearl.

In the next scene, the first of act 3, Jonson catches up another strand from act 1, but this time in a way less evidently logical and natural. This is the scene in which Mosca meets Bonario and invites him to Volpone's house to watch his father disinherit him. Upon that invitation, as John Dennis noted, "the whole plot turns."[8] There is no question but that Jonson needs this scene for the later part of the fable, since Bonario must be in the house in order to interrupt the rape

of Celia and thus precipitate the false climax of act 4. But there is
some question whether Bonario comes there simply in service of the
fable, to leap out at the appropriate moment, or whether his presence
may be understood as truly a coincidence of two unrelated schemes.

Jonson provides a colorable excuse for Mosca to do something
foolish—and the invitation to Bonario is at least foolish—by
directing our attention, by means of the speech in praise of parasites,
to his utter delight in himself. We are thus prepared to accept a Mosca
who overreaches himself through overvaluing his own powers. But
Jonson also suggests here that Mosca's intention to reveal the plans
to Bonario had been conceived earlier; for when he sees Bonario he
identifies him as "the person I was bound to seeke"
(3. 2. 2). We should, then, be able to discover a motive for Mosca's
action more precise than pride itself; we should, indeed, be able to
understand it as well as accept it.

Dennis found absurd Mosca's own explanation in act 3, scene 9,
that he had brought Bonario in the expectation that "the unnatural-
nesse, first, of the act, / And then, his father's oft disclaiming in
him / (Which I did mean t' helpe on) would sure enrage him / To doe
some violence upon his parent" (31–34). But Mosca's is the only
explanation the play provides, and Herford and Simpson insist, quite
properly, that we must take seriously its burden if not its precise aim.
"Corbaccio was attached to his son," they explain, "and, corrupt as
he is, had at first demurred to the prospect of disinheriting him. It is
Mosca's cue to prevent any recurrence of these scruples, and he takes
the course which he expects will promptly and violently alienate
father and son. What he meant to happen is substantially what he tells
Corbaccio has happened."[9]

That may be so, but it is difficult to find any particular reason in
the play why it should be so. Corbaccio's demurral in act 1 consists in
a single question—a slight foundation for so important an act—and
that question does not suggest that he has any special regard for
Bonario beyond their formal relationship: "And disinherit /
My sonne?" (1. 4. 95–96). He is thereafter enthusiastic about Mosca's
plans—so enthusiastic that he persuades himself they were his own
plans all along. Moreover, those plans have changed a bit and grown
more specific in the interval between acts 1 and 3. In act 1 no time was
fixed for the delivery of the will, nor was it clear that Corbaccio would
himself deliver it;[10] but at the beginning of act 3 Mosca clearly
believes that a time for its delivery has been agreed upon and that
Corbaccio will bring it himself. Thus, when he ushers Lady Would Be

offstage at the end of scene 5, he promises Volpone that his desire for
Celia will be satisfied, although he can tell him no more now because
"*Corbaccio* will arrive straight, with the will" (33).

That discrepancy suggests that elements in the play have different
faces for Jonson depending on whether they are regarded satirically
or comically. Act 1 is imagined satirically, and here Jonson needs no
more than Corbaccio's willingness to disinherit his son in favor of
Volpone in order to show that all feelings in Corbaccio have been
subordinated to the single feeling of greed. But when he draws
Corbaccio's willingness to disinherit into the comic fable, he must
particularize the circumstances of the delivery of the will because, in
the comic fable, Corbaccio's revised will becomes part of a chain of
events connected, at least nominally, by cause and effect and
dependent on the close timing of coincidence.

As the whole question of Corbaccio's will is developed in the
fable—that is, as an event with a particular meaning, to take place at a
particular time and in a particular manner—it seems to be chiefly a
creation of the fable itself, thrown up to provide the semblance of a
motive for an act the fable requires. The problem is not that Mosca's
reason for seeking out Bonario is intrinsically absurd, as Dennis
thought, but simply that it appears to be arbitrary, not founded in the
earlier development of the action. We can accept Mosca's invitation
to Bonario because we are now as buoyantly confident of his ability to
manipulate people as he is himself; but if we are to understand it as
part of a coherent sequence of action, we must supply its foundation
as generously as Herford and Simpson do.

That is the problem I had in mind earlier when I said that, once the
comic fable has been set going at the end of act 1, *almost* every stage in
its development follows logically and naturally from the one
preceding. The first scene of act 3 clearly does not. But, once past
Mosca's discovery to Bonario, the fable has clear sailing through the
end of act 4. And, as it proceeds, the fable continues to pick up and
animate, by means of Volpone's passion for Celia, other inert
elements of the situation defined in act 1.

The first of these elements is the postponed visit of Lady Would
Be, which finally occurs in act 3, scene 4. In one sense this scene, like
the earlier and later scenes involving Sir Politic and Peregrine, is a
satiric interlude, a gratuitous display of a pure and perfect fool,
contained and suported by the now strongly developed "motion of
the main plot." Lady Would Be's visit is almost wholly irrelevant to
the conduct of the fable, but Jonson makes her exhibition serve the

fable by having her arrive while Volpone writhes on his couch in anticipation of some word from Mosca about Celia. Her coming thus creates comic suspense at a crucial moment in the fable. And because of its timing we should see Lady Would Be as a foil for Celia, even if we were not pointedly directed to do so by the manner in which she is brought onstage. She knocks, and Volpone sends Nano to answer, sighing, as the dwarf goes off, "Now, *Cupid,* / Send it be *Mosca,* and with faire returne." Nano's shout from offstage is ambiguous: "It is the beauteous madam." But Volpone guesses from its tone: "*Would-Be*—is it?" (3. 3. 22–24). Then, as he settles himself on his couch, the Celia of his expectations having been metamorphosed into Lady Would Be, he breathes another sigh: "I feare / A second hell, too, that my loathing this / Will quite expell my appetite to the other" (27–29).

After so pointed a direction we should expect the two scenes—Lady Would Be's visit and the wooing of Celia—to play as point and counterpoint, as indeed they do. Both are designed around the same situation: a pious visit to a sickbed. Lady Would Be has ostensibly come to inquire about Volpone's health, like a grotesquely powdered and feathered hospital volunteer, and she stays to nurse him. The remedies she dredges up from the fantastic apothecary of her imagination—"Seed-pearle... boiled with syrrope of apples, / Tincture of gold, and corall, citron-pills, / Your elicampane roote, mirobalanes" (52–54)—are answered by the equally fantastic moral equivocation under which Corvino delivers his wife to Volpone's bed—"a pious worke, mere charity for physick" (3. 7. 65). Once Celia is delivered, of course, Volpone plays Lady Would Be's role, besieging Celia with words, urging her toward the couch, as he was himself confined to the couch and besieged by the "floud of wordes" from Lady Would Be. Celia's appeals to heaven recall Volpone's despairing citation of the classical poet who held "that your highest female grace is silence" (78). The pornographic fantasies with which Volpone attempts to woo Celia recall Lady Would Be's peculiarly sexless prattle about the more erotic Italian poets. And Celia's horror at discovering that her appearance has stirred improper desires answers Lady Would Be's anxiety that her own appearance may not stir them. Moment answers moment, until at last, in Celia's despairing cry to heaven, "O! just God!," we have an echo of Volpone's equally despairing prayer that "some power, some fate, some fortune rescue me!" (126). At that moment Bonario pops out to save Celia from rape, just as Mosca had earlier popped in to save Volpone from "torture."

Bonario's unexpected rescue of Celia sets off the second complica-
tion in the story of Volpone's pursuit of her (the first involved
Corvino's jealousy and how to get round it) and leads directly to the
resolution of the comic action that is informed by his desire. Up to
this point the fable has been animated by a single question refined
into successively more particular forms. The first was how to see
Celia, which issued in the mountebank scene; the second was how to
meet her, which led to the manipulation of Corvino's jealousy
following the mountebank scene; the third was how to bed her, which
led, through Corvino's threats and Volpone's lures, to the attempted
rape. Now, because Celia's unexpected resistance had forced Volpone
to that desperate measure, the question is not how to get Celia but
how to avoid the consequences of having sought her. And that is a
question that will ultimately exhaust the resources of the Celia fable
and set Jonson to discover new ways of animating the remainder of
the play.

The question is pursued at the *scrutineo* in one of those mad
convocations of fools before the seat of justice that Jonson delighted
in. And it is answered merely by allowing each of the fools to pursue
his natural bent. In the course of this sequence, Voltore, the first of
the fools to be introduced and the last to be drawn into the comic
action, organizes and carries off the largest of the transformations
wrought by avarice in the play, turning Venetian justice from truth to
falsehood. But those are terms accessible only to the chief antagonists,
Volpone and Mosca on one side, Celia and Bonario on the other. For
the lies they tell are never quite perceived by any of the fools precisely
as lies. "Each of 'hem," Mosca says later, "is so possest and stuft with
his owne hopes / That anything, unto the contrary, / Never so true,
or never so apparent / Never so palpable, they will resist it" (5.2.
23–27). Corbaccio, who would disinherit his son to gain Volpone's
estate, naturally has accepted Mosca's account of what took place in
Volpone's room, and he merely reproduces it in court. Corvino,
whose dedication to his hopes has led him to conceive Celia's refusal
to sleep with Volpone as an act of betrayal to be punished in just the
ways he had earlier threatened to punish sexual infidelity, merely
provides circumstantial embellishment for what he takes to be
essentially true: that Celia has betrayed him with Bonario because she
has allowed Bonario to keep her from Volpone's bed. And Voltore
merely provides a consecutive voice for the "formal tale" with which
Mosca has provided them all. On their side, Celia and Bonario have
only their innocence and their faith in heaven, neither of which, the

fourth *avocatore* tells them, is acceptable testimony in a Venetian court. And thus the *avocatori*, pursuing their own natural bent, have begun to find against Celia and Bonario even before Volpone is presented in court, once more in the costume and makeup of a dying man. The evidence of their own eyes—the least trustworthy evidence in the world of *Volpone*—persuades them. And as they order Celia and Bonario held for later sentencing, the circle of deception closes again, all within it safe.

Volpone does not, of course, bed Celia as Callimacho beds Lucrezia, and thus the resemblance between Machiavelli's comic *fabliau* and the comic fable of *Volpone* is not literally sustained. But Volpone's desire for Celia is ironically satisfied by the brilliant defense Mosca has concocted for him. That point is made in act 5, scene 2, when Mosca complains that Volpone does not seem sufficently delighted by the success of their strategies at court. Oh, but he is, Volpone replies, "more then if I had enjoy'd the wench: / The pleasure of all woman-kind's not like it" (10–11). In that way Jonson acknowledges the conventional ending of the comic fable even as he violates it.

But the very thoroughness with which Jonson pursues his comic and satiric logic is itself a problem; for he so manages the interplay of motive and self-deception that the only characters in possession of the information that could drive the comic fable forward are firmly committed to suppressing it. Thus, as act 4 ends, we find ourselves back in the dramatic predicament of act 1 before the mention of Celia, with a fully defined situation but without any particular line along which it is to develop. With Celia and Bonario clapped into prison, there may be a moral demand for the play to go forward, but there is no clearly defined reason, within the logic of the fable itself, why it should. Only the Peregrine–Sir Politic episode in act 4 establishes a salient that leads into act 5, and it is not a very distinct one. Peregrine merely observes, as Sir Politic and Lady Would Be go offstage, "Well, wise Sir Pol: since you have practis'd, thus / Upon my freshman-ship, I'le trie your salt head, / What proofe it is against a counter-plot" (4. 3. 22–24). We are thus prepared for the fourth scene of act 5, but the question is whether we are prepared for the first.

Dryden came at that problem from another angle, observing, as we have noted, that the action of the play comes naturally to an end with act 4 and that Jonson forces from it a new action in act 5. If we take it that by the "action" of the play Dryden means the action of the fable, there is no question, I think, that he is right and that his observation cuts a good bit deeper than Jonson's critics have lately been willing to grant. There is no point in arguing against Dryden that *Volpone* could not end with act 4, having merely returned to the situation of act 1 with its moral structure even more unbalanced,[11] for Dryden did not imagine that it could or that it should. Nor is there any point in saying that Dryden's criticism is a consequence of reading the play on one level only, as if, by attaching it to the fable, we could dismiss it as primitive and naïve.[12] However we choose to read the play, whatever we take to be its theme, the fact is that all of the levels on which we may approach *Volpone* are shaped by its comic fable. The very weight of Jonson's investment in the Celia fable, then, coupled with the clarity and firmness with which he pursues it, leads to a distinct break between the ending of that fable, the exhausting of its animating intention, and the development of what is virtually a new fable in act 5.

The intention that informs the new fable—Volpone's decision to plague his gulls by having it given out that he is dead and that Mosca is his heir—is neither crafty nor prudent, but it is not inconsistent at the level of character with the Volpone we have watched throughout the play. He has been an energetic schemer but not a wholly successful one—witness his loss of Celia. Moreover, the giggling elation he feels in the first scene of act 5, which develops naturally from the release of tension following the trial scene, lays an even more palpable groundwork in his character for a proudly foolish act than Mosca's speech in praise of parasites lays in his for the disclosures to Bonario, because we have been more fully persuaded of its emotional reality. The future had looked so bleak, but their defense had been so brilliant, their fools so sublimely foolish, that some grand, extravagant gesture must be found to set as a capstone on the whole enterprise. Voltore and the others demand "very richly— / Well — to be cozened" (5. 2. 46–47).

The gesture Volpone settles upon, then, is merely the perfection of a series of gestures he has made toward them during the play. For he and Mosca have not merely tricked Voltore, Corbaccio, and Corvino of their gold, their plate, and their jewels; they also put them through their comic paces, deliberately testing the lengths of folly to which their avarice could be made to lead them. And having found no limits, Volpone, buoyed up by his release from fear, simply proposes to demonstrate to them how vain, how perfectly foolish, their actions have been. This proposal itself is foolish, of course, for it means the end of his scheme for milking them of their wealth, it lays him open to the practices of Mosca, and it leads both to their falls. But as Dryden has observed, it agrees well enough with Volpone's established character as a voluptuary. The problem we encounter as we move from act 4 to act 5 is not, then, that Volpone's character is inconsistent, nor is it that the action taken up in act 5 is wholly new. It is simply that act 5 is organized around an action different from the one that has occupied us through the first four acts.

The Character of Volpone: Moral Voluptuary

It may seem curious to speak of the Volpone who sets out to plague his fools as a voluptuary, particularly since the story of his lust for Celia has just been concluded.[13] But to imagine Volpone's voluptuousness confined to his lusts or to the more obvious forms of sensuous pleasure is to imagine it much too narrowly. Volpone is from the beginning of the play what we might call an aesthetic voluptuary, perhaps even a moral one.

There is no question, of course, that Volpone is a voluptuary in the ordinary sense of the word. "The Turk is not," he boasts, "more sensual in his pleasures." But Volpone's pleasures must come to him in forms twice or thrice refined, spiced with an edge of the novel or the grotesque sufficiently excessive that one can see that it is the spice, not the meat, that chiefly delights him. Confirmation of this is easy to find in the play. Nano, Androgyno, and Castrone, his servants, are the handiest examples because they are not merely servants of his ease and pleasures; they are sports of nature, representing in miniature the whole range of human deformity. But another sort of example will allow us to come more quickly to the aesthetic and moral strains in Volpone's pleasures.

The passage I have in mind comes from the climactic moment of the Celia fable. Volpone has for two acts devoted all his energies toward getting Celia into his room. Now that she is there, he turns to describe what he intends to do with her:

> Our drinke shall be prepared gold, and amber;
> Which we will take, untill my roofe whirle round
> With the *vertigo*: and my dwarfe shall dance,
> My eunuch sing, my foole make up the antique.
> Whil'st we, in changed shapes, act Ovid's tales,
> Thou like Europa now, and I like Jove,
> Then I like Mars, and thou like Ericyne.
>
> . . . .

And I will meet thee, in as many shapes:
Where we may, so, trans-fuse our wandring soules,
Out at our lippes, and score up summes of pleasures,
   That the curious shall not know,
   How to tell them, as they flow;
   And the envious, when they find
   What their number is, be pin'd.

                                                              [3. 7. 217–39]

A good deal might be said about that passage, and I want to return to
it later; but what interests me at the moment is how relatively
insignificant Celia's role in the whole affair seems to be. Volpone's
vision of erotic paradise sounds like a theatrical performance,
complete with script, setting, costumes, and a drink or two before
going onstage. As in all theatrical performances, the extras—Nano
and the others, and the audience—the curious and the envious who
are to keep a tally of their encounters and be gratifyingly shocked, are
every bit as important to its success as the chief actors. For its success
is not measured by the pleasure of the principals but by the effect the
appearance of their pleasure has on the onlookers.

   The analogy between Volpone's erotic fantasies and a theatrical
performance suggests one reason why his desire for Celia is satisfied,
indeed more than satisfied, by the trial in act 4. The trial is finally a
better show than the one he had imagined, more daring in its premises
because his freedom was at stake, more brilliant in its execution
because the actors scarcely knew that they were actors. It delighted
him "more than if I had enjoyed the wench," Volpone says, "the
pleasure of all woman-kind's not like it." Here we can see clearly that
Volpone's voluptuousness runs more on aesthetic than on sensual
lines, derives more pleasure from a perfectly executed design than
from the consumption of its materials. But that is something Volpone
himself has told us in the first scene of the play, where he represents
himself as devoted to wealth to the point of worshiping it but as more
delighted by its "cunning purchase" than by its "glad possession."

   Jonson develops this distinction between the game and the candle
following each of the visits of the *captatores* in act 1. As they
successively exit, Voltore leaving behind his plate, Corbaccio his
gold, and Corvino his jewels, Volpone turns neither to plate, gold,
nor jewels, as we might expect someone animated by pure avarice to
do, but rather to Mosca, to praise him for something quite aside from
the collection of wealth. The rare skill with which Mosca has made
fools of them all simply delights him. "Contayne / Your fluxe of

laughter, sir," Mosca says, after the exit of Corbaccio; "you know, this hope / Is such a bait, it covers any hooke." "O, but thy working, and thy placing it!" Volpone replies, ignoring the *chequines* Corbaccio has left and embracing Mosca; "I cannot hold; good rascall, let me kisse thee" (1. 4. 133–37).

Volpone prizes his fools, then, not merely as sources of wealth; he prizes them also precisely as fools, because they provide him with the materials out of which comedies can be made. They are, to use an image of Mosca's, the "discords" out of which he and Volpone make "rare music." But Volpone's regard for them as fools is limned by a contempt for their folly that at times finds almost flatly moral expression and endangers the very comedy he is creating. It is in that respect that we might call him a moral voluptuary. His delight in Mosca's manipulation of Corbaccio, for example, leads him first to a moral formula: "What a rare punishment / Is avarice, to itself" (142–43). He then reflects for a half-dozen lines on the maladies of old age before turning to combine his formulation of avarice's power with those reflections to produce a formal, morally edged portrait of Corbaccio as a type of the old man whose avaricious folly has blinded him to his own mortality:

> Nay, here was one,
> Is now gone home, that wishes to live longer!
> Feeles not his gout, nor palsy, faines himself
> Yonger by scores of yeeres, flatters his age
> With confident belying it, hopes he may,
> With charmes, like Aeson, have his youth restor'd:
> And with these thoughts so battens, as if fate
> Would be as easily cheated on, as he,
> And all turns aire!
>
> [151–59]

What makes this example of Volpone's unexpectedly moral disdain especially interesting is the fact that his description of the corrective processes of fate, turning to air the false hopes of Corbaccio, parallels so closely his earlier description of his own practices against all of his gulls and anticipates the perfection of their cozening in act 5. He plays "with their hopes," he explains in act 1, just before the entrance of Voltore, feeding them, "letting the cherry knock against their lips, / And, draw it, by their mouths, and back againe" (1. 1. 85–90). And in act 5 he simply lets them see, as fate will let Corbaccio see, that their hopes have all been vain.

That parallel is sufficiently close that, if one were tempted by the play to psychologizing analyses of its characters, one might say that Volpone has deliberately adopted the role of fate, setting about to clarify men's motives and to reveal more quickly than fate does the ends to which they lead. Under that view we might almost speak of him as a soured idealist, a Jacobean malcontent who has gone beyond railing at the world to construct within it a *reductio ad absurdum* from the materials of latent foolishness it provides. Whether deliberately adopted or not, however, the creation of *reductiones* is a major part of Volpone's role, and of Mosca's as his agent, and in its execution the characters of Volpone and Mosca are transparently one with Jonson's purposes as a satirist.

The visits of the *captatores* in act 1 offer perhaps the clearest instances of this side of Volpone's character, particularly in their moments of what might seem to be incidental comic music. The moments I have in mind, really almost *lazzi,*, are those when Mosca, for example, takes advantage of Corbaccio's deafness simply to mock him:

> Mosc.: Your worship is a precious asse!
> Corv.: What say'st thou?
> Mosc.: I doe desire your worship, to make haste, sir.
> [1. 4. 130–31]

Or when, in the scene following, Mosca tells Corvino that Volpone is deaf so as to encourage Corvino to rail at him:

> Corv.:   [His cheeks]
> Are like an old smok'd wall, on which the raine
> Ran down in streaks.
> Mosc.: Excellent, sir! Speake out:
> You may be lowder yet; a culvering
> Discharged in his eare, would hardly bore it.
> Corv.: His nose is like a common sewre, still running.
> Mosc.: 'Tis good! And what his mouth?
> Corv.: A very draught.
> [1. 5. 60–66]

Each of these scenes has two recognizable purposes: one is the purpose of Volpone and Mosca to milk their gulls; the other is what we might call the purpose of the play itself, to reveal not only that Voltore, Corbaccio, and Corvino are avaricious but, more precisely, that their avarice has blinded them and made them fools. The confidence game Volpone and Mosca pursue serves this satiric purpose in a general way by showing that in their pursuit of gain the *captatores* can be deceived and bilked of their own goods. To that extent the two purposes coincide, and almost every advance by one is an advance by the other. But Mosca's *lazzi* of deafness are irrelevant to the aims of the confidence game; indeed, they endanger it, since any miscalculation of the extent of Corbaccio's deafness or Corvino's credulity might alert them to the fact that they are being deceived in other ways. What appears on the side of the care proper to the characters to be a needless risk is, however, on the side of Jonson's satiric rhetoric, a positive gain. For the very pointlessness of Mosca's taunting them merely emphasizes the fact that there is no limit to what Corvino will believe or Corbaccio fail to perceive when their eyes are on the main chance—Volpone's will.

The point is not, of course, that Corbaccio's deafness is caused by his greed. Regarded as a physical disability in a discrete character, Corbaccio's deafness and Mosca's fun with it are open to Dennis' objection that "personal defects cannot be amended and the exposing such, can never divert any but half-witted men."[14] But from the point of view of Jonson's satire, Corbaccio's deafness is an appropriate disability for a man animated by greed, as any disability that prevented him from perceiving the world accurately would be. And in emphasizing Corbaccio's deafness along with Corvino's credulity, Mosca's "pointless" *lazzi* provide comic examples of a satiric point he will later draw out in full:

> Each of 'hem
> Is so possest and stuft with his owne hopes.
> That anything, unto the contrary,
> Never so true, or never so apparent,
> Never so palpable, they will resist it —

"Like," Volpone adds, "a temptation of the divell."

That exchange takes place at the beginning of act 5. And Volpone sets about immediately to force his gulls to confront the diabolical temptation of truth by speeding up the processes of time and making them understand immediately that their hopes to be his heirs were all vain. Dennis objects to Volpone's plaguing his "bubbles...only for having been his bubbles."[15] But that is, of course, precisely the point. Volpone despises Voltore and the others even as he uses them, despises them for the self-induced blindness that enables him to use them. And to the end he retains, curiously, his capacity for wonder at their folly:

That, yet, to me's the strangest! how th' hast borne it!
That these (being so divided 'mongst themselves)
Should not sent some-what, or in me, or thee,
Or doubt their owne side.

[5. 2. 19–22]

At such moments Volpone stands sufficiently outside the "trans-changed" world of Venice to recognize that it is "transchanged."[16] In that respect, he has perhaps a better claim to be called the scourge of God in the narrow world of his play than Tamburlaine has in the larger world of his, for Volpone is explicitly aware of the ironically moral ends his knavery serves. The new action he sets about in act 5 is undertaken to perfect, for delight if not for profit, the proverb he had earlier touched on with musing wonder: "O, what a rare punishment / Is avarice to itself."

Mosca adds to that, "I, with our helpe, sir." And in doing so he raises a question. Does the play in fact dramatize avarice's punishment of itself? Mosca's comment, slyly directed toward the profit he and Volpone derive from the "punishment" of the gulls, points a fact. Avarice's punishment of Voltore, Corbaccio, and Corvino has, if it does not require, considerable help from Volpone and Mosca, who expend a good bit of effort and ingenuity on their schemes. It is true, nonetheless, that the eagerness with which Corbaccio and Corvino court their own deception—make their own such schemes as the disinheriting of Bonario and the prostitution of Celia—suggests that the efforts of Mosca and Volpone merely provide the occasion by which ravening greed and foolishness manifest themselves. "This plot / Did I thinke on before," Corbaccio says, after Mosca has suggested that he revise his will in favor of Volpone; and twice more he insists that it is "mine owne project." Corvino is similarly insistent on appropriating to himself the credit for Celia's prostitution, imploring Mosca to "tell him, with what zeale, / And willingnesse, I doe it: sweare it was / On the first hearing (as thou maist doe, truely) / Mine owne free motion" (2. 6. 92–94).

But that question takes a different form when applied to Volpone and Mosca themselves. For while their punishment at the hands of the *avocatori* is immediately occasioned by their mutual greed (dramatized in their whispered haggling over the division of Vol-pone's goods), they are, in any event, in a situation that can hardly be salvaged, and they have been put there because Volpone, acting as a moral voluptuary, set out to perfect his satirical design against

Voltore, Corbaccio,and Corvino. Ironically enough, it is not avarice that creates the situation leading to Volpone's fall; it is his decision to play the role of a moral fate.

THE CHARACTER OF VOLPONE: THE SATIRIC VICE

It may be tempting to see in Volpone's decision to play the role of fate the inverted moral passion of the malcontent, but *Volpone* is a play that scarcely admits, let alone invites, psychologizing analyses of its characters, all of whom are in the nature of caricatures. It is a species of morality play, the species moral satire, and so, for all its gritty substance, it is bound within the world of almost pure analytical reason inhabited by *The Castle of Perseverance.* Its form, of course, is different from the form of the *Castle.* But as Alan Dessen has shown, it is different in just the ways that the forms of such late moralities as *Like Will to Like, The Tide Tarrieth No Man, The Longer Thou Livest the More Fool Thou Art, All for Money,* and *The Three Ladies of London* are different.[17] All of them replace Mankind, the central figure of the *Castle,* with a reigning Vice and set round him a spectrum of characters representative of the diffusion and power of that vice in the world. They are all, that is to say, moral satires, concerned with tracing the consequences of a particular vice in society. Volpone occupies in his play the same position occupied by Corage in the *Tide* or by All for Money in the play that bears his name: he embodies in its purest and most intense form the greed that animates his world, and he sets in motion those who are moved by its promptings. Of the characters in the main fable, only Celia and Bonario are not paler images of Volpone himself, and they escape from the pole of greed only to slide, by a sort of rhetorical gravity, to a singular and similarly unreal purity, made necessary because their only function is to provide instances of the neglect and abuse of virtue—not a particular virtue but virtue itself—in Volpone's world.

Seen in that context, Volpone's passion to vex his gulls for his own delight while he swindles them for his profit recalls the passion the morality Vice has for bringing Mankind to the eternal vexations of hell for his own profit and delight. And Volpone's tireless interest in the moral teleology of greed, the guileless candor with which he sets about to reveal its consequences even as he depends upon its motions, thus seems of a piece with the similarly guileless exposition by the Vice of his own nature and the ends to which he leads. "His money brings him to pleasure," says the Vice in *All for Money,* "and pleasure sends him to me, / And I send him to damnation, and damnation sends him to hell quickly"(1317–18). Hell is not, of course, an issue in *Volpone,* except by implication in Celia's appeals to heaven, but one may find its shadow in Volpone's insistence on pushing his jest to its own inevitable end, perfecting it by stripping Voltore, Corbaccio, and Corvino of the happiness of being well deceived.

Thus, what seems to be a complicating moral edge to Volpone's voluptuousness when Volpone is regarded as a character seems, when we examine his place in the satiric strategy of the play, to be one of the conventional roles of the morality Vice. In that light, Volpone's passion to plague "his bubbles... only for having been his bubbles," which bridges the gap in the fable between acts 4 and 5, appears to be a consequence of the same sort of logic that leads the Vice to describe thoroughly his own viciousness or that enables Mankind to step out of his role in order to define for the audience the errors he has made within it. At such moments Mankind and the Vice speak directly for the preacher who stands immediately behind the dramatic world they inhabit, as Volpone at similar moments seems to act directly for Jonson. Of course, with the dispositions of character and the necessities or moral rhetoric both making claims on Volpone's actions, it is difficult to draw a line between mimetic and rhetorical logic. But I think Dryden strikes the proper balance. Volpone's decision to perfect his satire "agrees well enough with his character as a voluptuary," Dryden says, "and by it the author gains the end at which he aims, the punishment of vice and the reward of virtue." Dryden's rhetoric is appropriately slippery, for Jonson's is as well; but his point seems clear: Volpone's character provides a colorable excuse for his decision to play dead in order to see how Voltore and the others take the fact that they have been fooled by their own greed ("agrees well enough" with it), and that decision directly serves Jonson's larger moral aims.

If we understand Volpone in that way, however, it becomes more important than ever that we understand the action of the play to consist in a principle of moral teleology, one that includes Volpone himself. If we do not, we ought to convict the play, for all its evident toughness, of sentimentality, of juggling its way toward a morally satisfactory conclusion without a proper regard for the logic of its materials. For unless such a principle of action is securely dramatized before the beginning of act 5, all that we can say of the ending is that Volpone ran his head into a noose because he obediently played a role that Jonson cast for him.

THE COMIC AND SATIRIC STRUCTURES

I do not think that *Volpone* is quite sentimental, but it seems clear, on the basis of what has been said thus far of its structure, that we need to discover the principles of action around which it coheres in order to be able to maintain that it is not. Before we can do that, however, we will need to sort out its comic and satiric elements and come to some preliminary conclusions about the nature of that action, for one of the peculiarities of *Volpone* is that neither its comic fable nor its satiric thesis is developed coherently and consecutively to lead us to the second trial. Both founder on the second scene of act 5: its fable because act 5 marks the beginning of a new comic action and makes a clean break with the action that has animated the first four acts; its satiric thesis (which I take to be avarice's punishment of itself) because, in initiating the essentially comic movement of act 5, Volpone functions as the satirist of avarice and not the embodiment of its promptings, and thus his comic punishment turns on a rhetorical, not a moral, point.

There is, indeed, a stubbornly undramatic element in *Volpone* that resists consecutive development, an element that inheres in the nature of satire itself. It is an element that *Volpone* shares with other relatively pure moral satires, such as *All for Money,* that regard their characters as examples of perverse moral dispositions and set out to expose them along those lines. This element is simply that, having once exposed them, the play has accomplished its end, and, insofar as it continues to be imagined as a satire, has nowhere else to go, except, perhaps, to expose the same characters in other ways or to find new characters to expose in the old ways. The only action that pure satire of this sort admits—and by action I mean the tying-together of episodes into a single whole—is the action of repetition or variation. For satire regards those whom it attacks ontologically, not prudentially. Its concern is with fools and their folly, not with the ways in which fools may act on others. Thus it does not say that one ought to avoid being foolish because bad things may happen, as comedy does; it says simply that fools are ludicrous in themselves. It needs to say this, obvious though it is, because in the satirist's opinion society does a bad job of recognizing its fools. The creation of satire is thus the creation of a perspective on society that allows the satirist to share his special angle of vision in order to let us see beneath deceptive masks— those of the lawyer, the husband, and the father, for example—and to reveal the perverse folly they obscure. And its development is simply the filling-in of that perspective, the peopling of the world caught by it. The purest and most economical form of satire is invective, which, however long sustained, is a single rhetorical episode, resolvable into the cry "Fool!" And a sustained linear satire, a dramatic satire, is a series of such episodes, like a photograph album composed of pictures related to one another by a comic subject matter or a common point of view.

Thus, when the question of Corbaccio's will appears in the relatively pure satiric setting of act 1, it is only a question of fact, directed at revealing the depth of Corbaccio's avaricious folly: Will Corbaccio disinherit his son in order to advance his hope to be Volpone's heir? That is a centripetal question, and, once it is answered, Jonson is done with it in act 1. None of the centrifugal contingencies such as Bonario's reaction, the circumstances in which the decision is to be carried out—contingencies that could translate a discrete fact into an occasion for action—is even touched on there.

Yet it is these centrifugal contingencies that precisely determine the forms under which the question appears when it is taken up in act 3; for in the interim Jonson has begun to animate, by means of a comic fable, the satiric world he has defined, and comedy regards its materials as resources for action, focusing not on the making of decisions but on the process of carrying them out once they have been made. Where satire is ontological, then, comedy is prudential, involved in the world of contingent circumstances where men are happy or sad and their desires are satisfied or frustrated. In that respect the ends of satire are the beginnings of comedy; for in comedy the display of fools is preamble to their circumvention and their integration into, or exclusion from, a harmonious community in which real, not foolish, values prevail. If dramatic satire may be compared to a collection of discrete photographs, comedy is like a motion-picture film, each moment flowing into and shaping the one that follows as the plot develops from *turbulentia prima* to *tranquilla ultima*.

As we have seen, that formulation of the movement of comedy is ironically fulfilled in the Celia story with respect to the persons of the play who chiefly concern us, Volpone and Mosca. Volpone begins that part of the play troubled in the usual ways, and he ends it with all passion spent and the backwash of trouble stilled, "more [satisfied] than if I had enjoyed the wench." But Volpone and Mosca have been presented to us satirically, defined as the negatives of a comically approved society whose values are flouted in their comic triumph. The Celia fable, then, is itself a prolonged variation on the satiric displays of act 1. In its course we see that greed can turn Corvino's jealousy to pandering, as we had seen in act 1 that Corbaccio's greed was stronger than paternal love; we also see that Volpone's fools are perfectly willing to lie innocence into prison in order to preserve their hopes; and finally we see that Venetian justice is as easily gulled as any of Volpone's fools. In short, at the conclusion of the Celia fable, we have come to see—perhaps more clearly, certainly in different ways and with broader applications—precisely what we saw at the end of act 1: that Volpone's world turns upon greed and that those who inhabit it are blinded and made fools because their eyes are always on the main material chance.

Insofar as it makes the broadest application of that satiric point, including the institutions of Venetian society within the circle of those deceived by Volpone, act 4 marks the natural conclusion of the purely satiric structure of the play. As Celia and Bonario are led off to prison to await their sentences, darkness closes down as surely as it does at the end of Pope's *Dunciad,* and there seems to be as little hope that it will be lifted. But while the world of *Volpone* is imagined satirically, Jonson conceives the linear structure of the play comically, erring a bit against "the strict rigour of comick law," perhaps, but erring by design, "to put the snaffle in their mouths, that crie out, we never punish vice in our interludes."[18] The three relatively discrete episodes that compose the linear structure do indeed come loosely together to form a single comic action (as opposed to a single comic fable), which begins in trouble unrecognized, hidden by Volpone's guile and the blindness of Voltore and the others, and proceeds through successively wider revelations to the casting-out of the sources of trouble at the end of the second trial.

The judgment passed there on Volpone and his gulls is a comic judgment, but it is complicated by the fact that it is passed in a world Jonson continues to imagine satirically. Thus, while we can understand that Volpone and the others have been cast out of the society by law, we are given little reason to believe, and some to doubt, that the folly they represent has been cast out in fact. For as Volpone ripens toward his uncasing, the fourth *avocatore* ripens toward offering his daughter to Mosca. Both come to bear at the same moment, and the *avocatore* is prevented from making what he imagines to be a good match only because Volpone's confessional voice is, for the moment, louder.

Moreover, insofar as Volpone's punishment is comic, insofar as he is seized and cast out by the society of the play, the form of his punishment is slightly askew from the moral maxim the first *avocatore* extracts from it to close the play. "Mischiefes feed / Like beasts, till they be fat," he says, "and then they bleed" (5. 12. 151–52). But if we are to avoid succumbing to Volponeism on the strength of Volpone's comic punishment, we will need to imagine a more astute and searching system of justice than the *avocatori* lead us to expect— particularly if we are puzzled, as Volpone is, by the question of how he could have been so foolish as to have gotten himself into that situation in the first place.

There is another view, however. When Volpone uncases, the first *avocatore* exclaims, "The knot is now undone, by miracle!" (95). And Bonario echoes, "Heaven could not, long, let such grosse crimes be hid" (98). We may at first find such a reaction naïve. "Nothing could be less true," Edward Partridge writes, "because the Fox, refusing to be gulled, uncases himself....'Miracle' implies a Christian providence, which has as ineffectual a voice in the court as in the bedroom."[19] But I am not sure that one can judge in those terms whether providence had a hand in the outcome or not, unless one simply restricts the operations of providence to moments when no human motives are available, as if providence revealed itself only in a vacuum. Certainly, if one imagines the world to have been divinely created, one must imagine that nature and the men who are a part of it obey divine logic even when they have no intention of doing so. The question of whether Bonario's pious exclamation is also an accurate one thus becomes a question of whether the world of the play leads us to think that moral laws and their ends are immanent in the actions of men and that Volpone is uncased by the inexorable logic of nature itself. In short, is the world of *Volpone* one in which a sort of natural providence "shapes our ends, rough-hew them how we will"?

SATIRIC ACTION: VOLPONE IN THE LAND OF UNLIKENESS

I want to organize the answer to that question, as I believe Jonson does, around the figure of Volpone in "the land of unlikeness," not because there is any particular reason to believe that Jonson was familiar with *Parabola I* but rather because the satiric rhetoric of *Volpone* employs a set of visual and verbal images similar in kind and serving similar purposes. One of the basic themes of the play concerns the different forms taken on by Volpone and the others as they seek the satisfaction of their desires. And by manipulating the relationship between those forms and their natural forms, Jonson is able to characterize the souls of his Venetian grandees and to show that in their frantic and fantastical transformations they merely tread what Saint Bernard called "the sterile circuit of the impious," debarred from satisfaction by the very nature of their desires, just as Filius Regis is doomed to frustration in the land of unlikeness because the desires that brought him there are incapable of satisfaction. What we have in *Volpone,* then, is a parody of life's pilgrimage. Where the pilgrim is connaturally inclined toward God and journeys toward him in the spirit, Volpone is inclined toward "Riches, the dumbe god," and the course of his action clarifies and perfects his perverse inclination. Recognizing that the form of the body functions for Jonson, as it does in the Bernardine allegory, as a transparent opening on the form of the soul, we can see, I think, that the uncasing of the fox and his condemnation are latent from the beginning of the play in Volpone's disguises—with only the circumstances of their accomplishment to be satisfied later.

The most general of the characterizing images in the play, and perhaps the most theatrically evident, is provided by the allusions to the beast fables. According to their names, the persons of the play are a fox, a fly, three scavenger birds, two parrots, and a falcon. Too much can be made of that, however. To speak of the play as if it were itself a beast fable, a tour through a veritable zoo, seriously impoverishes it. For if we see Voltore as indeed a vulture and Volpone as a fox, there is nothing extraordinary about their behavior at all. It is in the nature of a vulture to hover around a dying fox, as it is, according to the bestiaries, in the nature of a fox to feign death in order to catch and devour scavenger birds. When we are reminded of the nature of those animals by the names of the characters and by the scattered allusions to the beast fable of the tricky fox, we are the more sharply reminded that it is unnatural for men to do either. And thus, as we watch Volpone feigning death and Voltore and the others creeping round his bed, offering him gifts only to snatch at his substance once he is dead, we are aware that these are men virtually taking on the natures of beasts, virtually transforming themselves into monsters.[20]

In Volpone's opening speech, Jonson locates the informing source of their transformations in the desire for gold, which Volpone hails as the "world's soule, and mine." As a piece of characterization, Volpone's mock *aubade* is perfectly straightforward, cast in the mode of frank moral confession familiar in the role of the Vice of the morality drama. Gold is Volpone's "god," he tells us; the pieces of gold heaped up in his "shrine" are "saints" and "reliques" manifesting the divinity; and he values all the world in terms derived from his religion of wealth. But Volpone's secular religion is not merely different from Christianity; it is, as Edward Partridge reminds us, "almost point for point the reverse of the Christian,"[21] ranking matter over spirit, gold over men, and hell with gold over heaven without it. And the form of Volpone's pursuit of it is almost point for point the reverse of the form of Christian life.

While locating the source of Volpone's transformed world in the disposition of his soul toward the "dumbe god" of gold, Jonson organizes the matter of Volpone's hymn to gold into a new account of creation and a new order of history, presenting them as they might be seen if gold were indeed the Holy Spirit. "More glad then is / The teeming earth, to see the long'd-for sunne / Peepe through the hornes of the celestiall *ram,*" Volpone cries—beginning with the beginning of a spring morning at the creation of both the day and the year—"Am I, to view thy splendor, darkening his" (1. 1. 3–6). The association of gold with the sun suggests to him the division of light from darkness at the time of creation and perhaps, as well, the light by which God led the nation of Israel through the wilderness: "That, lying here, / amongst my other hoords, / Shew'st like a flame, by night; or like the day / Strooke out of *chaos,* when all darknesse fled / Unto the center." After gathering up the gold into his arms to "kisse / With adoration, thee, and every relique / Of sacred treasure, in this blessed roome," suggesting a forgotten age of auric matyrs, he turns to redefine the Golden Age and to reinterpret the motives of the poets of antiquity who gave it its name: "Well did wise Poets, by thy glorious name, / Title that age, which they would have the best." From there he comes out into a modern world reshaped by its imagined history, all its natural values turned upside down: "Thou being the best of things: and far transcending / All stile of joy, in children, parents, friends, / Or any other waking dreame on earth" (7–18). The superior reality he attributes to gold in that line is matched by his attribution to it of the creative powers of the Holy Spirit: "Deare *saint,* / Riches, the dumbe god, that giv'st all men tongues, / That canst doe nought, and yet mak'st men doe all things." And by a perfectly logical process he arrives at last at a new eschatology, with heaven as hell and hell as heaven: "The price of soules; even hell, with thee to boot, / Is made worth heaven" (21–25).

In consequence of this new historical myth, Jonson is able not merely to universalize Volpone (as Saint Bernard universalized Filius Regis by associating his journey with the historical journey of the nation of Israel); he is able as well to suggest an area of consideration that the satiric mode of the play might otherwise not admit. That is the moral etiology of Volponeism, the way in which the disposition of the soul, Volpone's and his world's, away from the Christian God and toward the dumb god of gold flower into a monstrous parody of Christianity enacted by men who are themselves monsters.

These allusions to the historical movements of Volpone's spirit are muted during the first scene of act 1, but in scene 2 they are clarified and developed in a sequence that invites us to think directly about the movements of the soul and its relationship with the bodies it informs.[22] I have in mind the interlude Nano, Androgyno, and Castrone perform for Volpone, during which Jonson lays down many of the major thematic lines of the play. The subject of the interlude is the transmigration of a soul, from its origin in Apollo, through forms semidivine and heroic, into more simply human forms, then through various migrations in which the soul bounces around among men and animals, until at last it comes to rest in Androgyno, Volpone's hermaphroditic fool. In tracing the history of this soul, Nano, Jonson's interlocutor, is no more interested than Lucian, from whom Jonson took the skeletal fiction of the interlude, in the precise relationships among the various bodies animated by the soul on its downward flight. That is to say, the interlude does not present a spiritual process, in which subsequent forms of the soul are in some way logically related to preceding forms. The only consistently observed principle of disposition is the general one of the steady downward movement of the soul from divine to human and bestial forms. But the very lack of some principle of relationship among the bodies animated by the soul may itself be significant, since it suggests that distinctions among men, and between men and beasts, have been lost in the latter stages of the soul's journey. The central theme of the interlude is clearly degeneration, a theme underlined by its grossly cynical tone and falsely paced verse and by the fact that it is performed by a dwarf, a eunuch, and a hermaphrodite. The world of Volpone, we are told in the interlude, is a far cry from the world of gods and heroes and some fair distance also from the world of proper men. What was, in its origins, divine is now Androgyno.

Androgyno is, Jonson indicates, an objectification of an essential quality of Volpone's soul. For Volpone calls for Androgyno and the others, insisting as he does so that he is perfectly free to do whatever he wants. "What should I doe," he asks, after sending Mosca off to fetch his servants, "but cocker up my *genius,* and live free / To all delights, my fortune calls me to?" (1. 1. 70–73). Introduced in that way, as the objects of his free choice, the dwarf, the eunuch, and the hermaphrodite manifest the deformity, the sterility and the monstrous folly of Volpone's soul in the same way that one's answers in the game "What would you do if you had a million dollars?" reveal the direction and the poverty of one's material imagination. Volpone sends for them, when he could have sent for anyone, because they answer to something in his spirit. We can understand in light of that fact why Mosca later suggests that they are his natural children. Perhaps more important, we can see that, as early as the first scene of the play, Jonson intimates that frustration is inherent in the very composition of Volpone's soul because Volpone's soul does not seek its satisfactions within the bounds of nature.

In that respect, Jonson defines Volpone in the first two scenes of the play in much the same way as Lydgate defines the Pilgrim, when he is carried by his Youth to the broad plain of the world, by objectifying the tendencies of his spirit in a monstrous landscape whose deformity mirrors the deformity within. As it is for the Pilgrim, or Filius Regis, or Wit, or Richard, the consequence for Volpone of the perverted disposition of his soul is, in the language of the interlude, the loss of its divine form and its degeneration into the form of a monster and a fool. The first of these terms is clearly appropriate, for Volpone's delight in the capering of his servants marks him as spiritually monstrous. The second term, Volpone's folly, awaits clarification later in the play.

The interlude thus develops further implications of Volpone's hymn to his gold, this time using classical rather than Christian coordinates. But it has other, more properly dramatic uses as well, for it invites us to think explicitly about the relationship between the soul and the forms it inhabits. And, depending on the way in which we formulate its subject we may gain through the interlude a purchase on different aspects of the action of the play. We may say that the interlude is either about many bodies animated by a single soul or about the fact that a single soul animates many bodies. Either way, it is an emphatic restatement in usable dramatic terms—usable because it translates an apostrophe into a description of action—of the opening line of Volpone's hymn, "Haile the world's soule, and mine."

If we take the subject of the interlude to be many bodies animated by a single soul, we are concerned with the first term of that line, "the world's soule." Placed between Volpone's description of the *spiritus mundi* in scene 1 and the introduction of the first of the legacy hunters in scene 3, the interlude may be understood to suggest a hypothetical definition of the relationship between Volpone and his gulls, as the beast fable suggests a way to characterize that relationship. Are they all in fact animated by the same soul? That is a question Jonson spends a good part of the play answering, weighing Voltore's hopes to be Volpone's heir against his role as a lawyer, Corbaccio's hopes against the heritage of his son, and Corvino's against Celia and his jealousy, only to conclude that each of them is willing to give over the only relationship that identifies him, to sacrifice profession, son, and wife, in favor of his greed. Jonson's development of the Celia fable thus shows us that the fox and the scavenger birds are spiritually one, and by the end of the play we have been shown that Androgyno's equation of folly and monstrosity holds good for them all.[23]

The other tack is the more interesting and fruitful one, however; for if we think about the subject of the interlude as the passage of a single soul through many bodies, we are introduced immediately to one of the central patterns of action in the play, Volpone's adoption of a variety of disguises as he seeks to satisfy his desires. The interlude is interrupted by a knock on the door, and, in response to the knock, Volpone hastens to put on his makeup and costume, transforming himself from the vigorous and healthy figure of the first scene to the image of a sick and dying man. Thereafter we rarely see the Volpone of the first two scenes; instead we see the various guises Volpone assumes as he pursues his complicated designs. Throughout act 1 he plays the sick man, swathed in furs and robes, mouth agape, eyelids hanging, oil running from his eyes. In the second scene of act 2 he is Scoto of Mantua, strutting beneath Celia's window in a disguise so beautifully executed, Mosca assures him, that even Scoto himself might be fooled. In the fourth scene of act 2 he is Volpone again for some thirty-eight lines, during which he removes Scoto's costume. And he is himself again during the brief third scene of act 3, when he anticipates the delights of Celia. But with Lady Would Be's knock he hurries back into his robes and oils to play the dying man, and he does not remove that costume therafter until the beginning of act 5, although, during the scene with Celia, he plays within that costume a bewildering variety of other roles.

The scene in which Corvino delivers his wife to Volpone's bed is by far the richest scene of Volpone's transformations. For that reason I want to look at it closely. At the beginning of the scene Volpone lies on the couch in his basic disguise, fitting his voice to his makeup and both voice and makeup to a reassuring picture of impotency: "'Tis a

vaine labour, eene to fight, 'gainst heaven; / Applying fire to a stone:
(uh, uh, uh, uh) / Making a dead leafe grow againe" (3. 7. 83–85). The
pitiful image Volpone presents here is, of course, necessary to the first
part of his design, since Corvino's eagerness to prostitute his wife
depends in part on the rationalization that Volpone is, after all,
impotent. But when Mosca ushers Corvino out, Volpone leaps from
his couch, his voice and manner now those of the "real" Volpone. At
this point there are two "Volpones" onstage, one of costume and
makeup, the other of voice and movement. And, as Volpone presses
on, he recalls still others, created he says, by Celia's beauty:

> Why art thou maz'd, to see me thus reviv'd?
> Rather applaud thy beauties miracle;
> 'Tis thy great worke: that hath, not now alone,
> But sundry times, rays'd me, in severall shapes,
> And, but his morning, like a mountebanke,
> To see thee at thy windore. I, before
> I would have left my practice, for thy love,
> In varying figures, I would have contended
> With the blue *Proteus,* or the horned *Floud.*
>   [145–53]

When Celia resists him, Volpone imagines at first that she is repelled
by his apparent impotency; and just as he had offered to Corvino an
exaggerated image of impotency, to satisfy the first part of his desire,
he now, hoping to satisfy the rest of it, offers to Celia a slightly less
exaggerated image of vigor. He is still as vigorous, he assures her, as
he was

> when (in that so celebrated *scene,*
> At recitation of our *comoedie,*
> For entertainment of the great Valoys)
> I acted young Antinous; and attracted
> The eyes and eares of all the ladies, present,
> T' admire each gracefull gesture, note, and footing.
>   [159–64]

That is clearly an introduction to a dance turn. It is also an
introduction to the song "Come, my Celia, let us prove, / While we
can the sports of love," which Volpone presumably sings in the
manner in which he played Antinous, capering about the stage in a
parody of his youth while his cheeks sag and his eyes run with oil. If he
does (and why would Jonson have introduced the song with a
reference to his playing of Antinous if he did not?), there are now

three Volpones onstage, one dying, one in vigorous middle age, the third young and simpering. And the young one is an actor, playing at Antinous. Different aspects of his pursuit of Celia thus lead him to recapitulate all the ages of man. But these are by no means all of the forms of Volpone we discover in this scene. For as Celia continues to resist him, Volpone begins to tempt her, first with gifts—carbuncles, diamonds, earrings, meals of "the heads of parrats, tongues of nightingales, / The braines of peacoks, and of estriches" (202–3)— and then with prospects of what Volpone takes to be sensual splendor:

> my dwarfe shall dance
> My eunuch sing, my foole make up the antique.
> Whil'st we, in changed shapes, act *Ovid's* tales,
> Thou like *Europa* now, and I like *Jove,*
> Then I like *Mars,* and thou like *Euricyne,*
> So, of the rest, till we have quite run through
> And weary'd all the fables of the gods.
> Then will I have thee in more moderne formes,
> Attired like some sprightly dame of *France,*
> Brave *Tuscan* lady, or proud *Spanish* beauty;
> Sometimes, unto the *Persian Sophies* wife;
> Or the grand-*Signiors* mistresse; and, for change,
> To one of our most art-full courtizans,
> Or some quick *Negro,* or cold *Russian*;
> And I will meet thee, in as many shapes:
> Where we may, so, trans-fuse our wandring soules
> Out at our lippes, and score up summes of pleasures,
> *That the curious shall not know,*
> *How to tell them, as they flow;*
> *And the envious, when they find*
> *What their number is, be pind.*
>
> [219–39]

By the time that Bonario finally bursts in to save Celia from rape some twenty lines later, the prospect of endless metamorphoses having failed to seduce her, the stage has been filled with Volpones young, old, sick, healthy, in all forms, of all ages, from all times and all places. And all of them—the simpering youth, the impotent and dying man, the myriad roles taken from mythology and national typology, the erotic actor who has one eye on his role and the other on the audience, experiencing orgasms and keeping a tally of their number—all of them answer to different aspects of his desire for

Celia. These are the forms taken by Volpone's "wandring soule" as it seeks to satisfy that desire, and together these forms embody his desire in all its particularity.

The fact is, of course, that Volpone's desire for Celia is incapable of satisfaction, because, as we know from the forms it brings into being, his desire for her is self-contradictory. It requires that he be young *and* old, sick *and* healthy, actor *and* audience, god *and* man, Venetian *and also* French, Spanish, and Russian, Volpone *and also* the grand-Signior. His desire is so composed that it cannot be contained in any single form, nor can any of the forms he adopts to pursue its satisfaction be allowed to come to perfection. Volpone cannot be fully old and impotent because then he could not act; but neither can he be fully young and vigorous because then his scheme to cuckold Corvino would be revealed. He cannot be fully a participant in the erotic paradise he imagines for Celia but must also be stage manager and company accountant, an onlooker at the orgy, because the full satisfaction he seeks requires the proper setting, supernumeraries, an audience, and a tally of their orgasms to be presented to the envious so as to make them even more jealous. The composition of his desire requires that all of his roles coexist in uneasy contradiction, no one quite canceling out any other but each one frustrating the fulfillment of every other. Volpone's desire for Celia is thus literally as well as morally monstrous. His pursuit of its satisfaction through endless metamorphoses (and his vision of erotic paradise has almost infinite spatial and temporal reach) is at bottom what Saint Bernard calls "the sterile circuit of the impious," a foredoomed quest for a satisfaction that cannot be found.

Pursuing such a quest, Volpone bears out the equation of monstrosity and folly made by Androgyno during the interlude; for the monstrousness of Volpone's desire is a species of folly, insuring, as it does, his perpetual frustration. That point is clarified when Bonario pops out crying, "Forbeare, foule ravisher, libidinous swine" (267). For while the circumstances that led to Bonario's concealment in Volpone's inner room are troublesome at the level of the fable (and at that level one must simply allow Jonson the events that follow from his concealment), the consequence of his having been concealed is, in the moral structure of the play, the objectification and clarification of the sterility of Volpone's desire. When Bonario appears to snatch the cherry from Volpone's lips just as he snaps at it—in Volpone's own bedroom, after Celia had been brought there by her own husband, when all circumstances combined to make certain the accomplishment of Volpone's will—Bonario renders in action the conclusion merely implied in the visual and verbal imagery of the scene: that Volpone's desire is not to be satisfied in any circumstances. Bonario's entrance, which is weak as part of the fable, thus obeys a logic inherent in the very composition of Volpone's desire. And his stilted language, troublesome to Jonson's critics,[24] may be Jonson's unwilling acknowledgment that what he has dramatized is not a concrete coincidence but the conclusion of an abstract moral principle.

I have dwelt on this scene in part because it is the climax of the major episode in the play but mostly because it is emblematic of the uses of shape-changing in the play as a whole. Just as I have argued that in this scene Bonario's interruption of the rape is inevitable because it simply renders in action the conclusion implied by Volpone's transformations, so I would argue that the uncasing of the Fox in act 5–the end of a sequence every bit as troublesome at the level of the fable as the concealing of Bonario is here—simply clarifies the implications of the forms Volpone adopts to pursue the chief desire of his soul, the cunning purchase of wealth. Until Volpone reveals himself before the *avocatori,* we rarely see him *in propria persona.* Indeed, less than a third of Volpone's time onstage is spent outside the disguises he adopts to pursue his desires, and much of that skimpy third is spent in putting on and taking off the disguises. We see him as a dying man for almost half again as long as we see him in his own form, and together the roles of mountebank and *commandadore* occupy him for almost as long as does his own person.

The disguises reveal as much to the audience as they conceal from the *captatores,* developing different and deeper insights into Volpone as they are sustained. Volpone's pretending to be a dying man, for example, has at first a certain perversely enobling aspect. For if we are to take Volpone's inversions of heaven and hell not merely as bits of hyperbole or merely as the initial terms in the moral formula of error and recantation—if we are to understand that Volpone means it when he says "the price of soules, even hell, with thee to boot, / Is made worth heaven"—we need some indication that death is at least imaginatively real to him and that we are not to expect him to give over his views the first time that mortality raises its head. His cheerful exploitation of the physical minutiae of dying provides such an indication because it shows us Volpone confronting in imagination, indeed mimetically, the fact that he is mortal. His assumption of the role of the dying man thus gives to his absolutizing of wealth a different aspect from the absolutizing of wealth by, say, Mankind in *The Castle of Perseverance.* For where Mankind, like all morality heroes, is enraptured by wealth because he is only dimly able to conceive that he is mortal, Volpone perversely prizes gold in despite of hell. Where Mankind is presented as foolish and educable, then, the hero of a moral comedy and our own surrogate, Volpone is monstrous and settled and therefore altogether the object of satire.

But what gives a certain heroic cast to Volpone's avariciousness ultimately marks it as foolish and vain. For if we are to understand that in playing the role of a dying man Volpone is playing not another character altogether but rather himself at some future time, then we must understand that the play insists on the evanescent frailty of Volpone even as Volpone himself is insisting on the weight and importance of his schemes. Playing a dying man to deceive his gulls, Volpone functions as his own *memento mori,* reminding the audience continually that in the nature of things his apparent cleverness can come to nothing, that in the nature of things his mockery of Corbaccio must inevitably turn back on himself: Volpone, too, with visions of treasure "so battens, as if fate / Would be as easily cheated on, as he, / And all turnes aire."

While we must wait until act 5 for the perfection of these implications, there is a gradual clarification of them throughout the play. The man who asks, "What should I do but cocker up my *genius* and live free / To all delights, my fortune calls me to?" is, within a hundred lines, confined to the narrow boundaries of his couch, and there he remains, the prisoner of his own deceit, through the remainder of act 1, most of act 3, and all of act 4. The Celia episode is certainly a series of comic disasters for Volpone, in which his cleverness gets him twice beaten, tormented by Lady Would Be, frustrated of all his hopes, and finally terrified almost to death. In its course he proffers gifts with a far more liberal hand than any of his gulls, and at its climax he is treated by the course of events precisely as he had intended to treat them: the goal is snatched from him just as he grasps at it.

Volpone's disguise cuts deeper than a *memento mori,* however, to trace the very outline of his soul. Gold is Volpone's god; its cunning purchase is the motion of his soul; and the form of the dying man is the principal material form in which his soul seeks its end. Volpone's robes and furs and oils, the costume and makeup that allow him to play the dying man, have therefore the same function that the feathers and wings of a bird have or the fins and gills of a fish: they are the material forms in which Volpone's soul seeks its realization. The lameness and impotency, the slimy eyes and labored breath, all the physical symptoms of dying made possible by these theatrical devices, are literally the sensuous forms of Volpone's soul. The instrument through which Volpone exploits the vain hopes of his gulls is thus the same instrument through which Jonson reveals the spiritual horror, the emptiness, of Volpone's craft. Volpone's disguise in that sense does not simply recall the mortal limits to which all men are subject, implying the ultimate futility of his designs as a condition of life itself; his disguise is utterly transparent, a disingenuous expression of Volpone's interior reality. Volpone is truly a dying man because the cunning purchase of wealth in which he glories implies death, as any investment of the soul in objects that cannot endure implies death.

Volpone's manipulation of his *captatores* is thus a form of dying. That is a point Jonson suggests by having Volpone enact in play the stages of his own death. As he pursues his fraudulent designs against Voltore and the others, he pretends to have lost, in succession, not only each of his senses but his memory, his reproductive faculties, and, finally, his ability to accept nourishment; thus the progress of Volpone's schemes toward fulfillment is made to appear simultaneously as the progress of Volpone himself toward death.[25] That metaphorical pattern, lightly sustained during the first three acts, is perfected following the mock trial in act 4, when Volpone decides to perfect his design against the *captatores* and, in order to do so, has it given out that he is dead and that Mosca has been made his heir.

Volpone's point, of course, is to bring Voltore and the others to recognize—for his delight, not their profit—that their dreams of wealth have all been vain. It is thus altogether appropriate that, in order to get round and torment them while he is supposed to be dead, Volpone should adopt the disguise of the *Commandadore,* the sergeant of the court who summons offenders to the bar of justice, because Volpone's purpose is to summon his gulls to the more stringent bar of truth. Here too, however, the form through which he intends to deceive reveals the motions of Volpone's spirit in ways he does not intend. For in pursuing the role of the *Commandadore* he is led at last to summon himself to the bars of both truth and justice. In act 5 all of Volpone's pretenses, ironically apt all along, are translated into literal and apparent truths—and all through his own efforts. He sets out to reveal the vanity of avarice to his gulls, but he ends up by revealing in himself its telos, and the theatrical image of his ironic self-arrest is the image of an officer of the law.

A healthy skepticism might argue that the Fox uncases himself only because Mosca has attempted to defraud him and Volpone would rather pull down his whole scheme than become a gull like the others. That is true enough. But Mosca's attempted fraud against Volpone has its roots in Volpone's own actions, taken on Volpone's own initiatives, and those actions come at last to seem unintelligibly foolish even to Volpone. In consequence, the sequence of events that leads to Volpone's punishment is seen to grow out of a species of folly immanent in Volpone himself. *Praeceps et temerarius in prosperis,* like all of the pilgrims we have examined, Volpone has uncased himself.

On his own showing Mosca is an opportunist rather than a maker of sustained and original schemes. Like a satirical gardener, he merely brings to flower the seeds of folly his victims have carefully tended in themselves. There is not even a need, he assures Volpone, following the mock trial, to shield the *captatores* from the truth, for "Each of 'hem is so possest, and stuft with his owne hopes, / That anything, unto the contrary, / Never so true, never so apparent, / Never so palpable, they will resist it." Thus, when he turns against Volpone, a few moments after that speech, he simply allows Volpone's folly to take its own course. The bloom he plucks, the opening that allows him momentarily the upper hand over Volpone, is the product of the most deeply planted and carefully tended seed of all: it is simply and aptly the perfection of the principal form of Volpone's spirit. Volpone has sought the cunning purchase of gold by pretending to be dying. To set the capstone on his cunning, he pretends in game to be dead. And Mosca has merely to pretend to take his game for earnest: "Since he will, needes, be dead, afore his time, / I'll burie him, or gaine by him" (5. 5. 13–14). And in doing so Mosca draws out and objectifies the earnest truth implied by the forms of Volpone's deceit: the ultimate sterility of that motion of the spirit whose material form is the dying man.

While it takes some juggling in the fable to get to it, Mosca's appropriation of Volpone's goods is, then, like Bonario's interruption of the rape, simply a rendering in action of the end implied by the sensuous forms of Volpone's spirit. With rigorous metaphorical logic the dying man has died and his heir has come into his wealth. In *The Castle of Perseverance* that heir is I-Wot-Never-Who, the embodiment of the unknown and uncaring generations to whom all wealth inevitably passes. But Jonson's satire is more precise than the moral sermon that informs the *Castle,* for Volpone's "heir" and his betrayer is his own best servant, the chief of the instruments through which his soul sought its satisfaction. What Mosca calls "the Fox trap" is thus the final term in a moral formula whose first term is "Haile the world's soule, and mine." And its consequence is what Volpone calls with illuminating irony "the mortifying of a foxe."

It is toward that formula that the first *avocatore* points when he observes that "Mischiefes feed / Like beasts, till they be fat, and then they bleed." And it is, I would suggest, the providence immanent in the very disposition of men's souls that Bonario recognizes when he says that "heaven could not, long, let such grosse crimes be hid." In any event, it is only by means of such a formula that we can bridge the gap between acts 4 and 5 to discover that it is both appropriate and significant that Volpone should initiate his own punishment for avarice by setting out to play the scourge of avarice in others. For in having the illumination of all the fools turn on the perfection of the form in which Volpone sought the cunning purchase of wealth, Jonson shows in action that avarice is indeed a rare punishment to itself.

Recognizing that the play coheres around a teleological vision of avarice, we can recognize that the punishments meted out to those animated by it—acknowledged by Jonson himself to be troublesome in the comic structure of the play—are merely objectifications of judgments already rendered metaphorically by the characters themselves against themselves as they pursued their dreams of gold. What the *avocatori* ordain is simply that Volpone and the others continue to behave in the future as they have in the past, or at least as they have pretended to behave in the past—in short, that they realize fully the forms they have adopted in pursuit of gold. Thus the lawyer who has abandoned the law for greed is to be denied the law, sent into exile from Venice. The father who has disinherited his son and later disowned him is to have no son, and no goods either. The husband who pandered his wife in order to purchase more wealth is to give her up indeed and to be rowed around Venice as a cuckold. And Volpone, who had sought the cunning purchase of wealth by feigning disease, and who had earlier observed that to "be a foole born is a disease incurable," is simply to be locked in chains until he is "sicke and lame indeed" and to have all his wealth confiscated to the hospital of the

Incurabili. That, as Harriet Hawkins has noted, is where it has been all along: in the possession of one who suffered the incurable disease of folly.[26]

THE COMIC AND SATIRIC STRUCTURES OF VOLPONE

While the form of *Volpone* is comic, the only continuous logic in the play is thus the logic of moral satire. This is hardly the time to admit that I have not succeeded in uniting the comic and satiric structures of the play and making it a seamless whole. But it is true. I have not answered Dryden's criticism that the fable of *Volpone* is discontinuous, and I do not see that it is answerable. The comic fable of the play is clearly shaped to illuminate the teleology of avarice, but just as clearly Jonson has not discovered, or at least has not provided, a fable that manages to do that in a consecutive and probable fashion. In consequence, the structure of events in the fable appears to be at best the illustration of an action that can be fully revealed only symbolically. We are not persuaded, I think, of the circumstances of Volpone's punishment, because they depend on the "accident" of Bonario's appearance in his room and the new beginning Volpone makes in act 5; however, we are persuaded of the fact that punishment, at some time and in some fashion, is inherent in the composition of Volpone's spirit.

The gap between the comic and satiric structures of *Volpone* thus calls for an act of faith on the part of both its creator and its audience, for both must believe for the duration of the play that avarice is its own punishment without being able to make that probable in the affairs of men. At best the operation of moral providence, which is clear and intelligible in the metaphorical structure of the play, is apprehensible in the comic structure only through mysteries and foolish accidents. There is some support there for those of Jonson's critics who see Celia and Bonario as vapid and brainless,[27] for to see a moral imperative in the fable of the play may be a sentimental act, undertaken in spite of experience and common sense. It depends on supplying significance to events that have the logical status of accidents.

We are forced to depend on the metaphorical structure of the play to supply that significance, to fill in the gaps in the logic of the comic action. But the gaps themselves make it clear that the metaphorical structure of *Volpone,* the form taken in the play by the myth of the pilgrimage, is simply one way of interpreting an experience that nevertheless remains fragmentary and opaque. It is evident, then, that as plays became more minutely and concretely mimetic, it became more and more difficult—even for a playwright as thoroughly committed to notions of natural and moral law as Jonson—to sustain in probable action the forms of the pilgrimage myth. In that respect the gap between the comic and satiric structures of *Volpone* points toward the gap, indeed the deliberate divorce, between the skeptical and orthodox visions of experience around which Shakespeare has structured *King Lear*.

F I V E
The Skeptical Traveler:
King Lear and the End of
the Pilgrimage

> Thou shalt find
> That I'll resume the shape which thou dost think
> I have cast off forever.
>
> [*King Lear* (1. 4. 308–10]

THE MORAL PLAY OF *KING LEAR*

The author of Shakespeare's principal source for the story of King Lear, the anonymous *True Chronicle History of King Leir and His Three Daughters* (c. 1594), inherited from Holinshed and Geoffrey of Monmouth an abrupt and occasionally puzzling story, and he tried, with some success, to rationalize it by providing substantial and detailed motives for its strange events. Where Geoffrey and Holinshed go scarcely beyond "once upon a time," the *True Chronicle* explains carefully that a number of particular concerns, peculiar to the situation of King Leir, came together to persuade him to conduct a test of his daughters' love. He is, like Shakespeare's king, a very old man. His wife has died just before the play begins, and he is thinking about resigning his kingdom to his daughters so that he can prepare his own soul for death. That is in part why he wants to settle his daughters on good husbands, though he fears also that he is not able to care for them properly alone: "Fathers best do know to govern sons, / But daughters' steps the mother's counsel turns."[1] It is Cordella's stubbornness that brings Leir to reconsider a scheme he had rejected earlier, to distribute his kingdom among his daughters "as is their worth to them that love possess," because he begins to imagine that, if he can get Cordella to profess her love for him publicly, he can trap her publicly into marrying a suitor he has chosen.

Whether that scheme might have worked or not, it fails because Gonorill and Ragan, informed of Leir's plans by a courtier rather like Shakespeare's Oswald, concoct a scheme of their own. They are

151

jealous of Cordella, not because Leir favors her—there is no suggestion in the *True Chronicle* that he loves Cordella more than her sisters—but because, so they claim, she is proud, she outdoes them in fashion, and she buys popularity at court by pretending to be sober and demure. They plan to pollute the rhetorical atmosphere, to flatter Leir so outrageously that their fastidious sister will be unable to reply to his questions, and to promise to marry whomever he pleases so that Cordella will find herself in a "woeful plight": "For she will rather die than give consent / To marry with the Irish king: / So will our father think she loves him not / Because she will not grant to his desire" (1. 2. 187–90). As the author of the *True Chronicle* has developed the story, Cordella's "plainness" is not the expression of a naturally taciturn character, or not that alone, nor a sober statement of the office of a daughter that Leir misunderstands in his folly. It is engineered out of the discrete elements of a relatively detailed intrigue.

That is not Shakespeare's way with the story at all. When he took over the narrative line of the *True Chronicle,* he reformed it in ways very like those of a morality play,[2] pruning away the fussy intrigue so as to allow Cordelia's reticence and Lear's decision to disown her to stand alone, as substantive expressions of their states of mind, and introducing the parallel story of Gloucester and his sons so as to universalize and clarify the form of the action.[3] He aligned the subsidiary characters in the two stories into opposing groups whose moral affinities are illuminated as they are drawn closer together and whose moral qualities become simpler and clearer as the action proceeds. Goneril and Regan are not as strikingly evil, nor Cordelia as strikingly good, at the beginning of the play as they seem to be later on. And when Cordelia is joined by Kent, and Goneril and Regan begin to lust after Edmund, we see the two old men who are the centers of everyone's attention flanked by parties of unmistakable good and evil, much as Mankind had been. Shakespeare has also punctuated the major stages of the action with theatrical emblems familiar in the morality drama, such as Pity in the Stocks.[4] Perhaps most important, however, he has developed the action so as to draw out and clarify the hidden motives and implied ends compacted in that single moment of choice when Lear divides his kingdom. So where the Leir of the *True Chronicle* is at first foolish in his choice and later pathetic in his suffering, with no connection between the two states, Shakespeare's Lear is made to pursue in his suffering every particle of his folly. We might fairly say, then, that Shakespeare has deliberately restyled what he has taken from the old play so as to perfect the latent moral action at the heart of the story.

I will want to come back at the end of this essay to the general subject of *King Lear*'s relationship to the morality drama, but at the moment I want to focus on one element in it. That is Shakespeare's treatment at the beginning of the play of the relationship between Lear and Cordelia. With the exceptions of an unemphatic half-line in Geoffrey of Monmouth's telling of the story and what looks like a patch of syntactical confusion in Holinshed's version,[5] there is scarcely any suggestion in the sources that Lear has made a peculiar investment of himself in his younger daughter. The Leir of the old play is especially concerned about Cordella because she is troublesome; but Shakespeare's Lear is said to love Cordelia best, and of all the Lears only he plans to spend the rest of his life with her. His preference for Cordelia is so settled and widely known that, when he disowns her, Gloucester says that he has fallen from the bias of his nature; and we quickly come to understand how carefully that phrase has been chosen when we see that, having conveyed his kingdom and himself to Goneril and Regan, Lear has unsettled his own identity. So it is peculiarly true of Shakespeare's king, among all of the Lears, that his conduct of the love test leads him to act against his own deepest feelings.

We might want to ask, then, why Lear loves Cordelia best, what she appeals to in him, and thus what he turns from in himself when he disowns her. Taken at the full, that question is almost impossible. Lear's greater love for Cordelia may be imagined to be the indefinable accretion of thousands of moments in their lives together, half-remembered instances of tenderness and joy and pain. That is, after all, the ground of settled affection in life itself. But whatever may be imagined on the model of similar relationships in life, there is an abstracted and intelligible core in the relationships of dramatic characters; that is to say, it is the nature and purpose of these relationships to be *understood*. And we may fairly say, I think, that Lear loves Cordelia best for what Shakespeare tells us she is.[6]

What is true of Cordelia throughout the play, and what also characterizes other members of her party, Kent and Edgar, is that she is faithful to the formal bonds that relate her to her father. Her inability to answer Lear's question—"What can you say to draw / A third more opulent than your sisters?" "Nothing, my lord" (1. 1. 76–77)—has suggested to some readers that Lear's choice between his daughters involves a choice between self-interested flattery and a pure form of love, one not "mingled with regards that stands / Aloof from th' entire point."[7] But in a certain sense those regards are the entire point. Cordelia's reply may seem at first altogether different from her sisters' and admirably discreet. "Nothing" with which to purchase land. But her characterization of her love insists firmly on its roots in mutual exchange, and taken seriously it is far more grand than the professions of Goneril and Regan to love their father "more than words can wield the matter" (55):

> Good my lord,
> You have begot me, bred me, lovd me: I
> Return those duties back as are right fit,
> Obey you, love you, and most honor you.
>   [95–98]

What that amounts to is a claim that, because Cordelia has been altogether composed by Lear's love—"begot me, bred me, lovd me"—she is altogether composed of love for Lear—"obey you, love you, and most honor you." In the very formal syntax of her sentence, her obedience answers his begetting, her love his nurturing, her respect his love, all on the scale of that phrase "right fit," which expresses not merely the unspoken obligations that follow from nature and nurture but also Cordelia's embrace of those obligations in the office of a daughter. What Cordelia implies, then, is that to be properly herself is necessarily to love her father: to be Cordelia and to love Lear are one and the same.[8]

Later in the play Albany makes this commonplace notion—that one's identity is bound up with the fulfillment of one's office—both universal and explicit when he warns Goneril, who has stripped Lear of the dignity of his followers and turned him out into the storm, that "she that herself will sliver and disbranch / From her material sap, perforce must wither / And come to deadly use" (4. 2. 34–36). But we can see it beginning to emerge in a variety of ways early in act 1; for the outines of what Saint Bernard called the land of unlikeness begin to appear when Lear endangers his own identity by disowning his offices as father and king and Goneril and Regan begin to be characterized, as those led by appetite were often characterized, through images of animals. I will return in the next section of this essay to Shakespeare's development of that Bernardine trope.

Since all that we know about Cordelia in act 1 is that she loves her father as a daughter should, although she is naturally reticent and cannot "heave her heart into her mouth" to do more than bluntly tell him so, I think we can assume that what Lear loves in Cordelia, although he does not recognize it at the beginning of the play, is the fact that she is a faithful daughter. We can understand why that strikes so deeply into Lear's mind by looking at his first substantive discovery in the play. That is his discovery at the end of act 2 of what a man truly needs. When he is driven to realize that, he cannot express it, perhaps because he does not altogether understand it but certainly because the hysterical passion that has been rising in him endangers his balance. Goneril and Regan have been chipping away at him, holding him to narrow material standards. He should be acting like a proper old man, they tell him, humble and tractable. He does not need a hundred knights to serve him, or fifty, or one. Their minds run along the same course his took in posing the love test, confusing material things with matters aloof from that point, reducing him to their satisfaction as he had reduced them to his. And the reduction proves at last intolerable to him. If you think along material lines, he tells them, almost everything that we have is more than we need. "But for true need"—and there he breaks off to attend to his rising passion: "You heavens, give me that patience, patience I need" (2. 4. 270–71). What he was about to say, I think, or rather what the context of his thought implies is the standard of true need, can be summed up in a word like respect: a just regard for the needs that flow from the roles that define each person's place in the community and thus define his identity. What a man truly needs is what is due him not just as an animate creature but as a social one. It is that sense of need he is pursuing when he argues that he needs a hundred knights; it is not the material need for service—which the attendants of Goneril and Regan can fill just as well—but the need for a court to mark him out as a king. What he seems to fear is the loss of self that Marlowe's Edward II felt when he asked, "What are kings when regiment is gone / But perfect shadows on a sunshine day?" For needs generated by place are as powerful in the play as those generated by dumb nature. So Kent, relieved of his own place by his disguise as Caius, can tolerate being put in the stocks, even unjustly; but Lear in his role as king cannot tolerate having his servant stocked, justly or not: " 'Tis worse than murther / To do upon respect such violent outrage" (2. 4. 23–24). And all the onlookers recognize that that is so, except for Regan and Cornwall. It is to need at this basic, tautological level that Cordelia's bond speaks: by loving him as a daughter should she allows him his identity as a father.[9] Her bare expression of that bond does not satisfy Lear, because he expects to be flattered as more than a father, but his greater love for Cordelia than for her sisters and his plan to set his "rest on her kind nursery" seem to be expressions of a deeply rooted though dim intuition that she loves, and answers love, in a way that satisfies true need.

If that is so, we can recognize that the effect of Shakespeare's peculiar definition of the relationship between Lear and Cordelia is to place Lear, at the end of his life, at that crossroads where all the pilgrims we have talked about have stood early in theirs. Inclined by his nature and urged by reason to give himself into the care of a daughter with whom his identity is bound up, Lear is deceived by his passion into disowning her in favor of easier and cheaper pleasures. As we have seen, for the pilgrim to turn from reason and nature was to lose his resemblance to himself because reason was the faculty that characterized him as a man and taught him to perfect his nature. So Deguileville's Pilgrim is inclined even in the womb to seek the New Jerusalem; but he is carried away from the path of virtue by his Youth, who finds discipline troublesome, and set to wander in the land of unlikeness. The pilgrim in *Reason and Sensuality* is instructed by Nature herself that he must follow the path of reason if he is to become fully a man; but the sight of Venus knocks Nature's instruction out of his head, and his erotic passion sends him off to the Garden of Pleasure, where men are "ytourned to lyknesse / Of bestys and, makid bestial, / Los[e] hir reson natural." In the *Castle of Perseverance,* Mankind, born shortly before in "blody ble," prays that he may "folwe the aungyl that cam fro hevene trone"; but almost at once he turns to follow his Bad Angel off to meet the World. In *Wit and Science* this connatural knowledge of the good takes the form of Wit's romantic love for the Lady Science, in the possession of whom the perfection of his own identity consists; but Idleness is nearby and beguiling, and she transforms him into Ingnorancy. And Richard Plantagenet's love for Anne à Beame, who cherishes all of the qualities of political responsibility that would perfect in him the image of his father, is overshadowed by the gaudy delights of Bushy, Bagot, and Greene, which will cost him his crown.

Seen in that company, Lear's love for Cordelia and his intention to set his rest on her seem to be one more form of what Saint Thomas called the law of nature: man's connatural knowledge of what he ought to embrace in order to be himself. Shakespeare has made the instruction of reason toward that end transparent to everyone but Lear. To turn from Cordelia, Kent warns Lear, is folly and madness.

"Reason without miracle" could never persuade France that Cordelia has done anything worthy of being disowned. Lear's own response, when he begins to recognize his mistake, is to "beat at this gate that let thy folly in / And thy dear judgment out" (1. 4. 270–71). Even Goneril and Regan acknowledge "with what poor judgment he hath now cast her off," and at the end of the scene they are preparing to protect themselves against Lear's "long-engraffed rashness" and the "unruly waywardness that infirm and choleric years bring with them" (1. 1. 283).

When the pilgrim chooses between reason and passion, he does not, of course, choose between alternatives separate from himself; they are simply facets of his own psyche. The dramatic landscape of a play like *The Castle of Perseverance* is the psyche of Mankind, spread out in a single plane upon the stage. In that setting Mankind himself appears in the figure of his own will, while the psychological forces that press upon the will have been abstracted from him and embodied in separate characters, guides or tempters who urge him to go in one direction or the other. So in choosing one rather than the other, Mankind chooses to realize in action potentialities that are present in his own mind, and by doing so he clarifies their ends both for himself and for his audience.

I am not going to claim that Goneril and Regan are simply the promptings of Lear's own heart. They are literally his daughters, flesh and blood. And for all of my emphasis on the ways in which Shakespeare has reformed the story along the lines of a morality play, I want to insist in a moment that there is a stubbornly literal and skeptical strain in its composition that dramatic allegory finally cannot tolerate. But the fact that they are literally his daughters is itself significant in a way that, for example, the fact that Hamlet is old Hamlet's son is not. For the relationship between parent and child— what it means, what it obliges parents and children to do—comes in for a good deal of sustained and explicit attention in the play itself. As Cordelia points out, to say that they are his daughters is to say that they have grown from his seed and been shaped by his nurturing. So both physically and mentally they are objective images of Lear himself, and Shakespeare uses them to clarify, in relatively pure forms, discordant elements mingled in Lear's character, much as Jonson uses Volpone's "children" to clarify facets of his character. Their opposed qualities, the willful selfishness of Goneril and Regan and the formal, irreducible love of Cordelia, are reconciled only in Lear, who is their author and who would be their sole object. The

Lear implied in the love test may be said to dissociate into his daughters, as William Elton has observed;[10] by denying his own office as a father, he disowns Cordelia, and, simultaneously, freeing Goneril and Regan into his political kingdom, he frees in himself the elements in his character to which they appeal.

In a way peculiar to Shakespeare's telling of the story, then, the kingdom Lear conveys to Goneril and Regan is not only a political kingdom; it is also a moral and psychological kingdom. And, both politically and psychologically, Lear's kingdom is divided against itself. In his political kingdom Lear is, like Richard II, to be the king and yet not the king. He, too, has "farmed out" his body politic. Goneril and Regan and their husbands are to have the "power, / Pre-eminence, and all the large effects / That troop with majesty"—that is, the substance of kingly authority; but Lear is to keep for himself the name of king and all the forms of respect that flow from that authority. And in his psychological kingdom he denies the office of a father and disowns Cordelia to embrace appetite, but at every collision between himself and his remaining daughters he is drawn toward the formal defenses that that office provides against appetite. He will expect boundless toleration from Goneril simply because she is his daughter, and he will pretend not to recognize her when she calls his disorderly behavior to account, for proper daughters do not call their fathers to account. Fleeing from Goneril, he will confidently expect from Regan the "offices of nature," though the Fool warns him that she will taste as like Goneril "as a crab does to a crab." Finally, fleeing from both into the storm, he will fantasize that he can reduce his daughers to proper order if he can only bring them before officers of justice, but he has given all the offices of justice into the keeping of his daughters.

The self-contradictions compacted in Lear's choice are also imaged in another detail, one that only Shakespeare employs. That is Lear's decision, once he has given up his intention to set his rest on Cordelia, to live with Goneril and Regan by monthly turns. Taken in itself this living arrangement is unwieldy and absurd, but, like other absurdities in the play, it has the ring of a familiar and apposite moral trope. In this case the trope is the figure Saint Bernard calls the "sterile circuit of the impious." Traveling in a circle, endlessly round and round, is for Saint Bernard a model of the experience of those who try to find satisfaction in things of this world. Because he was made in the image of God, man's nature can be satisfied only by God. So when he turns from God to the world for satisfaction, he condemns himself to perpetual frustration, to a fruitless search in the world for what can be found only in God. Having fallen from the bias of his own nature, Lear's endless circuit between Goneril and Regan expresses a similar point; for the rest he seeks in them can be found only in the daughter he has disowned. And it is the business of the first two acts of the play to trace his sterile circuit between them.

WHEN MAJESTY FALLS TO FOLLY: KING LEAR IN THE LAND OF UNLIKENESS

When the Fool enters for the first time in act 1, he tells Kent, now disguised as Caius, that Lear has "banish'd two on's daughters, and did the third a blessing against his will" (1. 4. 102–3). Since Lear has "banish'd" only one of his daughters and has appeared to do the other two a blessing in giving them his kingdom, modern editors have sometimes glossed "banish'd" as "alienated," suggesting that the Fool means that Lear has made Goneril and Regan independent of himself.[11] That is not a meaning of "banished" that the *OED* recognizes, nor is it a meaning that Shakespeare uses elsewhere, and I suspect that his audience, and ours, is likely to take the Fool's expression much more simply as a nonsensical inversion of the facts set round a kernel of truth: that Cordelia is better off outside Lear's topsy-turvy kingdom. But the fact that the Fool echoes another and equally strange use of "banished"—one that cannot simply be attributed to habitual or professional nonsense—suggests that Shakespeare may have had something else in mind.

When Kent himself left the stage in scene 1, banished by Lear for the crime of honesty, his parting words to Lear were, "Fare thee well, King; sith thus thou wilt appear, / Freedom lives hence, and banishment is here" (1. 1. 180–81).[12] By Lear's "appearance" Kent means the whole set of attitudes he has displayed and acts he has performed: disowning Cordelia, dividing his kingdom between Goneril and Regan, and refusing to listen to Kent's just reproaches. Lear has thus acted tyrannically, and "freedom," in two older and closely related senses, no longer inhabits his kingdom. One of these senses pertains to Kent, whose energetic candor (freedom in the sense of a willingness to speak and act openly) Lear has just banished; the other, corollary, sense pertains to Lear, whose unwillingness to listen to just reproaches indicates that he has also banished the kind of integrity and generosity of spirit (freedom in another of its meanings) that distinguishes nobility. What I think Kent is saying, in a form characteristically gnomic at this point in the play, is that Lear has banished from his kingdom virtues that formerly marked it, with the result that the kingdom has paradoxically become a place of exile from itself, habitable only by those in exile from themselves. We cannot understand most of what that means until we see, later in the play, that only those who are false to themselves can live freely in Lear's new kingdom while those who are true to themselves are either sent away, like Cordelia, or forced to adopt disguises, like Kent and Edgar, in order to stay. But we can see almost at once the outlines of what it means for Lear. Alienated from Cordelia and himself, become a king without power in his own country, condemned by his own act to wander ceaselessly back and forth across the face of what had been his home, Lear has made his home a far country and made himself an exile there.

I think this is what Shakespeare had in mind when he had the Fool say that Lear had "banish'd two on's daughters": by the edict of his gift he has sent them into the alien place that England now is. The Fool enters at a telling point, just after a series of puzzling frustrations for Lear has erupted briefly into violence. Lear's own entrance at the beginning of the scene (1. 4)—the first time he has been onstage since he divided the kingdom and set off on his circuit between Goneril and Regan—has been prepared by Goneril's complaint in the preceding scene that his knights are riotous and "himself upbraids us on every trifle" (1. 3. 6–7). The question between them, for her at least, is who is to rule, and she is determined, now that she has power, "not to be overruled"—especially in her own house. But Lear comes onstage giving orders, and throughout the early part of the scene he fires them off in all directions, although few of them are obeyed and those tardily. One would give a good deal to know just who that attendant is that editors since Nicholas Rowe have blandly sent off on Lear's bidding ("Let me not stay a jot for dinner; go, get it ready. [*Exit an Attendant*]"). Is he part of Goneril's household, practicing "weary negligence," or part of Lear's own retinue? If we knew whose servant he is, we could judge immediately whether the king's dignity has already been undermined by his own disorder or simply denied by an ungrateful daughter, because the attendant never returns. It is clear nonetheless that Lear's gestures of authority are empty now, that he tries to play a role that has been hollowed out by its own contradictions. In the new kingdom Lear has created, his expectation that he can retain the "name and all the additions to the king" is foredoomed because the "additions" are not secured by the formal obligations that lie outside material wealth and power. So to

Goneril he has already lost the names of father and king and has become merely an "idle old man / That still would manage those authorities / That he hath given away." And to an audience watching gestures still in royal form but empty of effect, he might well begin to seem a parody of himself; as in the title of John Fletcher's play, he is a King and no King.

The exchange with Oswald that immediately precedes the Fool's entrance provides a measure of this self-parody. Once again, as in the opening scene, Lear is braved by a subordinate; but where his response there, however wrongheaded, had been kingly, here it is small, crude, and ineffectual, with more the quality of the schoolyard than the court. When Kent defied him, his impulse to strike out physically had been checked by the decorum of the court and channeled instead into the order banishing him. But now formal constraints have themselves been banished, and the gesture checked at court is completed in debased form when Lear slaps Oswald. To no effect. Oswald says merely, "I'll not be strucken, my lord" (1. 4. 85), and Lear can discipline this insolence only when Caius/Kent trips Oswald up by the heels and drives him out of the room—a playground exercise that merely confirms Lear's impotence, since it gets rid of Oswald without subordinating him. So when Lear tosses Kent a purse in reward, the gesture is a pathetic parody of kingly favor, and Shakespeare has it answered immediately in the entrance of the Fool: "Let me hire him, too: here's my coxcomb" (95).

The Fool's point is that Kent is a fool for serving Lear because Lear himself is a dependent now. Shakespeare's point in having the Fool enter here, on such a line and with such a gesture, is to establish visually the parallel between Lear and the Fool that the remainder of the scene, up through the entrance of Goneril, merely explicates. Thus it seems likely that Lear tosses his purse to Kent with a distinctive motion and that the Fool repeats it when he gives Kent his coxcomb.

The Fool is Lear's zany, and, like the *zanni* of the *commedia dell'arte,* who strut behind Il Dottore, aping his pompous walk, his job is not merely to make fun for Lear or fun of him in a general way; it is, more precisely, to clarify the forms of folly that lie buried beneath the pompous and, later, pathetic surfaces of Lear's acts. Kent had said that the honorable man was bound to be plain "when majesty falls to folly" (1. 1. 148–49), but "folly" then had been a rhetorical extravagance, the expression of a judgment not altogether peculiar to Kent but not altogether self-evident either. But now that the kingdom has been transferred to Goneril and Regan, and Kent's prophetic judgment is in the process of being realized in the failures of Lear's expectations, we are never allowed to see Lear alone without the Fool's parody of the forms of his acts, a parody that locates the folly in even the most pathetic of them. "O me, my heart! My rising heart! But down!" (2. 4. 121), Lear cries when, recognizing that Regan is as unkind as Goneril, he begins to feel hysteria rising in him. But Shakespeare will no more allow that pathetic gesture to stand alone than he will allow Lear's pompous gestures to stand alone. The Fool immediately reduces the naïveté that expected anything else of Regan, and the futility of trying to suppress the pain of that recognition, to the absurdity of the cockney who thought live eels would lie still to be cooked:

> Cry to it, nuncle, as the cockney did to the eels when she put em i' the paste alive; she knapped 'em o' th' coxcombs with a stick and cried, "Down, wantons, down!"

When the laugh at that line starts to die away (and one is clearly expected), Shakespeare has the Fool cap it with a reference to another *naïf* that is at once so theatrically deft in milking the audience with an old joke and yet so morally incisive that it is hard to think of a better example of the genius of the popular theater: "'Twas her brother that, in pure kindness to his horse, butter'd his hay"(122–26). Empson is led at this point to think first of rogues, since the most common form of the old joke turned on deceitful ostlers, and then, by strained connections, to suspect the cockney of bawdry;[13] but the point—the Fool's? Shakespeare's?—is surely that Lear's superfluous kindness was as naïvely mistaken as the cockney's brother's and that his gift of a kingdom will prove no more nourishing than buttered hay to a horse.

The Fool is thus a caricaturist, and his art lies in the relationship between his original—Lear overlaid with all his illusions—and his comic imitations of the significant forms these illusions take. His art is nominally practiced for Lear; but Lear so rarely understands it or attends to it that it seems more to the point to think of this part of the Fool's role as an element in the play's analytical perspective on Lear that leads us to recognize that Lear himself is playing the fool. I do not mean this simply as a judgment of the quality of Lear's acts. In a more important sense, it is a statement about Shakespeare's theatrical rhetoric. For the image of Lear that the play steadily insists on is a complex image, literally a confused one: not of Lear alone but of Lear shadowed by the Fool's theatrical caricature of the forms of his folly. "Who is it that can tell me who I am?" Lear asks sarcastically when Goneril begins to rate him about the behavior of his knights, and the Fool's answer, unattended, is "Lear's shadow." "I would learn that," Lear goes on, "for by the marks of sovereignty, / Knowledge, and reason, I should be false persuaded / I had daughters," and here the edge of his angry sarcasm, his whole posture of calling to account an erring child, is blunted by another of the Fool's answers that no one but the audience seems to hear: "Which they will make an obedient father" (1. 4. 230–35). That sounds a bit like the perverse cross-talk of low clowns, willfully turning meanings around for a laugh; but its nearer antecedent is Marlowe's treatment of Faustus, none of whose postures, prideful, angry, or defiant, is complete without the clarifying mockery of Wagner and the clowns. And behind Marlowe's treatment of Faustus lies the directly symbolic method of playwrights like John Redford, who objectifies the loss of Wit's likeness to himself by having Idleness blacken his face and dress him in Ingnorancy's gown.

Like Redford, Shakespeare exploits the gap between figure and likeness, between the various normative roles that define Lear's identity—chiefly as king and father—and the quality of Lear's performance of them. Toward that end, Lear's formal Fool entraps him in riddles, draws from him the punch lines of old jokes (which prove "thou wouldst make a good Fool"), and casts him in the part that is indispensable to all theatrical fools, the literal-minded straight man, always a beat or two behind the understanding of the audience, but now in a serious vaudeville with a single theme:

FOOL: ... Nuncle, give me an egg, and I'll give thee two crowns.

LEAR: What two crowns shall they be?

FOOL: Why, after I have cut the egg i' th' middle and eat up the meat, the two crowns of the egg. When thou clovest thy crown i' th' middle and gav'st away both parts, thou bor'st thine ass on thy back o'er the dirt. Thou hadst little wit in thy bald crown when thou gav'st thy golden one away. If I speak like myself in this, let him be whipt that first finds it so.

"Fools had ne'er less grace in a year,
For wise men are grown foppish,
And know not how their wits to wear,
Their manners are so apish."

LEAR: When were you wont to be so full of songs, sirrah?
FOOL: I have used it, nuncle, e'er since thou mad'st thy
       daughters thy mothers; for when thou gav'st them
       the rod and put'st down thine own breeches,

> "Then they for sudden joy did weep,
>   And I for sorrow sung,
> That such a king should play bo-peep
>   And go the fools among."
>   [1. 4. 155–78]

I quote this passage not merely because it shows Lear playing the
straight man but also because it provides a cluster of verbal images of
Lear in which one can see the survival of Saint Bernard's useful
paradox of the image that has become unlike its original. In the
Fool's mockery Lear is not simply a fool who has given away a crown
and become no longer a king; he is a mock king with an eggshell for
his crown, a wise man grown foppish, a father who has become a child
to his daughters. Through each image we see the original figure,
which Lear imagines he has retained, transformed into its opposite.
The matter of the Fool's jokes is all the same: Lear has lost his likeness
to himself. Looking at that loss from another point of view, Regan
will later urge him to bring his appearance into line with her own
narrow version of reality: "I pray you, father, being weak, seem so"
(2. 4. 201). And when Lear begins to recognize what sort of kingdom
he has created, he threatens, in one of a series of impotent boasts, to
recapture his lost likeness: "Thou shalt find," he warns Goneril and
Albany, "that I'll resume the shape which thou dost think / I have
cast off forever" (1. 4. 308–10)—meaning, presumably, the shape of
the king. But at the moment the bite of all of the Fool's jokes depends
on the fact that Lear, like Wit in a similar confrontation with reality,
does not recognize how he has changed. The old child continues to act
like a father, and the mock king thinks the eggshells are made of gold.

We need the Fool's shadowing caricatures in act 1, then, for much
the same reason that we need the parodies of Wagner and the clowns
in the first movement of *Doctor Faustus:* we need them because, in
act 1, Lear's illusions are still intact. His gestures, though empty now,
are still regal in their forms: the imperious demand for dinner,
apparently ignored, the purse tossed to Kent, the haughty question to
Oswald, "Who am I, sir?" (1. 4. 78), which really means, "I am the
king and you had better mind your manners." And though Oswald's
answer, like the indifference of Lear's attendants, suggests another
sort of world from the one Lear imagines, one in which Lear's identity
derives from Goneril, Lear's illusions govern sufficiently that we need

the Fool to point through them toward their immanent comic forms. But when Goneril enters, toward the end of the scene, and brings the matter of Lear's knights and his authority in her house into question, Lear's illusions begin to break down, the contradictions enfolded in his actions begin to be realized, and he himself begins to seem, in equal measure, pitiable and directly and theatrically ridiculous in his attempts to sustain the roles he has foregone.

Lear's cue is baffled impotence. When Goneril comes to complain about the behavior of his knights and to threaten that if he does not discipline them she will, Lear responds with an elaborately sarcastic performance:

> Are you our daughter?
> . . . .
> Does any here know me? This is not Lear.
> Does Lear walk thus? speak thus? Where are his eyes?
> Either his notion weakens, his discernings
> Are lethargied — Ha! Waking? 'Tis not so.
> Who is it that can tell me who I am?
> . . . .
> I would learn that; for by the marks of sovereignty,
> Knowledge, and reason, I should be false persuaded
> I had daughters.
> . . . .
> Your name, fair gentlewoman?
>
> [1. 4. 218-36]

There has been some tendency in productions of the play, and among its critics, to sentimentalize this passage, to play it on a note of rising panic, as if Lear really had begun to wonder who he was.[14] Such a reading is important to the developing theme of Lear's passage through the land of unlikeness, and those who have read the play in light of Renaissance texts on the subject of *nosce teipsum* have pointed out that Lear here, at least nominally, takes the first step on the road to self-knowledge by recognizing that he does not know himself.[15] But to put the matter thus baldly is to falsify the tone of the passage, the state of Lear's progress, and the complexity with which Shakespeare sets out both. For what Lear really means here is just the opposite: he is not saying that he does not know who he is but that Goneril seems to have forgotten who she is and what she owes him. What Lear's performance seems to aim at—and it is clearly a performance, complete with theatrical gestures, commentary from the Fool, criticism from Goneril, and a return to Lear's own nakedly passionate voice in, "Degenerate bastard, I'll not trouble thee" (253)—is to exact from Goneril an embarrassed confession that she has been presumptuous. "Look at me, father," she is supposed to say, while Lear's friends laugh indulgently, "I'm really your daughter, though I recognize now that I have not seemed daughterly." In that respect, his performance is as rhetorically insensitive as is Goneril's own way of talking to him as if he were a child. And in keeping with Lear's presumptions about his authority, it is rhetorically presumptuous as well, especially if we remember that the farthest reach of the land of unlikeness is the region of damnation, where man's will has become so unlike God's will that God can no longer recognize his image in man. Lear's prayers to nature to execute his will suggest this presumption in another form. But if there is some feeling in Lear that his will ought to be as normative as God's, what we can see in his performance is not divine dignity but rather a grotesque and pathetic clownishness; for his elaborate sarcasm lands far from the mark. His own knights may grant him the laugh at which his whole performance seems to aim, confirming the illusion of authority implied by the form of the joke, but Goneril will allow him neither one. Her reply is brief and contemptuous, and her diction draws into literal action the Fool's earlier joke that Lear has made his daughters his mothers: "This admiration, sir, is much o' the savor / Of other your new pranks" (237–38).

I do not mean that Lear is ridiculous here simply because Goneril says that he is. Taken in itself, his sarcastic performance might suggest several contradictory adjectives: "overblown," "insensitive," "pathetic," even "deserved"; similarly, the charade he later plays for Regan, kneeling before her in Gloucester's courtyard, might seem, taken in itself, a just comment on her advice that he go back and apologize to Goneril:

> Do you but mark how this becomes the house!
> "Dear daughter, I confess that I am old;
> Age is unnecessary. On my knees I beg
> That you'll vouchsafe me raiment, bed, and food."
> [2. 4. 153–56]

But neither can be taken simply in itself, for both are elaborate rhetorical acts aimed at immediate practical ends, and both fail to achieve their ends. Like the Red Queen in Wonderland, Goneril and Regan are the arbiters of language in Lear's new kingdom, and Lear must submit himself, however clumsily, to their verbal authority. He can no longer assume that words like "respect" and "obedience" will mean what they used to mean or that the qualities to which they refer will be found where common wisdom says they ought to be found, in the relations of parent and child; nor does the "name and all the additions to the crown" now mean what it should, for in disowning Cordelia he has disowned the authority of formal relationships. Love due, owed, paid, secured by the forms of identity, of father and daughter, seemed cold to him then compared to what seemed the love freely given by Goneril and Regan. So it is particularly ironic, a measure of the contradictions enfolded in Lear's choice of Goneril and Regan over Cordelia, that, coming to Regan from Goneril, he depends on and urges on her the formal defenses against individual appetite he had disowned in Cordelia: "The offices of nature, bond of childhood, / Effects of courtesy, dues of gratitude" (2. 4. 178–79). And it is a measure of how alien are the values of his new kingdom, how foreign its language, that Regan simply dismisses them all as irrelevant in her declarative question: "Good sir, to th' purpose" (181).

In giving his kingdom over to Goneril and Regan, Lear has made himself into a rhetorical monster, like Wit in the costume of Ingnorancy. He is now a petitioner king, an alien in the land he nominally rules. In the terms I have borrowed from Saint Bernard, he has retained his image—the outline of his identity in the roles of king and father, which he continues to assume; but the image has lost its likeness to its original, and the extravagant violence of his language is a measure of how lost it is, combining, as it does, the habits of power and the assumptions of place with the realities of powerlessness and placelessness. Goneril and Regan habitually refer to him generically as the "old man," denying him even the names of "father" and "king." And, as he speaks to them, one can hear, in his curious, often childlike turns of phrase, both the king who knows what is due him and the dependent who must beg for it. Authority and weakness are briefly poised in his reply to Goneril's charge that his followers are "so debosh'd and bold / That this our court, infected with their manners / Shows like a riotous inn" (1. 4. 242–44), for the memory of authority is present in his rage, but there is a tacit acknowledgment in the piling up of superlative adjectives that, finally, it is Goneril, mistress of the house, who must be persuaded:

> Detested kite, thou liest.
> My train are men of *choice* and *rarest* parts,
> That *all* particulars of duty know,
> And in the *most exact* regard support
> The worships of their name.
>   [262–66; emphasis added]

When he comes to Regan from Goneril, he spells out painfully the relationships that should command the appearance and respect of his daughter and her husband: "The king would speak with Cornwall; the dear father / Would with his daughter speak, commands, tends service" (2. 4. 101–2). And when Gloucester tells him they will not come, reminding him of how stubborn and hot-tempered Cornwall is, Lear, lacking any material power to enforce the authority of king and father over baron and daughter, any power to give to those terms their former meanings, erupts in impotent anger. He will get a drum, he says, and beat it outside their chamber door "till it cry sleep to death" (119). This is reminiscent of Hotspur's threat to teach a starling to cry "Mortimer" and give it to Bolingbroke to keep him from sleep, and the similarity is not fortuitous; for Lear's is as much a "huffing part" as Hotspur's, as much shaped, Wilson Knight reminds us, by the forms of comedy, though laughter itself may be checked by pathos.[16]

Because it is no longer tempered by real authority, Lear's language, never measured in the best of times, turns to fustian and rant as he tries to enforce through the violence of language alone what he can no longer enforce in material and ethical terms. His characteristic rhetorical figures during this movement of the play are invocations and apostrophes, empty commands to great and shadowy powers. When his daughters and their servants prove disobedient, he orders the powers of nature and the gods to take his vengeance on them, much as Richard II, though more limply, assumes that nature and God will sustain his kingly authority. But there is a common thread running through all these commands, great and small, connecting the trivial and domestic—

> Let me not stay a jot for dinner, go, get it ready.
> Where's my knave? My fool? Go you, and call my Fool hither.
> You, you, sirrah, where's my daughter?
> [1. 4. 9, 42–43, 44]

with the awesome and cosmic—

> Hear, Nature, hear, dear goddess, hear!
> Suspend thy purpose if thou didst intend
> To make this creature fruitful.
> [1. 4. 275–77]

All the stor'd vengeance of heaven fall
On her ungrateful top! Strike her young bones,
You taking airs, with lameness!

[2. 4. 162–64]

And thou, all shaking thunder,
Strike flat the thick rotundity o' th' world!
Crack nature's moulds, all germains spill at once
That makes ungrateful man!

[3. 2. 6–9]

That common thread is their futility. No one listens and no one obeys. His attendants, Oswald, the thunder, the gods, all go about their own business. And as his voice grows louder and his commands more sweeping, we see more and more clearly that he has become the strange creature he chose to be, a king and no king.

As the gap between Lear's illusions and the reality of life in his new kingdom becomes clearer, there is a new emphasis on his physical weakness and there are changes in his physical appearance. Regan had complained toward the end of act 2 that, being weak, he did not seem so. But now, stripped of his followers and locked out in the storm, he does. He has only the Fool and Kent with him now, at least until Poor Tom bursts out of the hovel to become the philosopher of his madness and to become, as well, the visible model of the state toward which he is moving, as the Fool had been the visible model of his earlier state. Throughout act 3 Lear's theatrical image is confused with Tom's, as it was, earlier, with the Fool's; he embraces Tom and trades mad antiphonal fantasies with him.[17] For all his blustery defiance of the storm, he is progressively more helpless, literally unable to care for himself in the simplest ways. His age and distraction tell. He needs to be physically shepherded around the stage, guided into shelter, put to bed, and, finally, carried off on a litter. His costume is a matter for the designer, of course; but it seems reasonable to assume that, whatever he wears when he rushes from Gloucester's castle into the storm, it will mark out his illusion that he has retained royal dignity along with the name of the king, because that has been his contention throughout the scene. If so, there are several indications, early in act 3, that Shakespeare intends us to see this illusion unravel. Whatever other business an actor might invent to make the point, it seems clear, for example, that Lear is to strip off his outer garment at the words "take physic, pomp. / Expose thyself to feel what wretches feel" (3. 4. 33–34). And, later on, when he has slipped into madness and thinks he sees in Poor Tom the image of natural man himself, he tries to tear off the rest of his clothes. What we see onstage, then, are transformations in Lear's appearance—from king toward naked madman—as telling as the transformations in Volpone or, perhaps closer to the point, as telling as the transformation of Wit into Ingnorancy. For the effect of Lear's next appearance on stage, decked in weeds, full-blown in madness, announcing "I am the King himself" (4. 6. 84), is similar in kind if not in quality to the effect of Wit's appearance to Lady Science in Ingnorancy's motley, his face blackened, claiming to be himself. Each has become in a very precise and significant way his own opposite.

The chief difference between Shakespeare's image and Redford's is its greater complexity. For Poor Tom presents Lear with a model of natural man that he must accept as his own, if only in part, before he can come to terms with himself, just as he must feel his kinship with the "naked wretches...who bide the pelting of this pitiless storm" before he can again put on his pompous robes. While Wit's progress toward Ingnorancy is simply the perversion of his identity, then, Lear's progress toward the mad king of a fantastical kingdom that he portrays in act 4, scene 6, is at the same time a progress toward a deeper understanding of himself and his real kingdom. Before I can take up that strain in the play, however, I will need to follow Lear still further into the land of unlikeness.

Lear's madness has no single cause. His suffering, his naïveté, his corrosive self-pity, his temperament, all combine to topple his mind.[18] But there is a sense in which his madness merely draws out and objectifies the cast of mind—naïve, rash, self-indulgent—that found Goneril and Regan's flattery more immediately satisfying though he loved Cordelia best. And in the forms of his madness the confused roles we have been tracing are finally dissociated and clarified. The king he imagines himself still to be withdraws to a fantasy kingdom in his mind, there to arraign his daughters in a cracked trial, leaving the placeless old man he has become to be tended by Kent and the Fool.

The kingdom over which Lear reigns in his madness is shaped by his desire for revenge and by a solipsistic self-pity that projects the collapse of his own illusions out on to all the world. Because he was betrayed by the daughters he trusted, everyone in a position of trust appears to him to be deceitful. So it is not only a mad kingdom; it is also a parody of a sane one, all the institutions of a sane kingdom being now inverted and deformed. Everywhere he looks there are only predators and prey; there is no room for integrity, for faithful service like Kent's or for love like Cordelia's, both of which exist in reality but have been banished from his inner and outer kingdoms. Poor Tom, huddled in his blanket, must have been betrayed by his daughters, he insists, for "nothing could have subdu'd nature / To such a lowness but his unkind daughters." And radiating from that imaginative center there is in Lear's mind a kingdom populated with creatures like his daughters, whose hidden desires belie their innocent appearances and whose acts belie their offices.

Lear's exploration of his mad kingdom provides a running commentary on the degeneration of the real kingdom, in which he has lost "the name and all the additions to a king."[19] To understand why that should be so, why the kingdom of Lear's fantasies should mirror the downward progress of the kingdom in which he has empowered Goneril and Regan, we need to remember that in Elizabethan political philosophy the king was a twin person. He was first of all himself, individual and mortal; but he was also the will that animated the laws and institutions of the immortal body politic. Laws and institutions were the limbs of his extended body, realizing the motions of his political spirit as the limbs of his mortal body realized the desires of his soul. So it was customary to speak of the kingdom itself as the body of the King and to speak of the king himself as the state. Ideally, the king's two bodies were to be thought of as complementary, indeed, as interdependent, since the authority of any individual king derived from the laws and institutions of the body politic, while the laws of the body politic could be actualized only by an individual king. We saw in *Woodstock* how the relationship between the king's two bodies could be imaginatively exploited to show the parallel degeneration of his bodies natural and politic when the king turned to self-indulgence, and Shakespeare's treatment of the form of Lear's body politic proceeds along similar lines. Having dissociated the king from the King by giving the administration of his body politic over to Goneril and Regan and their husbands, Lear lost his own likeness. And having been conveyed by the king to those animated by appetite, his body politic loses its likeness to itself as the forms of its institutions erode.

Perhaps the most compelling evidence that the mirroring of the king's two bodies is part of Shakespeare's design is the fact that Goneril and Regan do not emerge full-blown in evil until Lear retreats to his mad kingdom. In the temporal structure of the play their clarification runs parallel with his. As they evolve toward the harpies who scream, "Hang him instantly!" "Pluck out his eyes!" in anticipation of their revenge on Gloucester for sending Lear to Dover, he evolves toward the madman crowned with weeds we see in act 4, scene 6, the king of a nightmare in which evil is so pervasive it can no longer be distinguished from good. Shakespeare's presentation of what Lear sees in his fantasy kingdom, then, provides surreal images of what we see happening in his real kingdom. Thus the cracked trial in act 3, scene 6, in which Lear arraigns his daughters, is echoed immediately in scene 7 in the more grotesque perversion of the institution of justice we see in the trial of Gloucester.

The two trials are arranged as intricate distorting mirrors of each other. The defendants in each are addressed at first as foxes ("Now, you she-foxes!" [3. 6. 22]; "Ingrateful fox, 'tis he" [3. 7. 28]). Goneril and Regan, absent from Lear's trial except in his own fantasy, are present at Gloucester's—Goneril for part of the time, Regan through-out; and the indictment that Lear tries to bring against them in his fantasy ("she kicked the poor king, her father" [3. 6. 47]) is pursued in reality by Lear's double, Gloucester, with terrible irony: "I would not see thy cruel nails / Pluck out his poor old eyes, nor thy fierce sister / In his anointed flesh rash boarish fangs" (3. 7. 56–58). But Gloucester's complaint is overborne by their charge, straight from the wonderland of Lear's own imagination, that Gloucester has been a traitor because he has been loyal to his king. The shouts and howls of pain as they tear out his eyes echo the cacaphonous accompaniment the Fool and Poor Tom provide for Lear's trial. And, finally, both trials collapse in unforeseen disorder before they end, Lear's because "Regan escapes," Gloucester's because Cornwall's servant rises up in revulsion and kills him.

According to Heilman, the chief point of these intricate parallels is to provide a foundation for the paradox that "a trial that goes on in a madman's mind may embody a closer approximation of justice than an apparently legal procedure by the constituted authorities."[20] If that is so, however, it is only in the very precise sense that the madman is careful about the forms of judicial procedures; for Lear's fantasy never gets much beyond them, while the "constituted authorities" cynically disdain them. Almost all of Lear's lines concern the arrangement and formal conduct of the imaginary trial. He twice settles Poor Tom and the Fool—who seem to be hopping around the stage—on what he imagines to be their judicial benches; he then deputizes Kent as a member of the commission, decides on the order of the arraignments, and calls for the presentation of the evidence—in short, he conducts in his mind a formally punctilious trial, though the audience can perceive its form only through the obvious disorder of the theatrical scene. On the other hand, Gloucester's trial is disorderly, both within and without. Cornwall brushes aside the very notion of the forms of justice at the beginning of the scene so that his and Regan's power may immediately do a "courtesy to [their] wrath" (3. 7. 26), and he speaks of what they do to Gloucester simply as revenge. Gloucester's "punishment" is itself an emblem of disorder; physically revolting and having no relation to his supposed crime,[21] it is chosen by Cornwall in what is made to seem merely an angry whim (to Gloucester's "I shall see the winged vengeance overtake such children," he replies, "See't shalt thou never" [65–67]). Shakespeare will not let us blink away its sheer physical horror, no matter how discreetly the scene is staged, because the language is insistently concrete. The most immediate effect of Gloucester's blinding is to shatter existing order, for Cornwall's lifelong servant rebels against him. Those left onstage after Regan has helped Cornwall off see the order of society itself at stake in the punishment of these offenders:

> [2]SERV.: I'll never care what wickedness I do,
>   If this man comes to good.
> [3]SERV.:   If she live long,
>   And in the end meet the old course of death,
>   Women will all turn monsters,
>
>   [99–102]

It is here, in the relationship between order and justice, that the issue between the two trials is most sharply joined. Neither trial really approximates justice, but Lear's arraignment of his daughters contains the capacity for it. For the forms of justice—which Lear in his fantasy attends to but Cornwall brushes aside in his anger—may be exasperating, easy to mock, open to perversion by devious men, and sometimes even productive of injustice themselves, but they are finally society's only barriers, however rickety, against the chaotic individual appetite to set things right according to its own lights. The purpose of the forms of justice is not to do a courtesy to wrath but to dissipate it in the law's delay and the trappings and decorum of a trial and thus to subordinate individual passion to the symbolic judgment of the community.

Remembering that, we can recognize in the contrast between the two trials—one a disordered expression of anger, the other a chaotic expression of order—the latest instance of the dialectic that has been developing since the beginning of the play: the dialectic between individual appetites of all sorts and the social forms that seek to constrain them. We see its first terms in the bonds of Cordelia's love and the unbounded flattery offered by Goneril and Regan, the office of a daughter and the appetite for power. Thereafter we see it in all the mutual attempts by Lear and his daughters to satisfy their own appetites by reining the appetites of others within normative bounds. A psychomachia between appetite and order also goes on within Lear himself. His notion that Goneril and Regan ought to behave like proper daughters, grateful and obedient, collides with the refusal of his own passions to submit themselves to the offices of a father. Out in the storm the psychomachia is carried on through the opposed pairs of revenge and justice. Grotesque schemes for getting back at his daughters jostle in Lear's mind against reflections on social and divine justice. For example, immediately before he decides to arraign Goneril and Regan, he imagines having "a thousand with red burning spits come hizzing in upon 'em" (3. 6. 15–16), and when Cordelia's attendants catch up with him in act 4, scene 6, he is still hatching schemes to satisfy his anger instantly and theatrically:

> It were a delicate stratagem, to shoe
> A troop of horse with felt. I'll put't in proof,
> And when I have stol'n upon these son-in-laws,
> Then kill, kill, kill, kill, kill, kill!
> [184–87]

It is not, then, Lear himself who stands opposed to Cornwall, embracing justice rather than revenge; what is represented is merely the oscillation within his mind of the form of the dialectic.

By this point in the play other institutions, formal and informal, have collapsed and are collapsing as the form of Lear's body politic is eaten away by appetite. At the heart of it all is the inversion of what Hooker speaks of as the first form of the state, that is, the family. In casting Lear as both father and king, all versions of the story at least touch on the overlap between these twin foundations of social order, but only Shakespeare's pays attention to the consequences in the larger community that follow from the overturning of the smaller one. Both families in the play have now been taken over by duplicitous children, loyal siblings have been banished, fathers have been turned out, and the process of this overturning has sent out waves that have begun to erode other institutions. Goneril's desire to force the question of authority into the open leads her to license her servants to "put on what weary negligence [they] please" in attending Lear. Once licensed, discourtesy spreads—through Oswald's insolence, the calculated rudeness of Regan and Cornwall, the stocking of Kent, the betrayal of Gloucester's hospitality—to one unlooked-for fulfillment in the rebellion of Cornwall's servant and also to another one, more congenial to Lear's daughters, in the rise of Edmund. With the failure of courtesy, the bonds that hold individuals in community decay. Betrayal is prized, and loyalty becomes treason. Shakespeare has kept Albany out of the events of acts 2 and 3 and thus unchanged by them; so Albany's reaction to these events at the beginning of act 4, described by a bewildered Oswald, serves to measure how thoroughly the values and expectations of those aligned with Lear's daughters have been inverted:

> I told him of the army that was landed;
> He smil'd at it. I told him you were coming;
> His answer was, "The worse." Of Gloucester's treachery,
> And of the loyal service of his son,
> When I informed him, then he call'd me sot,
> And told me I had turn'd the wrong side out,
> What most he should dislike seems pleasant to him;
> What like, offensive.
>
> [4. 2. 4–11]

It is Edmund's "loyal service" that overturns the order of his family, elevating him from bastard to earl and bringing him into the way of Goneril's lust. What she takes to be Albany's weakness has saved the affair for some readers ("I must change names at home, and give the distaff / Into my husband's hands...O the difference of man and man" [4. 2. 17–18, 26]).[22] But there is no blinking away the deep lawlessness of her passion. Marriage is no more an impediment to her desires than the forms of justice are to Cornwall's anger, nor are the forms of justice. She solicits Edmund to murder Albany so that they can be together, and, when she is found out, she simply asserts that she is her own law: "The laws are mine. Who can arraign me for it?" (5. 3. 156–60). When she discovers that Regan has the same itch in her loins, she poisons her. And when Regan, already feeling the poison, lays claim to Edmund, the perversion of the forms of sexual relations in Lear's new kingdom is summed up in Albany's savage joke:

> For your claim, fair sister,
> I bar it in the interest of my wife;
> 'Tis she is sub-contracted to this lord,
> And I, her husband, contradict your banes.
> If you will marry, make your loves to me,
> My lady is bespoke.
>
> [5. 3. 84–89]

In a thorough going way, then, the shape of Lear's extended body has changed. The forms of all the relations that characterize the body politic, from the most private to the most public, have been twisted in service to appetite.

Animal imagery has played around Goneril and Regan since early in act 1, when Lear called Goneril a "kite" and threatened that Regan would flay her "wolvish visage." There the images spoke more to Lear's rhetorical excesses than to anything perceptibly animal-like in Goneril's behavior, but here, with the restraints on appetite that characterize civilized communities gone or going, such terms are more appropriate. Goneril and Regan have grown into Lear's metaphors, as it were, just as Lear has grown into Kent's description of him as mad. And, as part of the same process, Lear's kingdom has come in metaphor to resemble the regions of unlikeness found in the *Pilgrimage of Human Life* and *Reason and Sensuality*—countries of sensuous desire inhabited by monstrous figures, where men are "ytourned to lyknesse of bestys, / And, makid bestial, los[e] hir reson natural."

There may indeed be some reason to believe that, as the animal imagery becomes increasingly apposite to the behavior of humans who are abandoning their humanity, that process also becomes theatrically evident through changes in their appearance. Albany, at least, who has not been part of any of the changes and so measures them, seems insistent at the beginning of act 4 that Goneril looks different. She has been mocking him as a "moral fool," too weak to defend his own interests, when Albany tells her to look at herself:

> ALB: See thyself, devil!
>   Proper deformity shows not in the fiend
>   So horrid as in woman.
> GON.:   O vain fool!
> ALB.:   Thou changed and self-cover'd thing, for shame
>   Bemonster not thy feature. Were't my fitness
>   To let these hands obey my blood,
>   They are apt enough to dislocate and tear
>   Thy flesh and bones. Howe'er thou art a fiend,
>   A woman's shape doth shield thee.
>   [4. 2. 59–67]

This is generally taken to mean the opposite of what it seems to mean; that is, it is interpreted to mean that Goneril's appearance has *not* changed. Perhaps readers are reluctant to imagine that Shakespeare might be so simple and direct, so old-fashioned, as to have Goneril's appearance alter along with changes in her moral state. The key term is "self-covered," which some editors gloss flatly as "disguised,"[23] as if Albany were saying that, while Goneril has grown ugly within, she is still deceitfully attractive on the outside. But the term in itself need mean nothing more than that Goneril is responsible for her own appearance. And it is reasonable to imagine that her appearance has changed in the direction of a revealing ugliness, that what has been "self-covered" is the morally more complex, less easily defined Goneril of the beginning of the play; for Albany has been saying in a variety of ways throughout the scene that Goneril has degenerated, has been "disbranched / From her material sap," become more barbarous than a bear, been deformed from her proper self. Since Albany has already told her that she is deformed, it seems likely that his prefix *be,* in "bemonster not thy feature," is an intensive; if so, what Albany means is not "Don't look like a monster" but rather "Don't look even more monstrous"—presumably because Goneril has been smirking at him as she speaks the words "O vain fool." This reading at least has the advantage of making the line a concrete exclamation in an ongoing quarrel rather than an airy and somewhat oblique wish that she not look like what Albany has already told her that she is. If it is accurate as well—if Albany does mean that her grimacing makes her look even more monstrous—then it would seem that what he calls her deformity lies in some marked change in her expression, some coarsening of her look that reflects what she has done. That sort of change in her appearance would be natural enough, even expectable in the theater, where appearances are so important a part of an author's vocabulary. And, if Goneril, then surely Regan, who helped to pluck out Gloucester's eyes and killed Cornwall's servant. So we might reasonably imagine that Goneril and Regan, like the figures who serve their appetites in *Reason and Sensuality,* though more subtly, have been "ytourned to lyknesse of bestys"—a change we might appreciate even more if the way they look early in the play conveys the narrow concern for respectability that leads Goneril to urge Lear to retain only "such men as may besort your age."

Whatever we conclude about the looks of Goneril and Regan, however, the details of Lear's appearance in act 4, when he catches up all its transformations into a last searing image of his body politic, seem clear enough. Cordelia tells us that he has been seen "crown'd with rank femiter and furrow weeds, / With hardocks, hemlock, nettles, cuckoo-flow'rs, / Darnel, and all the idle weeds that grow / In our sustaining corn" (4. 4. 3–6)—plants that have been identified as "bitter, biting, poisonous, pungent, lurid and distracting...[and so] emblematic of the sources and variety of the diseases under which he labours."[24] If Cordelia means by "crown'd" that the plants have been plaited into a crown and not merely strewn in his hair, we can recognize immediately at his entrance that Lear has now become altogether a parody king, not only the king of sorrows but also the perfection of all the Fool's jokes ("Who is it that can tell me who I am?" "Lear's shadow."). We can see the image in which he was made in his bearing and in the structure of his fantasy ("I am the king himself"), just as we can see Wit's true form through Ingnorancy's motley, or Volpone's through the disguise he adopts for Celia. But Lear is, otherwise, point to point the reverse of the assured monarch we saw at the beginning of the play: for his golden crown he has one of bitter weeds; for his robes, rags; for his mastery of the law, outlawry; for the illusion of sanity, open madness; and, for England, the mad kingdom of his fantasies, to which he has been reduced.

Lear's description of the inhabitants of his fantasy kingdom is, among other things, a bitter satirical portrait of the state of England. Lear does not know, or at least we have no reason to believe that he knows, about the blinding of Gloucester, or Goneril's adulterous affair with Edmund, or anything that has happened to the other characters since the end of act 2; yet all of it appears refracted through his madness. His meditations on his own injuries seem to have carried him imaginatively along the same course that his daughters have taken in fact. Like Queen Anne in *Woodstock,* numbering the poor of England, Lear has special insight into the state of his kingdom by virtue of his role as its embodiment. So, like England, the kingdom in his mind is preparing for war, impressing soldiers, maneuvering with pikes, practicing archery. As in England, its judicial institutions are corrupted by wealth and subservient to appetite. Like England, it teems with lechers. And, like England, Lear's mad kingdom seems to have lost the distinction between animals and men. When Lear compared his daughters to animals earlier in the play, he assumed that humans and animals occupy different spheres of creation and that to say that human behavior is animal-like is to identify it as self-evidently abhorrent. Such assumptions seem now to have been foregone; the behavior of animals seem now to be the model for human behavior. In his fantasy Lear can see no reason to punish an imagined adulterer before his imaginary court because "the wren goes to't, and the small gilded fly / Does lecher in my sight" (4. 6. 112–13), and a barking dog seems to him "the great image of authority" (158).

While many of the things that Lear says about his mad kingdom are commonplaces of Renaissance political skepticism,[25] we ought not to allow them too broad a reach. Lear gains necessary, though partial, insight into the state of man in society through his vision of a community whose institutions are hollow masks for vices everyone shares. But there is finally as much impertinency as matter in this vision, particularly in its form and in the conclusions Lear derives from it. The two are intricately entwined. Lear's mistake about Edmund is obvious enough, for example, but he combines it with an equally obvious truth—that Goneril and Regan are in any event unkind—to produce a universal and false conclusion: that copulation ought to be allowed to thrive because a bastard has proved kinder than Lear's legitimate daughters. Meanwhile, Edgar cradles Gloucester in his arms, and Cordelia has landed in England on her father's business. The effect is rather like the effect achieved at the end of act 2 of *As You Like It,* where Jacques' theatrical cynicism and Amiens' song about man's ingratitude are played against Orlando's tender and loving care of Adam. Lear's other observations are similarly contextualized and qualified by wider perspectives than his own. Thinking about his daughters immediately leads him to "see" in his fantasy the mincing dame "whose face beneath her forks presages snow" but who goes to it more lustily than a polecat or a soiled horse. She is not precisely Goneril, but she does combine what Lear knows of Goneril, her cold respectability that "shook the head to hear of pleasure's name," with what we know of her and he can only intuit, her corrosive lust, to lead him to another universal conclusion: that all women are like her, hypocritically divine to the waist and fiendish beneath. From our larger perspective, however, Lear's dame no more represents all the women in the play than his "great image of authority" represents all the transactions between those in office and those who obey them. Time-servers like Oswald may take on the interests of anyone above them, however venal; but Kent shows that, for him, the highest form of loyalty to his master is loyalty to the truth. The trouble is that Kent and Cordelia have been banished and, with them, discriminating loyalty, chastity—all the virtues that give life to the dead institutions in which the vices of both of Lear's mad kingdoms flourish. Lear has sent them away from his larger kingdom, and so he cannot see them in his smaller kingdom; they exist in the play but not in his world. What Lear sees in his fantasy, then, is not the state of man in society as the play would have it understood, namely, as universal viciousness disguised by hypocritical social distinctions; it is instead a perfected image of the England he created, the land of unlikeness. The forms of its institutions are intact, but their substance has been eaten away. It is a parody of itself.

Recognizing the limitations of his vision, we can recognize that then the absolution Lear pronounces on his mad kingdom is as much an act of unwarranted despair as Gloucester's attempted suicide is in a world that seems to him "all dark and comfortless." "None does offend," Lear says, "none, I say none," meaning, ironically, that his kingdom is so shot through with offense that legal distinctions between good and evil are meaningless. Let copulation thrive, then, and, along with it, usury and cozening and theft, not because Lear embraces those vices or even forgives them—his attitude toward humanity is disgust rather than acceptance—but simply because there seems to be nothing in his kingdom to leaven vice. So the injunction that traditionally follows a pardon, "Go, thou, and sin no more," is replaced by Lear's despairing indulgence: "I'll able 'em" (168). Let them go and sin with impunity.

This parody of a pardon, spoken by a parody king in a parody kingdom, is answered within moments by Cordelia's own pardon of Lear. There is some tendency among the play's critics to see the two pardons as complementary. "Shakespeare has led Lear to compassion for sin as well as suffering," Granville Barker said.[26] Cordelia's "forgiveness," Michael Long explained, "completes and crowns the movement through which Lear himself has gone to 'None does offend.'"[27] But I would argue that precisely the opposite is true, that Lear's indulgence for evil, spoken from within the land of unlikeness, is the mirror image of Cordelia's pardon, its opposite in every way except for the similarity in their skeletal forms. Both are pardons; but where Lear, out of despair, licenses what he know to be evil, Cordelia forgives, *a poena et a culpa,* out of love. "No cause, no cause" dissolves both the penalty Lear offers to endure and his wrong. Nicholas Brooke says that it is an emotional gratuity, a loving grace note that helps us to endure a world in which there is no enduring order, because Cordelia has undeniably been wronged.[28] We can see in Perillus' explication of Leir's faulty reasoning in the *True Chronicle,* however, a sense in which the very notion of wrong might be irrelevant for Cordelia. She will never receive me, the old Leir complains, much more flat-footedly than Shakespeare's, for "she did find my love was not to her / As should a father bear unto a child." "That makes not her love to be any less," Perillus assures him, "If she do love you as a child should" (3. 5. 1720–23). According to that line of reasoning, Cordelia's wholehearted embrace of Lear, far from being emotionally gratuitous, is simply the expression of her own identity as his daughter. It is what she cannot fail to do and continue to be herself. Lear's imaginary negation of the laws and institutions of his body politic, on the other hand, is a denial of his identity as its king, just as any act of despair is a denial of the capacities of the self, because the king is a creature of the law. "None does offend," neither adulterer, cozener, nor thief: this is what Lear cannot say and continue to be himself. Thus, when Lear announces at the beginning of the scene that he is the "king himself," the very construction of his fantasy seems to invite as a judgment on that illusion the line repeated by Richard II's minions at the abduction of Gloucester, when Richard subverted his own body politic and came to the outer boundaries of the land of unlikeness: "You're still deceived, my lord, the king's not here."

RESUMING HIS SHAPE: THE PILGRIMAGE OF KING LEAR

While Cordelia's role in *King Lear* is brief (scarcely 100 lines in all), she is crucial to its structure, which turns on the three sequences in which she appears onstage with her father. The first, in which he abandons the bias of his nature and disowns her, points toward the second, a *scene à faire* in which they are reconciled; but the peace he finds there is shattered in the last sequence, in which she is murdered and he falls back again into madness. The imperative that drives Lear through the play is the need to understand and properly value Cordelia, to come to terms with her, first alive and then dead, and with her way of loving.

In the event, of course, Lear, to understand Cordelia, must come to understand a great deal more. Her way of loving is part of a network of relationships that stretch, or seem to, from earth to heaven, and to pursue Cordelia is to touch them all. Shakeseare's reconstruction of the relationships between Lear and his daughters, then, opens up the literal and discrete events of the Lear story to questions as far-reaching as those explicated in *The Pilgrimage of the Life of Man,* questions of social and divine justice and of the nature and necessities of men. In the course of his pilgrimage Lear must discover the nature and function of social offices and the fact that his identity is bound up with them. And, most of all, he must come to understand himself, as king, as father, and as a man. As Rolf Soellner has observed, no other play of Shakespeare's announces so clearly that its subject is self-knowledge.[29]

Self-knowledge is also a major concern in all of the imitations of the pilgrimage we have examined. The pilgrim's journey through his life is shaped by his lack of self-knowledge, and that journey regularly brings him toward a more precise and substantial understanding of himself. At first, whatever his guise—as the Young Man of *Reason and Sensuality*, as Wit, as Richard—the pilgrim knows himself only schematically. His completed identity lies before him, like a theatrical role whose outlines he can see but whose individual speeches have yet to be memorized and performed. The Young Man knows that he is distinguished from the rest of creation because he has a rational soul, and he vows to follow the path of reason, "which doth a man to heven lede." Richard knows that he looks like his father, and he promises that, "as we are his body's counterfeit, / So will we be the image of his mind." All know what they are *in potentia*, but none of the pilgrims can sustain the vision of his perfected identity against the subtle entanglements of each moment. They are, to recall Saint Bernard's spiritual ages of man, *egens et insipiens*, yearning toward what they might be but distracted from it by folly, just as Lear, *egens et insipiens*, inclines toward Cordelia but chooses instead to give himself into the keeping of Goneril and Regan.

While Lear stands at the end of his life, not at its beginning, his grasp on his identity, focused in the roles of father and king, is as loose as that of any of the pilgrims. He is regularly surprised by the ordinary conditions of life—that the rain wets, that the wind chills, that the lot of the poor is hard, that nature goes its own way no matter how loudly you shout at it to do your bidding. Like Shakespeare's Richard II, Lear seems never to have learned that kings are first of all men, subject to all the infirmities of mortal bodies. And Mack is surely right when he suggests that we are to understand that Lear's kingdom is far too swathed in robes and furred gowns to be altogether healthy.[30] Lear must come to understand, then, that beneath the robes that insulate him from nature he is weak and vulnerable. But that knowledge is not itself the goal of his pilgrimage, as it is the goal of Renaissance manuals of self-knowledge. *King Lear* is a profoundly social play, concerned with man's nature chiefly as it shapes his relations with other men, and what Lear learns about the lot of humanity is steadily related to his place in the social scheme. The trouble is that Lear knows no more about his place in society than he does about his humanity. He is a father and a king, the pivot of the interlocked communities of family and state. Like the Young

Man's nature or Richard's resemblance to his chivalric father, these are at once roles already granted to him and at the same time roles he has yet to achieve. One may become a biological father or an anointed king in a moment, but the offices that attach to that moment, the responsibilities that distinguish fathers and kings from other men and so underpin the authority and deference they command, have still to be fulfilled through all the entanglements of every day.

Those responsibilities are not systematically defined in the play, although Cordelia briefly recalls the office of a father when she defines her filial office, and Lear comes later on in the play to recognize particular ways in which he has failed against the office of a king. Still, one can see almost at once that Lear has misconceived the forms of his offices: "Better thou / Hadst not been born than not t'have pleas'd me better," he tells Cordelia, summing up the narrow self-absorption that has led him, through "Which of you shall we say doth love us most?" and "Here I disclaim all my paternal care," to his resignation of all the "cares and business" of the throne while attempting to retain its dignities. He has converted both his roles from responsibilities to others into opportunities for self-gratification and, by doing so, has drained them of their ethical authority.[31] And without that authority his relations with his daughters and with the subjects of his kingdom, except for those who remain stubbornly loyal to their own offices in spite of all that he does to drive them away, are governed by the Fool's maxim: "Fathers that wear rags / Do make their children blind, / But fathers that bear bags / Shall see their children kind" (2. 4. 48–51).

Skeptical, worldly wisdom of this kind is the first and simplest of Lear's lessons. If he is ever to understand himself and properly value Cordelia, he must come to understand that the dignities of fathers and kings are granted to them by those who are subject to their authority, either simply because of their power and worldly wealth or, more securely, because of the bonds of mutual obligation that hold families and states together. As Lear passes into and through the land of unlikeness, his illusion that he has an absolute and irreducible right to deference and obedience is drawn out and clarified in all the harrowing details we have just examined. The parody king we see in act 4, scene 6, surveying a kingdom marked by the hollowness of its offices, is implied in the hollow exercises of royal and paternal authority we see in act 1, scene 1, just as Wit's abandonment of Reason implies his appearance later on in the costume and makeup of

Ingnorancy. Having chosen to be a father and king in name only, Lear inevitably discovers that he is only nominally a father to his daughters and only nominally a king.

It would be too much to say that Lear comes to understand fully that he is a king only because others are subjects or that he is a father because Cordelia is a daughter. There is nothing systematic and very little that is cumulative about Lear's pilgrimage. *Praeceps et temerarius in prosperis* (Kent and Goneril agree on that), he disowns Cordelia and gives himself into the keeping of his older daughters, and thereafter his insights come either in flashes of anger or refracted through his madness. Lear grows and learns passionately.

And from the first moments of his disillusionment, he begins to feel as much as to understand his dependence on the integrity of others. His sarcastic address to Goneril that begins "Are you our daughter?" rests on the self-evident premise—self-evident to him and assumed in his sarcasm—that daughters simply cannot treat their fathers as she is treating him. There are limits, he implies, to the behavior of daughters (and so, of course, to the behavior of everyone)—limits beyond which they cannot stray and continue to be themselves; and when, burned already by Goneril, he comes to Regan, he is careful to remind her of them: "The offices of nature, bond of childhood," etc. Beyond these limits there is social and psychological chaos, and the form of his sarcastic words to Goneril poses for him a question that he comes to feel more and more deeply as his mind shuttles between his daughters' ingratitude and the edges of madness. It is not merely "Who am I?" but the whole of the thought that locates the problem of his identity within the network of his relations with others: "Who is it that can tell me who I am? / I would learn that, for by the marks of sovereignty, / Knowledge and reason, I should be false persuaded / I had daughters." While it is merely sarcastic overstatement that here links self-knowledge and the integrity of his senses with the integrity of his daughters, Lear's overstatement is prophetic; for later on in the play, when hysterical passion threatens to overwhelm his reason, it does so at the moments when his mind is dwelling on what he calls the unnaturalness of his daughters.

Adversity was said by the manuals of self-knowledge to be a teacher of humility to the proud, and certainly it serves Lear in that way. Stripped of his dignities by his daughters and locked out in the storm, he begins to learn the "art of our necessities," which "makes vile things precious" (3.2. 70–71). He discovers bonds of common humanity with the Fool, whom he addresses for the first time as "my fellow" when he discovers that he and the Fool are chilled by the same storm. Wet and cold, he feels, for what seems to be the first time, compassion for the "naked wretches... / That bide the pelting of this pitiless storm," and in that compassion he discovers that he has failed in his office as their king. The discoveries that he makes are the sorts of discoveries that the manuals of self-knowledge argue that men in high places must make to rid themselves of the illusions engendered by their high estate. And they are effective. It is when he finds that he is not "ague-proof" that Lear sees through the flatterers who told him he was everything.

But these discoveries sometimes appear in such shifting and equivocal contexts that it is difficult to settle on a single meaning or value for them.[32] When one of the naked wretches appears in the guise of Poor Tom, Lear thinks he has found an image of "the thing itself," natural man, unaccommodated by the social trappings that hide men from themselves, and he tries to strip down to his natural state. But ironically, of course, Tom is a sophisticated courtier, accommodated by his nakedness against Edmund's intrigue, and his true nature is the more deeply hidden precisely because it seems so disingenuously open. While Lear imagines he can see in Tom the hidden truth of mankind, in fact he cannot even recognize the open features of his own godson. That being so, I suspect we stop short if we merely applaud Lear's new and humbling insight into the fragility of man (a "poor, bare, forked animal"). We come closer to Shakespeare's point, I think, if we go on to recognize that, in the scheme of the play, taking man's fragile body for man himself, trying to distinguish man's nature from the accommodating web of society that provides him with a peculiarly human identity, is a reductive illusion suspiciously like his daughters' illusion that Lear himself might easily be stripped of the trappings of royalty and served merely according to his natural needs, which Lear himself equates with making "man's life cheap as beast's." Shakespeare seems regularly to treat conceits like this, which are skeptical about the dignity of man and his institutions, ironically, as partial truths that, taken for the whole, lead to despair. Edmund is their chief spokesman, and the images of animals that cluster around Edmund and Goneril and Regan are consistently associated in the play with less-than-human behavior. So here, as later, in act 4, scene 6, Lear's insights are contextualized and qualified by perspectives larger than his own. Even as he tries to strip down to the animal within, Lear is protected from his enthusiasms, as he is from the violence of the storm, by Kent and the Fool, both of whom act out of a more comprehensive image of what it means to be irreducibly human.

Lear's newfound sense of his own fragility suggests the third in Saint Bernard's spiritual ages of man: Rash and thoughtless in prosperity, Saint Bernard said at the end of *Parabola I,* man becomes fearful and trembles when he falls into adversity (*trepidus et pusillanimus in adversis*). Of course nothing is simple or simply presented in Lear's pilgrimage, least of all the successive states through which he passes. He does not move from one spiritual condition to another, from pride to humility or thoughtlessness to fearful self-examination, as emblematic characters do. There is a realistic integrity in Shakespeare's presentation of Lear's growth toward resuming his shape, a blending and blurring-together of all the contradictory and mutually qualifying impulses in Lear's mind, those that are fading away and those that are not yet fully grasped. Humbling insights are jostled by boozy self-pity, and he veers from moments of compassion for others to grotesque schemes for revenge against his daughters which suggest that, if circumstances were different, he might still be as vicious as they. At his worst moments he is preserved by his awesome energy and buoyancy. He is literally fearful only of madness: "O, let me not be mad, sweet heaven! / Keep me in temper, I would not be mad" (1. 5. 46–47). And for two acts he skirts the edges of it, encountering madness unexpectedly at the ends of thoughts that start out in other directions: "O Regan, Goneril! / Your old, kind father, whose frank heart gave all — / O, that way madness lies, let me shun that. / No more of that" (3. 4. 19–22). But the drift of his thought and feeling, in sanity and in madness, is toward a sort of bewildered and chastened anxiety. His last huffing speech, the one that begins "Let the great gods / That keep this dreadful pudder o'er our heads, / Find out their enemies now," ends in a diminuendo, a blustery whimper: "I am a man / More sinn'd against than sinning" (3. 2. 49–51, 60). His exchanges with others are governed now by questions—solicitous, mad, and finally unanswerable: "Then let tham anatomize Regan, see what breeds about her heart. Is there any cause in nature that makes these hard hearts?" (3. 6. 76–78). The end of that drift is despair. He is kept from Cordelia, Kent tells us while Lear is offstage, by a "sovereign shame" that venomously stings his mind. And when he reappears in act 4, scene 6, crowned with the flowery images of his shame, his vision is bleak and almost altogether hopeless.

The effect of Shakespeare's presentation of Lear's drift toward a despairing parody of himself is unique among all the versions of the Lear story in the structural weight it gives to Cordelia. Always before, Lear had sought out his youngest daughter when he had learned the truth about the older ones; he had done this reluctantly and shamefacedly, but the initiative had always been his, and Cordelia had always merely responded to it. Only Shakespeare's Lear is so burdened with guilt that he refuses to see Cordelia, and so only Shakespeare's Cordelia is made to hunt her father down and recover him in spite of himself.

There is thus a peculiar quality of grace about Cordelia's reconciliation with her father. It is not the Calvinist grace of unmerited salvation but the more traditional notion of grace that we see in Augustine's *Confessions* or embodied in Grace Dieu in Lydgate's *Pilgrimage:* the power freely and steadily offered to man to elevate and perfect his own nature. By his own unaided efforts Lear has come to despair, but along the way he has accumulated, as it were, the elements of a new and more realistic conception of himself. And now, in grave and ceremonious fashion, which is underlined by the music that accompanies the scene, Cordelia organizes these elements and confers on Lear his lost identity as father and king. She has had Lear dressed while he slept, presumably in something distinctively royal, because she is careful throughout the scene to treat him like a king. So we can see at once, even before he wakes, that she has brought him to resume his "shape." And when he does wake, she leads him step by step, back from the fantasies of sleep and madness, to assume it. Her formal language and the gestures it implies recreate in her tent the royal court abandoned by Lear in the opening scene. He is once again "my royal lord," "your majesty," "your highness," installed once again in his "own kingdom" at the center of a solicitous assembly. Cordelia wakes him with a prayerful kiss, repeatedly calls him "dear father," kneels for his formal blessing—in short, leads him back to assume his offices by acting, herself, as daughter and subject.

If she is the old Cordelia, however, rearticulating and reconstructing their formal bonds, he is a different Lear, no more the blustering tyrant but now a man groping toward a more realistic grasp on himself. Throughout the scene of their reconciliation he slowly awakens in several senses: literally from his healing sleep, metaphorically from what he calls "the grave," psychologically from false notions of his own self-sufficiency. Though he has not yet been perfected in the domain of love—the last of Saint Bernard's spiritual ages—he begins to recognize, before his pilgrimage is cut short by the political forces he has unleashed, its first principles. His language is appropriately tentative, his gestures unsure and aborted but nonetheless telling, since they reveal his new awareness that the relations between fathers and daughters need to be governed by mutual exchanges. So when Cordelia kneels to get his blessing, for example, he tries to kneel to her for pardon, thereby echoing and answering that earlier moment when he had knelt mockingly before Regan to show her how foolish and degrading it would be if he were to beg pardon of his own daughter. And when next we see him onstage, two scenes later, after the French assault has failed and he and Cordelia are being sent off to prison by Edmund, he imagines their imprisonment as an idyllic retreat from a slippery world, where he and Cordelia will shower blessings on each other and take on themselves "the mystery of things, / As if [they] were God's spies."

IS THIS THE PROMISED END?

The speech in which Lear assures Cordelia that they will transform their prison into a retreat is defined as sentimental fancy even before he makes it. At the end of act 5, scene 1, Edmund had promised that if Lear and Cordelia came into his power he would kill them; and as soon as they leave the stage in scene 3, guarded, he sends the captain off with orders for their deaths. If we set that aside for a moment, however, just as Shakespeare does by means of the distracting interlude of Goneril and Regan's bickering over Edmund, which is followed by the combat between Edmund and Edgar and their mutual confessions, we can see that Lear's fancy is one of the promised endings of the play. His failure to value Cordelia's plain expression of love properly had led to all the imbalances in the narrative—Cordelia's banishment and Kent's, as well as Lear's impulsive transfer of all that he had to Goneril and Regan—and now that failure has been corrected and most of the imbalances have been set right. Lear has discovered that to be loved according to the bond that unites him with his daughter is not to be loved coldly and grudgingly, as he had thought, but to be loved constantly and inexhaustibly. And so he has come to value Cordelia above all the world.

Still holding Edmund's counterplot at bay, we can see that there are other senses in which the state of restored and enhanced happiness expressed in Lear's fancy is also promised. Alan Young has argued, for example, that the promise is made in one form by all the cognate stories in folklore that end happily and so establish a generalized expectation, triggered as soon as we recognize the form of the Lear story, that Shakespeare's play will also have a happy ending.[33] The fact that every other version of the Lear story ends happily leads F. T. Flahiff to imagine that Shakespeare's original audiences must have felt "shock and surprise... when they did not witness Lear's happy restoration to the throne, his peaceful death, or his succession by Cordelia." The title given to the play in the quarto edition *(M. William Shakespeare: His True Chronicle Historie...)* implies for Flahiff that his audiences were "invited to attend Shakespeare's reworking of familiar history," only to see instead his "disaccommodation of history."[34]

There are also reasons closer to home, within the play itself, why one might conclude that shock and surprise were the ends at which Shakespeare deliberately aimed. As soon as it becomes clear that Goneril and Regan mean to reduce Lear to their authority or dispossess him, we begin to hear that Cordelia is coming to rescue him, and these assurances become more specific, more pointed and weighty, as we move toward their reconciliation. So the roots of the structural association of Cordelia with redemptive grace are planted early and grow throughout the narrative. The letter that Kent reads in the stocks early in act 2 is no more than a vague promise ("shall find time from this enormous state—seeking to give losses their remedies"); but at the beginning of act 3 we hear that the French have indeed landed and are almost ready to show themselves, and two scenes later Gloucester assures us that "these injuries the king now bears will be reveng'd home; there is part of a power already footed." Even "tied to the stake" by Regan and Cornwall at the end of act 3, he is confident that he will "see / The winged vengeance overtake such children." We may find ourselves to be as confident as he that justice will prove out (with the same ironic result), encouraged as we are by the idealizing language that plays around Cordelia like a corona, absolutizing her virtues and implicitly associating her with Christ ("O dear father, / It is thy business that I go about"), with redeemed souls ("Thou art a soul in bliss"), and with redemptive grace ("Thou hast one daughter / Who redeems nature from the general curse / Which twain have brought her to").

These implications fail at last, but, before they do, the verbal and structural associations of Cordelia with Christian grace function in another way; and to my mind the most telling promise made by the play that its ending will be in some sense happy is the promise implied by Shakespeare's detailed restructuring of the old story around the action of life's pilgrimage. In every other version of the story, the Lear who suffers at the hands of his daughters is merely a pathetic victim; only in Shakespeare's is his suffering treated as part of a spiritual pilgrimage in which, by pursuing all his follies to the disillusioning ends they imply, he discovers what his nature truly requires. From the beginning our understanding of the story is guided along familiar lines by Kent and the Fool, by Edgar, even by Goneril and Regan, who, no less than the others, keep us aware of the familiar forms of moral action that shape Lear's pilgrimage. Regan's remark when Lear rushes out into the storm, that "to willful men / The injuries that they themselves procure / Must be their schoolmasters," though it convicts her as smug and coldhearted, given the circumstances, is a moral commonplace we have often heard before. And when the storm persuades Lear that he has taken too little care of the poor, and when Gloucester, blinded, discovers that "our means secure us, and our mere defects / Prove our commodities," it turns out to be true in precisely the same sense in which it has always been true—though that sense is more profound than Regan could have imagined.

Set to think along familiar lines by the pattern of changes Shakespeare has made in his sources, we are, I believe, positively encouraged, as part of the design of the play, to expect that these lines will be played out to their familiar ends: that, having brought him through suffering and repentance to the beginnings of understanding, Lear's pilgrimage will end, not with everyone living happily ever after, perhaps, but with some sort of assurance that he has won through to a secure spiritual state. Even Lear's fancy that he and Cordelia, imprisoned, will take on "the mystery of things" and "wear out... packs and sects of great ones / That ebb and flow by th' moon" may seem to further this expectation in a curiously teasing fashion. For the Pilgrim, Filius Regis, and Mankind are all sent off to secure castles after they have been recovered from the land of unlikeness, and there they are sequestered from the world and provided with knowledge of eternal things. These castles, too, are assaulted and even breached, as we know that Lear's prison/retreat will be breached by Edmund's order; but the assaults all fail in the end because the strength of the castles—which is to say the integrity of the moral knowledge they enclose—is secured by the grace with which Cordelia has been associated. So even Edmund's plot against

Cordelia's life, flatly revealed to us, may be ironically encouraging and lead us further down the garden path.

But not for long. Within two hundred lines, scarcely fifteen minutes' playing time, Lear enters with Cordelia dead in his arms, shattering whatever expectations the form of the story may have generated. He has fallen back into madness again, deeper and more terrible than the madness from which Cordelia had recovered him, because, where that had come from the loss of illusions, this comes from the loss of a painfully acquired truth. And, fifty lines later, he dies himself, asking what sense there is in Cordelia's death.

This has long been the crux of every interpretation of *King Lear*—the relationship between the action, as it is developed through the reconciliation of Lear and Cordelia, with all the formal expectations generated by that development, and the tragic ending that Shakespeare, in distinction from everyone else who has told the story, finds appropriate for it. Explanations of the sense to be found in Cordelia's death cover the whole philosophical spectrum, from Christian optimism to the bleakest nihilism;[35] but almost everyone who has commented on it has noted some element of misdirection, even of gratuitousness, in its presentation. Bradley said that Cordelia's murder seems "especially designed to fall like a bolt from a sky cleared by the vanished storm,"[36] and there has been little disagreement about that. Lear's anguished death is rooted in Cordelia's, and hers seems unarguably an expression of a vision that what is inescapably tragic is not life lived foolishly or badly, as in the allegorical tradition that Shakespeare drew on in constructing the play, but simply life lived, even to the highest pitch of integrity. The world revealed at the end of *King Lear* seems to have been constructed as a challenge to the earlier part of the play; as such, it indirectly challenges the rational and optimistic assumptions that underlie the figure of life's pilgrimage, for in the world of *Lear* it is possible to follow the pilgrim's route to the very end only to have everything snatched away by what is made to look very much like an accident. Shakespeare moves the responsibility for Cordelia's death around like a pea in a shell game, obscuring it almost as soon as he has revealed it. Edmund considers his intention to have Lear and Cordelia killed only toward the end of act 5, scene 1, about forty lines before he sends the captain off to do it. And by the time we learn that his order has been carried out, he no longer wants them dead but is urging Albany to hurry and save their lives. Moreover, the scheme that Edmund has now disowned is given a chance to work only because Albany's attention has been deflected from Lear and Cordelia, first by Edmund's presumption and then by the combat between Edmund and Edgar. The result, when Albany is recalled to the major issue of the play by Kent's inquiry for Lear, may be the most astonishing cue for a tragic entrance to be found in any literature: "Great thing of us forgot!"

Of course, the whole sequence might have been as plausibly handled in a different manner. But Shakespeare's use of Albany in the design of the scene seems clearly intended to throw into high relief the quality of accident in Cordelia's murder: committed after the man who ordered that it be done has repented; permitted only because the objects of a great battle were simply forgotten in its aftermath. With will and purpose canceled in advance and the occasion provided by inadvertence, Cordelia's death and Lear's are left almost opaque, challenging attempts to reduce them to form and order.

The problem of making sense of events, particularly moral sense, is thus built aggressively into the tragic ending of the play. In truth, of course, the problem has been there all along, a softly whispered and diffused threat of a different and bleaker end; but it is only in the last scene that we are forced to confront it. As Shakespeare has constructed it, Lear's entrance with Cordelia's body forms the final term in a dialectic between different ways of understanding experience, medieval and modern, broadly Thomist and even more broadly Calvinist, that has been woven lightly through the narrative from the first. On one side there are characters who imagine that good will regularly come from good and evil from evil, who expect, with Aquinas and Hooker, that they will find in the form of experience itself the evidence of a divine and intelligible order. On the other side there are the strange twistings and turnings of events that sometimes directly, more often indirectly, challenge that expectation by implying that, if there is a divine order, it may not easily or certainly be known. An assumption that the values of the gods are regular and knowable and woven as laws into the tissue of human experience shapes the common language of characters like Lear and Kent and Albany, revealing itself in inferences and judgments, blessings and curses, that turn out either not to be answered at all, as in Lear's case, or answered in ironic and equivocal ways. Kent's benedictory wish in act 1, scene 1, that "the gods to their dear shelter take [Cordelia] / That justly think'st and hast most rightly said," seems to be answered directly when France's love is "kindled to inflamed respect" by Cordelia's virtue and he makes her his queen, and it appears to be answered even more fully when she is reconciled with her father. But her accidental murder calls everything into doubt. An ironic answer to Kent's wish that "the gods reward" Gloucester for helping Lear comes more swiftly—Cornwall and Regan pluck out his eyes in the very next scene, while Gloucester swears by the "kind gods"; but it turns out to be no less equivocal a reply when Gloucester discovers that he "stumbled when he saw" but that blind, he recognizes his true son. Are the gods indifferent or malevolent? Or do they answer in their own obscure ways, providing, in the words of the *Book of Common Prayer,* what is "most needful" for men? Uncertainty about that is built into even the verbal rhythms of the play. When Albany is told that Cornwall was mortally wounded by his own servant after he had plucked out one of Gloucester's eyes, he takes that revolt from within Cornwall's extended body to be evidence of the swiftness of divine justice, as might any Elizabethan steeped in the Scholastic doctrine that the punishment for evil is immanent in the act itself. But then he is told that Cornwall went on, nonetheless, to pluck out the other eye. Edgar extracts from the fates of Gloucester and Edmund an example of moral economy that Hooker might have seen as a fair poetic image of the working of natural law: "The gods are just, and of our pleasant vices / Make instruments to plague us: / The dark and vicious place where thee he got / Cost him his eyes." But as Rosalie Colie notes, that "dark and vicious place" will, in less than a hundred lines, cost Cordelia her life and Lear his peace.[37] Patterns that seem to reveal an immanent moral order may dissolve in a moment to challenge it. This equivocal irony is brought into direct and theatrical focus when the dead bodies of Goneril and Regan and Cordelia are laid side by side on the stage. The corpses of Goneril and Regan provide Albany with an image of the awesome "judgement of the heavens," but, fifteen lines later, his complementary prayer, that the heavens defend Cordelia, is answered only by Lear's "howl" as he enters with her body.

The dialectic remains unresolved. Life as it is imagined by the play may be inescapably tragic, even, on the evidence of Cordelia's murder, randomly tragic; yet there is clearly some sort of retributive force at work in the play, and its operations are regularly pointed out to us. This force may not seem to be economical or precise, but it is sufficiently sure to warrant Albany's belief that there are justicers above and thus, by implication, to underpin the social order that seemed imperiled when it seemed that Goneril and Regan were triumphant. The wages of evil are certainly death. But what the gods do not guarantee, either within the world of the play or by any clear implication beyond it, are the wages of virtue. They are paid, if at all, only in the hazard that being true to oneself may be more likely to succeed than being false. There is no hint of transcendence or affirmation in Cordelia's death, no clue as to what we are to make now of those teasing allusions to grace. We are directed instead toward its finality: "She's dead as earth." "She's gone for ever." She will "come no more, / Never, never, never, never, never."

There are critics who have suggested that to find the manner of Cordelia's death morally significant is naïve. We all know, they remind us, as Shakespeare's contemporaries did, that life has never been fair. But to take Cordelia's death as merely realistic, no more a challenge to moral perception than tragic accidents in life,[38] is to trivialize it as art, which has the advantage over life of being free of accidents. Accidents in art are not morally indigestible lumps of experience; they are inevitably part of the complex perception of moral order that a work embodies, positive assertions that experience cannot be completely digested by rational moral categories.[39] The passage that Bradley thought summed up the meaning of the play— "'The gods defend her.' [*Enter Lear with Cordelia in his arms.*]"[40]—is the clearest form of a challenge, made over and over in the play, to those who think they know exactly what the gods will reward, shelter, cherish, and defend; it teases them out of thought, disarms authority, leaves them only with what they feel, not what they ought to say. While it may be going too far to conclude, as one recent critic has put it, that Shakespeare has "broken the Elizabethan dramatist's teleological link between the world of the play and a beneficent divine order, and set the play world terrifyingly adrift,"[41] there seems every reason to think that our capacity to see and to understand that link is made problematic by the play's design.

King Lear may, indeed, be Shakespeare's most Shavian play in the way that it turns a familiar dramatic form against itself and the assumptions it embodies. Just as Shaw appropriates the narrative conventions of nineteenth-century melodrama in order to bring melodramatizing thought to the surface and set its romantic fictions against reality, so Shakespeare reworks the Lear story along the lines of dramatic moral allegory and draws out the forms of thought associated with it, only to confront allegory with tragic reality. The result is that what we once thought of as moral allegory we must now think of as moral romance.

The problem posed by Shakespeare's peculiar construction of the ending of *King Lear* is thus essentially an epistemological problem, and the terrible poise with which the play addresses this problem dramatizes the epistemological crisis of its time. The Scholastic image of the universe and man's place in it, the image assumed and articulated by Aquinas and Hooker and embodied in all the plays we have been examining, was in the process of being dismantled at the turn of the century—in philosophy by a resurgent nominalism, in religion by the voluntarism of Luther and Calvin and the skeptical materialism of Bacon and Montaigne. Aquinas' God, whose justice was immanent in the laws of man's nature—the God assumed in the Bernardine figure of the land of unlikeness—had begun to retreat behind the clouds of his heaven, driven there by Calvin's insistence that for men to imagine they could trace his ways further than he had explicitly chosen to reveal them was presumptuous: God's ways are just simply because they are his ways; but "the reason of the divine justice," Calvin said, "is too high to be measured by a human standard or comprehended by the littleness of the human mind."[42] So, for Montaigne, "it is enough for a Christian to believe that all things come from God and to receive them with acknowledgement of his divine and inscrutable wisdom," but to go further and expect that his wisdom will make itself scrutable to man is to diminish and falsify God, who "allots and handles the fortunes and misfortunes of the world according to his occult disposition."[43] It is this hidden and inscrutable disposition of whatever gods rule the world of the play that we are made to confront in the final tableau—not a terrible void or an imbecile universe but a puzzle that has come to be all too familiar. The dominant rhetorical mode of the last moments of the play is interrogative, and the questions are all variations on one: What are we to make of this? It is in that sense, I think, that *King Lear* is, not a moral tragedy but a tragedy of a moral system. Lear's entrance with Cordelia's body virtually marks the end of a long-lived way of understanding experience and of the dramatic form created to express it.

ABBREVIATIONS

CD	*Comparative Drama*
EETS	Publications of the Early English Text Society; o.s., original series; e.s., extra series
ELH	*English Literary History*
HLQ	*Huntington Library Quarterly*
JAAC	*Journal of Aesthetics and Art Criticism*
MP	*Modern Philology*
PMLA	*Publications of the Modern Language Association*
PQ	*Philological Quarterly*
RenDr	*Renaissance Drama*
SEL	*Studies in English Literature*
ShS	*Shakespeare Survey*
SP	*Studies in Philology*
SQ	*Shakespeare Quarterly*
TAPA	*Transactions of the American Philological Association*

N O T E S

INTRODUCTION

1. Robert Potter, *The English Morality Play* (London and Boston, 1975); Bernard Spivack, *Shakespeare and the Allegory of Evil* (New York, 1958); David Bevington, *From Mankind to Marlowe* (Cambridge, Mass., 1962); Willard Farnham, *The Medieval Heritage of Elizabethan Tragedy* (Berkeley, 1936); W. Roy Mackenzie, *The English Morality Plays from the Point of View of Allegory* (Boston, 1914).

2. To sample a very broad field: The Aristotles of S. H. Butcher *(Aristotle's Theory of Poetry and Fine Art)*, Walter Jackson Bate *(Prefaces to Criticism)*, Francis Fergusson *(The Idea of a Theatre)*, John Jones *(On Aristotle and Greek Tragedy)*, and O. B. Hardison ("A Commentary on Aristotle's *Poetics,*" in *Aristotle's Poetics,* trans. Leon Golden) seem to me incompatible, and all of them differ from the Aristotle used by the group Kenneth Burke called the Neo-Aristotelians: Ronald Crane, Elder Olson, and Norman Maclean.

3. I have used Leon Golden's translation of the *Poetics* (Englewood Cliffs, N.J., 1968), chapter 9. Hereafter I will give chapter numbers in my text following significant quotations.

4. So, at the end of chapter 6, Aristotle says, "spectacle, to be sure, attracts our attention but is the least artistic and essential part of the art of poetry. For the power of tragedy is felt without a dramatic performance and actors. Furthermore, for the realization of spectacle, the art of the costume designer is more effective than that of the poet."

5. For a discussion of the problems involved in supporting the traditional readings of the catharsis clause from the text of the *Poetics,* see Gerald Else, *Aristotle's Poetics: The Argument* (Cambridge, Mass., 1967), pp. 224–32. Else's own view (developed in pp. 423–50) is that the catharsis clause should be read as the purification of pitiable and fearful incidents, and by "purification" he would understand the act of making clear through the plot that the tragic events are the results of *hamartia* and so are to be pitied rather than condemned.

6. H. D. Goldstein, "Mimesis and Catharsis Re-examined," *JAAC* 24 (1966): 567–77.

7. Leon Golden, "Catharsis," *TAPA* 93 (1962): 51–60.

8. The distinction between mimetic and didactic poetry is developed by Elder Olson in "William Empson, Contemporary Criticism, and Poetic

Diction," included in *Critics and Criticism,* edited by R. S. Crane (Chicago and London, 1952), pp. 65–68.

9. G. R. Owst, *Literature and the Pulpit in Medieval England,* 3d ed. rev. (New York, 1961), pp. 526–45.

10. The term *sermo corporeus* was first applied to the plays by E. N. S. Thompson in "The English Moral Play," *Transactions of the Connecticut Academy of Arts and Sciences* 14(1910):320. Joanne Kantrowitz argues that associating the plays with sermons at all suggests that they are less than fully dramatic ("Dramatic Allegory, or Exploring the Moral Play," *CD* 7 [Spring, 1973]: 68–80). See also Michael Kelley, *Flamboyant Drama* (Carbondale and Edwardsville, Ill., 1979), pp. 25–27. My own view of the relationship between the plays and sermons is set out more fully at the beginning of chapter 1.

11. Spivack, *Shakespeare and the Allegory of Evil,* p. 102.

12. Critics have tended to assume that the basic metaphor of the morality drama is the psychomachia. This view is shared by E. K. Chambers (*The Medieval Stage* [Oxford, 1903], vol. 2, p. 154), Robert Lee Ramsay (Introduction to Skelton's *Magnificence,* EETS, e.s. 98 [London, 1908]: cxlix–cliii), Thompson ("The English Moral Play"), Spivack *(Shakespeare and the Allegory of Evil),* and Bevington *(From Mankind to Marlowe),* although Ramsay and Spivack acknowledge that the conflict between vice and virtue does not aequately explain the dramatic structure of the play. Robert Potter *(The English Morality Play)* takes a more rhetorical and, to my mind, more productive approach by arguing that the plays are shaped to the common purpose of moving their audiences to repentance.

13. Such arguments have been made, of course; see Mabel Keiler, "The Influence of *Piers Plowman* on the Macro Play of *Mankind,*" *PMLA* 26 (1911): 339–55. W. Roy Mackenzie proposed *Reason and Sensuality* as a source for *Nature* in "A Source for Medwall's *Nature,*" *PMLA* 29 (1914): 189–99. H. N. McCracken offered *The Mirror of the Periods of Man's Life* as a source for Mundus et Infans in "A Source for Mundus et Infans," *PMLA* 23 (1908): 488–96. And recently Alan Nelson has argued that the *Mirror* is a close analogue of *The Castle of Perseverance;* see his "'Of the Seven Ages': An Unknown Analogue of *The Castle of Perseverance,*" *CD* 8 no. 1 (1974): 125–38.

14 In addition to the poems mentioned in note 13, a list of the prominent English poems might include the numerous translations of Deguileville's trilogy, Gavin Douglas' *Palace of Honour* (1501) and *King Hart* (before 1512), Stephen Hawes' *The Example of Virtue* (1503–4) and *The Pastime of Pleasure* (1507), Stephen Batman's *The Travayled Pilgrim* (1569), William Goodyear's *The Voyage of the Wandering Knight* (1581), a translation of Jean Cartigny's *Le Voyage du Chevalier errant* (1557), Nicholas Breton's *Pilgrimage to Paradise* (1592), Anthony Copley's *A Fig for Fortune* (1596), and, of course, Spenser's *Faerie Queene* (1590).

15. In quoting from the Bible, I have used the King James translation.

16. For example, Saint Bonaventure's *Itinerarium Mentis in Deum,* the anonymous *De Septem Itineribus Aeternitatis,* and Walter Hilton's *Scala Perfectionis.* In 1400 Jean Gerson, bishop of Paris, designed a set of spiritual exercises as a "pèlerinage d'équivalente durée" for those who were unable to

make a pilgrimage to Rome for the Jubilee; see Joannes Gerson, *Initiation à la vie mystique,* edited by Pierre Pascal (Paris, 1943).

17. Samuel Purchas, *Hakluytus Posthumus, or Purchas, His Pilgrimes* (Glasglow, 1905–7), vol. 1, p. 138.

18. Saint Thomas Aquinas, *Summa Theologiae,* edited and translated by the Dominican Order (New York and London, 1964), 1a, 2ae, Q. 94, art. 2. All citations will refer to this edition.

19. *The Pilgrimage of the Life of Man,* EETS, e.s. 77 (London, 1899), 83 (London, 1901), and 92 (London, 1904).

20. *Lydgate's Reason and Sensuality,* edited by Ernst Sieper, 2 vols., EETS, e.s. 84 (London, 1901) and 89 (London, 1903).

21. "So in regard to particular acts reason's judgement is open to various possibilities, not fixed to one. It is because man is rational that such decisions must be free" (*Summa Theologiae,* 1a, Q. 83, art. 1).

22. The characterization of youth as universally headstrong and improvident is, of course, a commonplace in formulations of the ages of man. For example, William Bond writes that "after the example of the chyldren of Israel, whan we come to the yeres of discretion, we be as rebellys to God and ydolteres, coveyting the things of this world" (*The Pilgrimage of Perfection* [London, 1520], vol. 1, p. 2).

23. Saint Bernard of Clairvaux, *Opera Genuina,* edited by Jean Mabillion (Paris, 1839), vol. 3, p. 446.

24. The figure appears in book 7 of Augustine's *Confessions:* "And I perceived myself to be far off from Thee, in the region of unlikeness *[regione dissimilitudinis],* as if I heard this Thy voice from on high: 'I am the food of grown men, and thou shalt feed on *Me;* nor shalt thou convert *Me,* like the food of thy flesh, into thee, but thou shalt be converted into *Me*" (translated by Edward Pusey [New York, 1957], pp. 117–18). Saint Bernard used the figure in a similar way in the forty-second sermon of *De diversi,* where the region all men inhabit because of original sin is called *regio dissimilitudinis.*

25. Saint Bernard of Clairvaux, "De gratia et libero arbitrio," quoted in Etienne Gilson, *The Mystical Theology of Saint Bernard,* translated by A. H. C. Downes (New York, 1955), p. 49. My reading of Saint Bernard is everywhere indebted to Gilson.

26. *Reason and Sensuality,* vol. 2, p. 4.

27. Castles of virtue are attacked in *King Hart* and *A Fig for Fortune,* while in the *Pilgrimage to Paradise, The Example of Virtue, The Pastime of Pleasure,* and *The Faerie Queene* the pilgrim must survive an attack in order to reach the castle.

28. O. J. Campbell, "The Salvation of Lear," *ELH* 15 (1947): 93–109.

CHAPTER ONE

1. E. K. Chambers, *The Medieval Stage* (Oxford, 1903), vol. 2, p. 201.

2. Works concerned with theatrical matters are Richard Southern's *The Medieval Theatre in the Round* (London, 1957), T. W. Craik's *The Tudor Interlude* (Leicester, 1962), and, more recently, Sumiko Miyajima's *The Theatre of Man* (Avon, Eng., 1977).

3. The characters are all given Latin speech tags in the manuscript but are called by their English equivalents in the body of the play. I have chosen to

use their English names because "Humanum Genus" seems to me to gloss over an important equivocation in the play about the reach of Mankind's character.

4. Mark Eccles, ed., *The Macro Plays*, EETS, o.s. 262 (London, New York, and Toronto, 1969), p. xi. I have used this edition of the *Castle*, and I will give line numbers in citing from it in my text.

5. The argument is developed by Jacob Bennett in "*The Castle of Perseverance:* Redaction, Place, and Date," *Medieval Studies* 24 (1962): 141–52.

6. G. R. Owst, *Literature and the Pulpit in Medieval England*, 3d ed. rev. (New York, 1961), pp. 77–85. See also Roberta Cornelius, *The Figurative Castle* (Bryn Mawr, Pa., 1930), and Morton Bloomfield, *The Seven Deadly Sins* (East Lansing, Mich., 1962).

7. Bernard Spivack, *Shakespeare and the Allegory of Evil* (New York, 1958), pp. 71–84.

8. See M. D. Anderson, *Drama and Imagery in English Medieval Churches* (Cambridge, Eng., 1963), pp. 80–83, and Ernst Tristram, *English Wall Paintings of the Fourteenth Century* (London, 1955), p. 97.

9. Cf. Aquinas, *Summa Theologiae*, 1a, 2ae, Q. 65, art. 2: "And so it is evident that infused prudence cannot exist without charity, nor in consequence can the other moral virtues, since they cannot exist without prudence."

10. Ibid., 1a, 2ae, Q. 65, art. 5.

11. In discussing man's need for the theological virtues, Aquinas writes, "First, with regard to his intellect there are added certain supernatural beginnings which he holds to in a divine light; these are the truths to be believed, and he does this by faith. Secondly, his will is adapted to this end, both in its reaching out for it, the movement of intention toward what is attainable, and this is the work of hope, and in a certain spiritual union whereby his will is, so to speak, transformed into the end, and this is the work of charity" (ibid., 1a, 2ae, Q. 62, art. 3; cf. 1a, 2ae, Q. 66, art. 6, and 3a, Q. 7, arts. 3 and 4).

12. For example, the state of mind expressed in the speech of Mankind beginning at line 2505.

13. The questions of whether the scaffolds had curtains and how they were likely to have been arranged are taken up by Southern in *The Medieval Theatre in the Round*, pp. 111–13.

14. What I have in mind are plays like the one in the Fleury Playbook that gives free rein to the skepticism of Mary Magdalene and John about the Resurrection. The Fleury play can be found in David Bevington, ed., *Medieval Drama* (Boston, 1975), pp. 39–44.

15. Southern imagines that the audience stood in the middle of the playing area and that the traffic lanes were kept clear by the "stytelerys" mentioned in the stage plan appended to the manuscript. His reconstruction of the stage has been challenged by Natalie Crohn Schmitt, "Was There a Medieval Theatre in the Round? A Re-examination of the Evidence," *Theatre Notebook* 22 (1968–69): 130–42; 24 (1969–70): 18–25, and by Sumiko Miyajima, *Theatre of Man*, pp. 157–68.

16. Sermon 19 in *Middle English Sermons*, edited by Woodburn Ross, EETS o.s. 209 (London, 1960), p. 111. Ross dates the sermons in the latter half of the fourteenth century and the early part of the fifteenth, so they are roughly contemporary with *The Castle of Perseverance.*

17. The passage seems to dramatize Aquinas' explanation of how hope is transformed into despair when one is made to dwell on present sufferings: "Now an arduous good has a two fold aspect: *qua* good it attracts us and arouses the emotion of hope; *qua* arduous it repels us, and arouses the emotion of despair" (*Summa Theologiae*, 1a, 2ae, Q. 23, art. 2.).

18. See Eccles, *The Macro Plays*, pp. XVII–XVIII.

19. In medieval literature the debate usually dramatizes the heavenly reasoning that led to the Incarnation and Redemption, although its place in the scheme of salvation varies somewhat. In the *Ludus Coventriae* it comes just before the Incarnation, while in *Piers Plowman* it is placed just before the Harrowing of Hell. But its resolution is almost always associated with some event in the life of Christ because its resolution marks the moment when God reveals his mercy. In English it is only in the *Castle of Perseverance* and the later *Castell of Labour* that the debate comes at the time of the Last Judgment. The literature is surveyed by Hope Travers in *The Four Daughters of God* (Bryn Mawr, Pa., 1907), and by Samuel Chew in *The Virtues Reconciled* (Toronto, 1947).

20. So Aristotle in chapter 25 of the *Poetics:* "If neither of the above is the case, the criticism must be met by reference to men's opinions, for example in the myths that are told about the gods."

21. *Myroure for Lewde Men*, quoted in Owst, *Literature and the Pulpit*, p. 103.

22. Cf. Henry Medwell's *Nature* (1490–1501), *John the Evangelist* (1517–18), *Wit and Science* (1535), and *Lusty Juventus*, (c. 1547), all of which use travel metaphors in much the same way.

23. Southern (*Medieval Theatre in the Round*, p. 156) argues that this, or something like it, is necessary, given the circumstances in which the play was performed.

24. Ibid., p. 96.

25. Mankind's absence from the stage during this, the most complete version of the psychomachia in the morality drama, is interesting in light of Spivack's observation that "in the logic of the Psychomachia metaphor man himself cannot appear in the action because he is the battleground on and for which the battle is fought or the castle besieged and defended" (*Shakespeare and the Allegory of Evil*, p. 92). Spivack goes on to explain that Mankind appears merely as a "convention" of the drama (ibid., p. 95).

26. Ibid., p. 101.

CHAPTER TWO

1. I have used the text of *Mankind* given in *The Macro Plays*, edited by Mark Eccles, EETS, o.s. 262 (London, New York, and Toronto, 1969). All citations in my text are to this edition.

2. The relationship between *Reason and Sensuality* and Medwall's play

was pointed out by W. Roy Mackenzie in "A Source for Medwall's *Nature,*" *PMLA* 29 (1914): 189–99.

3. For a detailed analysis of the emergence of literal drama during the middle of the sixteenth century, see Bernard Spivack, *Shakespeare and the Allegory of Evil* (New York, 1958), pp. 206–414.

4. For *Wit and Science* I have used the text given in *English Morality Plays and Moral Interludes,* edited by E. T. Schell and J. D. Shuchter (New York, 1969). All citations in my text are to this edition.

5. Spivack, *Shakespeare and the Allegory of Evil,* p. 220.

6. Werner Habicht reads the scene as a test of Science's character: see his "The Wit Interludes and the Form of Pre-Shakespearean Romantic Comedy," *RenDr* 8 (1965): 80.

7. For *The Marriage of Wit and Science* I have used the text given in *A Select Collection of Old English Plays,* edited by W. Carew Hazlitt, vol. 2 (London, 1876; reprinted New York, 1964). The quotation here is from page 330. Because lines are not numbered in this edition, I will give page numbers for all quotations from this play.

8. We might say, of course, that Science represents an organized body of knowledge that exists in the community itself, as distinct from its existence in any particular mind; but then we would have to understand Wit as a particular sort of student, not as intellectual capacity itself.

9. Redford's Wit is also "son to Dame Nature" (690).

10. Grace Dieu explains to the pilgrim that the temporal journey of life is merely a segment in a larger circular journey that brings man back to the ground of his being: "thow off God...art thymage and creature," and, therefore, "to hym off verray ryht certayn / Thow must resort and tourne ageyn, / As by mevyng natural / Ageyn to thyn orgynal" (12251–54).

11. I rely here on Etienne Gilson, *The Mystical Theology of Saint Bernard,* translated by A. H. C. Downes (New York, 1955).

12. Habicht, "The Wit Interludes," pp. 80–81.

13. The comparison is drawn by T. W. Craik, *The Tudor Interlude* (Leicester, Eng., 1962), p. 85, note.

14. For example, W. Roy Mackenzie comments, "there is not a scene, with the exception of Ignorance's lesson in spelling *(sic),* that is not a distinct and significant step in the progress of the allegory" (*The English Morality Plays from the Point of View of Allegory* [Boston, 1914], p. 160).

15. Richard Southern, *The Seven Ages of the Theatre* (New York, 1961), p. 137.

16. They are also physically detached from the text of the play itself in the manuscript in which it has been preserved.

CHAPTER THREE

1. Edward Hall, *The Union of the Two Noble and Illustre Famelies of Lancastre and Yorke* (London, 1809; reprinted, New York, 1965), p. 46.

2. *Woodstock, A Moral History,* edited by A. P. Rossiter (London, 1946), p. 47. I have used this edition of the play, and in my text I will refer quotations from the play to it. Like everyone who writes on *Woodstock,* I am deeply indebted to Rossiter's scholarship. He has gone thoroughly into

Woodstock's relations to its sources in both the chronicles and the homiletic drama, and I have done little more with these subjects than build on his foundations. I am sure that more debts will appear than I have been able to acknowledge. But I differ with Rossiter on the largest matter. As he reads the play, it is about Woodstock rather than Richard; hence his title.

3. Raphael Holinshed, *Chronicles of England, Scotland and Ireland* (London, 1807; reprinted, New York, 1965), vol. 2, p. 837. This is a reprinting of the 1586 edition. Rossiter concluded that "the main source of *Woodstock* is certainly Holinshed," pieced out by some details from Stowe and Grafton, and he includes selections from all three. There were other views of Woodstock's character, of course. He is described in Grafton as an "honorable and good man" (Rossiter, p. 250), and in *Mum and the Sothsegger* Woodstock appears as one of Richard's "best frendis," and his arrest is characterized as a "fals dede" (quotations from *Mum* are from the volume edited by Mabel Day and Robert Steele, EETS, o.s. 199 [London, 1936], Passus 1, lines 98–109).

4. Wolfgang Keller, "Richard II, Erster Teil," *Jahrbuch der Deutschen Shakespere-Gesellschaft* 35 (1899): 27–32. Cited by Rossiter, p. 39.

5. Holinshed, vol. 2, p. 849.

6. Ibid., p. 794. The year was 1388.

7. Ibid., p. 868.

8. Ibid., p. 836. The conspirators met in 1397 at Arundel Castle. "The earle Marshall that was Lord deputie of Calis, and had married the earle of Arundel's daughter, discovered all their counsell to the king, and the verie daie in which they should begin their enterprise." Richard was at first skeptical, but after consulting with his council he decided to arrest Woodstock.

9. Ibid., p. 839.

10. Quoted by Ernst Kantorowicz in *The King's Two Bodies* (Princeton, 1957), p. 7. This particular formulation of the theory comes from the arguments of crown lawyers in a case involving the ownership of the duchy of Lancaster, as reported in Edmund Plowden's *Commentaries or Reports*. The author of *Woodstock* was at least familiar with Plowden's *Reports* if not with this formula; for, just before the text breaks off, Nimble says, "I have plodded in Plowden and can find no law" (5. 6. 34–35). But I am not concerned to show that he knew Plowden or this formula so much as I am to show that the play can be illuminated by this legal version of the doctrine of the king's two bodies.

11. Holinshed, vol. 2, pp. 735–36. The tax had been levied to support a grant made in Parliament for "the king's use, and toward the charges of the armie that went over into France with the earle of Buckingham" (p. 734).

12. For example, these three consecutive sentences from Holinshed's account of 1387: "About the same time, Robert Tresilian lord chiefe justice of England came to Coventrie, and indicted there two thousand persons. The king and the queene came to Grobie, and thither came by his commandement the justices of the realme. There were also with him at the same time Alexander archb. of Yorke, Robert Veere duke of Ireland, Michaell de la Poole earle of Suffolke, Robert Tresilian, & his fellowes; of whom it was demanded if by the lawes of the realme the king might revoke the ordinances

made in the last parlement, to which he had given his assent in manner by constraint; and they made answer that he might" (ibid., p. 781).

13. Between this and the next line, the text includes a passage of seven lines explaining why Richard's father was called the Black Prince. The passage was marked for cutting in the manuscript.

14. Rossiter, note to line 45, p. 182.

15. The date is wrong, of course; Richard was born in 1367. Rossiter speculates that the playwright took the superscript number 1365 to refer to the wrong column in the edition of Holinshed he was using.

16. Kantorowicz, *The King's Two Bodies,* p. 149.

17. Thus the blank charters occupy the same place in *Woodstock* that the disinheriting of Bolingbroke occupies in Shakespeare's *Richard II.* That too is an act that implies the unkinging of Richard, as the duke of York points out: "Take Hereford's rights away, and take from Time / His charters and his customary rights; / Let not tomorrow then ensue today; / Be not thyself; for how art thou a king / But by fair sequence and succession?" And Shakespeare clarifies this logic by giving all the verbal initiatives in the march toward Richard's deposition to Richard himself.

18. In act 5, scene 2, Woodstock refers to them corporately as the state: "I compared the state (as now it stands— / Meaning King Richard and his harmful flatterers)" (31–32).

19. Quoted in Kantorowicz, *The King's Two Bodies,* p. 50.

20. Quoted ibid., p. 156.

21. "On Princely Government," *Selected Political Writings,* edited by A. P. d'Entrèves, translated by J. G. Dawson (Oxford, 1959), vol. 1, pp. 1–3.

22. Quoted in George C. Herndl, *The High Design: English Renaissance Drama and the Natural Law* (Lexington, Ky., 1970), p. 79.

23. Rossiter also thinks that the passage was "politically unsafe in the emphasis on kingly willfulness" (Text Notes, p. 198). But I cannot imagine how kingly willfulness could be more strongly emphasized than by having Richard assent bit by bit to the transfer of every one of his prerogatives and every inch of his land.

24. Holinshed, vol. 2, pp. 836–37.

25. This speech neatly illustrates how closely and carefully the playwright worked with his sources. It is composed of two different incidents reported by Holinshed. In 1386, during one of Richard's quarrels with his recalcitrant Parliament, Holinshed (vol. 2, p. 775) reports him as saying, "Well we do perceive that our people and commons go about to rise against us: wherefore we thinke we cannot doo better than to aske aid of our cousine the French king, and rather submit us unto him than to our owne subjects." Rossiter quotes a parallel passage from Grafton. This incident was drawn together with a rumor that circulated in 1388, when Richard was about to go on a pilgrimage to Canterbury, "that he meant to steale over into France, unto the French king, having promised to deliver up into his hands, the towne of Calis, with the Castle of Guisnes" (ibid., p. 785).

26. When the battle has been won, Lancaster says: "Thus princely Edward's sons, in tender care / Of wanton Richard and their father's realm, / Have toiled to purge fair England's pleasant field / Of all those rancorous weeds that choked the grounds / And left her pleasant meads like

barren hills (*Woodstock*, 5. 6. 1–5). Historically their victory meant a return to the Good Parliament of 1387.

27. Richard seems to be referring to the murder of an Irish Carmelite in 1383. If so, the playwright has him omit the circumstances that favored Lancaster. Holinshed (vol. 2, p. 763) reports that the friar had falsely accused Lancaster of treason, and it was while he was in prison, awaiting clarification of the affair, that he was murdered—not by Lancaster but by John Holland, the king's half-brother, and one Henry Greene. Since Lancaster does not defend himself, even against "ungracious deeds and practices," it seems clear that the playwright wants Richard's charge to stand so as to limit the moral stature of Richard's uncles.

28. Holinshed, vol. 2, p. 869.

CHAPTER FOUR

1. For *Volpone* I have used the text given in volume 5 of the eleven-volume edition of Jonson's works edited by C. H. Herford and Percy Simpson, *Ben Jonson* (Oxford, 1925–52).

2. Freda Townsend, *Apologie for Bartholmew Fayre* (New York and London, 1947), p. 59.

3. Dennis's letter to Congreve is reprinted in Herford and Simpson, 11:555.

4. Jonas Barish, "The Double Plot in *Volpone*," *MP* 51 (1953): 83–92.

5. *Essay of Dramatic Poesy* in *Essays of John Dryden*, edited by W. P. Ker (New York, 1961), vol. 1, p. 73.

6. Ibid., p. 70.

7. Jonson's relationship to Machiavelli is explored in Daniel Boughner's *The Devil's Disciple* (New York, 1968), esp. pp. 113–37.

8. Dennis's letter to Congreve, in Herford and Simpson, 11:555.

9. Commentary on the plays, in Herford and Simpson, 2:62.

10. The only reference to its delivery is Mosca's line, "This will, sir, you shall send unto me."

11. As Freda Townsend does (*Apologie*, pp. 61–62).

12. This argument is made by John Weld, "Christian Comedy: *Volpone*," *SP* 51 (1954): 184.

13. The idea apparently seemed so odd to Robert Knoll that he turned Dryden's meaning around. Dryden, he writes, "observed two actions in it. The first, dealing with the Fox's voluptuary qualities, ends naturally with the fourth act; the second, dealing with his covetousness, ends in the fifth" (*Ben Jonson's Plays* [Lincoln, Neb., 1964], p. 81).

14. In Herford and Simpson, 11:555.

15. Ibid., p. 556.

16. The term comes from the quarto edition of *Every Man in His Humour*. For a discussion of its use as a key to Jonson's satirical strategy, see Edward Partridge, *The Broken Compass* (New York and London, 1958), pp. 63–69.

17. Alan Dessen, *Jonson's Moral Comedy* (Evanston, Ill., 1971), pp. 70–104.

18. The quotation is from Jonson's dedicatory epistle to Oxford and Cambridge.

19. Partridge, *The Broken Compass*, p. 105.

20. Partridge emphasizes the transitional state of the characters (ibid., pp. 82-83), as does Alvin Kernan in the Introduction to his edition of *Volpone* (New Haven and London, 1962), p. 19. On the other hand, John Enck, complaining of the overdelicacy with which Herford and Simpson treat the play's allusions to animals, says flatly, "here the men are animals," and he goes on to imagine the actors costumed and directed in animal-like ways (*Jonson and the Comic Truth* [Madison, Wis., 1957], pp. 116-18).

21. Partridge, *The Broken Compass*, p. 76.

22. Harry Levin sees a similar function for the interlude: "The play within the play presents the point of view from which the play itself is about to launch its satirical attack." But he develops that function toward a different end ("Jonson's Metempsychosis," *PQ* 22 [July 1943]: 238-39).

23. The relationship between folly and monstrosity is explored by Barish in "The Double Plot in *Volpone*."

24. It has especially troubled Wallace Bacon, who describes Bonario's entrance as "the hero leaping through the door to save the little seamstress from the clutches of the villain" ("The Magnetic Field: The Structure of Jonson's Comedies," *HLQ* 19 [1956]: 137). Alvin Kernan characterizes the virtue of Celia and Bonario as "mechanical" and their language as "wooden" in *The Cankered Muse* (New Haven, 1959), pp. 184-85.

25. The pattern is traced by Alvin Kernan in his Introduction to *Volpone*, pp. 22-23.

26. Harriet Hawkins, "Folly, Incurable Disease, and *Volpone*," *SEL* 8 (1968): 335-48.

27. Boughner is perhaps the most scornful (*The Devil's Disciple*, pp. 118-19), but even Herford and Simpson complain that they are "almost as insipid as they are innocent" (2:63-64).

CHAPTER FIVE

1. I have used the text of *The True Chronicle History of King Leir* given by Joseph Satin in *Shakespeare and His Sources* (Boston, 1966).

2. A. C. Bradley described the skeletal moral structure of the play almost a century ago (*Shakespearean Tragedy* [London, 1904; reprinted London, 1965], pp. 198-276), and since then its relationships to the morality drama have been worked out by a number of critics, among them O. J. Campbell, "The Salvation of Lear," *ELH* 15(1947): 93-109; Irving Ribner, *Patterns in Shakespearean Tragedy* (London, 1960); Virgil Whitaker, *The Mirror up to Nature* (San Marino, Calif., 1965); Maynard Mack, *King Lear in Our Time* (Berkeley and Los Angeles, 1965); and Robert Potter, *The English Morality Play* (London and Boston, 1975). Potter quotes the *Gesta Romanorum* to show that the skeleton of a moral allegory was recognized in the story almost from the beginning:

> Dere Frendes, Thes Emperour may be called ech worldly man, the which hath thre doughters. The first doughter...is the worlde...the second doughter...is thi wife, or thi cheldryn, or thi kyn...and the third doughter...is our lord god.

[P. 153]

3. Shakespeare's use of the Gloucester story to clarify the issues in the Lear story is explored by Bridget Lyons, "The Subplot as Simplification in *King Lear,*" in *Some Facets of King Lear,* edited by Rosalie Colie and F. T. Flahiff (Toronto and Buffalo, 1974), pp. 23–38.

4. These emblems are studied by Russel Fraser, *Shakespeare's Poetics in Relation to King Lear* (London, 1962), and by John Riebantz, "Theatrical Emblems in *King Lear,*" in *Some Facets,* pp. 39–51.

5. The passage in Holinshed reads: "When this Lear therefore was come to great yeres, & began to waxe unweldie through age, he thought to understand the affections of his daughters towards him, and preferre hir whome he best loved to the succession over the kingdome" (Raphael Holinshed, *Chronicles of England, Scotland and Ireland* [1586] [New York, 1965], vol. 1, p. 447).

6. The issue is complicated by the fact that Cordelia has seemed to many readers to be strangely cold and unyielding. Coleridge's remark that she suffers "some little faulty admixture of pride and sullenness" (*Coleridge's Writings on Shakespeare,* edited by Terence Hawkes [New York, 1959], p. 183) has colored subsequent discussions, and readers who have not been content merely to criticize her answer to Lear have invented ingenious explanations for its peculiarity. S. L. Goldberg, for example, argues that Cordelia's refusal to compromise her integrity forces Lear to confront reality (*An Essay on King Lear* [Cambridge, Eng., 1974], p. 19), and Ivor Morris contends that the language of her refusal is carefully framed by Cordelia to present Lear with an ironic image of the nature of his own fault ("Cordelia and Lear," *SQ* 8, no. 2 [Spring 1957]: 141–58). But the fact is that no one onstage, except for Lear, seems to notice anything odd in what she says or how she says it. Indeed, Kent, who takes it on himself to criticize the exchange, says that she "most justly think'st and hast most rightly said"(1. 1. 183). In quoting from *King Lear,* I have used the text given in *The Riverside Shakespeare,* edited by G. Blakemore Evans (Boston, 1974). All citations in my text will refer to this edition.

7. For example, Robert Heilman (*This Great Stage* [Seattle, 1963], p. 162), says that Cordelia "refuses to translate the nonmarketable into a currency that can buy property."

8. Cordelia's integrity in this and other respects is explored by John Danby in *Shakespeare's Doctrine of Nature* (London, 1951), pp. 125–40, and the relationship between office and identity assumed in Shakespeare's plays is investigated by Thomas van Laan in *Role-Playing in Shakespeare* (Toronto, Buffalo, and London, 1978), pp. 21–42.

9. In all the earlier versions of the story Cordelia clearly recognizes need in this sense. So when Lear comes to ask her help, after Goneril and Regan have turned him out, she has Lear dressed and attended as a king should be before she receives him.

10. William Elton, *King Lear and the Gods* (San Marino, Calif., 1966), p. 280.

11. For example, Russel Fraser in his edition of the play for the New American Library (New York and Toronto, 1963), and David Bevington in his revision of Hardin Craig's edition of *The Complete Works of Shakespeare* (Glenview, Ill., and Brighton, Eng., 1973).

12. Rosalie Colie (*Paradoxica Epidemica* [Princeton, 1966], pp. 461–81) weaves this paradox into the complex pattern of paradoxes she finds in the play.

13. William Empson, *The Structure of Complex Words*, 3d ed. (London, 1977), p. 133.

14. Productions are described by Marvin Rosenberg, *The Masks of Lear* (Berkeley and Los Angeles, 1972), pp. 117–20. The tendency is so common in the criticism that it seems pointless to survey it. Rosalie Colie may illustrate how even a very good reader of the text may go off the tracks by taking striking lines out of their context: "In the huge task of self-identification, Lear's courage is terrifying. 'Who is it that can tell me who I am?' he asks after Goneril's first descent upon him, only to hear the Fool respond, 'Lear's shadow.'" She then goes on to pursue the resonances in the word "shadow" (*Paradoxica Epidemica*, p. 477). But the fact that Lear does not acknowledge the Fool's comment in any way, even by the slightest deflection in the course of his speech, makes it difficult to believe that he hears it in any meaningful sense.

15. The relevance of these Renaissance texts is explored by Paul Jorgenson in *Lear's Self-Discovery* (Berkeley and Los Angeles, 1967), and by Rolf Soellner in *Shakespeare's Patterns of Self-Knowledge* (Columbus, Ohio, 1972).

16. Wilson Knight, "Lear and the Comedy of the Grotesque," *The Wheel of Fire* (Oxford, 1930), pp. 175–93.

17. It is at Tom's entrance that Lear's sanity finally gives way.

18. Lear's madness has been studied in terms of Elizabethan psychology by Lily B. Campbell, *Shakespeare's Tragic Heroes* (New York, 1952), and in terms of modern psychology by Norman Holland, *Psychoanalysis and Shakespeare* (New York, 1964).

19. Mack points out that the language of the play may often be sharply individuated but that it "is always yet more fully in service of the vision of the play as a whole than true to a consistent interior reality" (*King Lear in Our Time*, p. 68).

20. Heilman, *This Great Stage*, p. 149.

21. However, Gloucester's blinding may be symbolically appropriate in another sense. Heilman develops its significance (ibid., pp. 41–53), and Mack sums it up neatly: "the blindness is not what will follow from adultery but what is implied in it" (*King Lear in Our Time*, p. 70).

22. See, for example, Rosenberg, *The Masks of Lear*, pp. 251–53.

23. See, for example, Frank Kermode in *The Riverside Shakespeare*.

24. The quotation is from a note in *A New Variorum Edition of Shakespeare*, edited by H. H. Furness (Philadelphia, 1880), vol. 5, p. 257.

25. The contemporary literature is surveyed by Elton, *King Lear and the Gods*, pp. 231 ff.

26. Granville Barker, *Prefaces to Shakespeare*, vol. 1 (Princeton, 1947), p. 297.

27. Michael Long, *The Unnatural Scene* (London, 1976), p. 211.

28. Nicholas Brooke, "The Ending of *King Lear*," in *Shakespeare 1564–1964*, edited by E. A. Bloom (Providence, R.I., 1964), p. 87.

29. Soellner, *Patterns of Self-Knowledge*, p. 281.

30. Mack, *King Lear in Our Time*, p. 94.

31. The reciprocal relationship between service and authority is explored by Jonas Barish and Marshall Waingrow in "Service in *King Lear*," *SQ* 9, no. 3 (1958): 347–55.

32. Lear's encounter with Poor Tom has been read in diametrically opposed ways. Elton (*King Lear and the Gods,* p. 191), Jorgenson (*Lear's Self-Discovery,* pp. 117–18), Soellner (*Shakespeare's Patterns of Self-Knowledge,* p. 313), Knight (*The Wheel of Fire,* p. 183), and Marcus Charney ("We Put Fresh Garments on Him," in *Some Facets of King Lear,* pp. 77–78), all take it that Lear comes upon unequivocal truth when he finds in Tom an image of "the thing itself." But Colie (*Paradoxica Epidemica,* pp. 473–74), and Danby (*Shakespeare's Doctrine of Nature,* pp. 28–30) recognize in different ways that his insights are profoundly equivocal.

33. Alan Young, "The Written and Oral Sources of *King Lear* and the Problem of Justice in the Play," *SEL* 15 (1975): 309–19.

34. F. T. Flahiff, "Edgar: Once and Future King," in *Some Facets of King Lear,* p. 226.

35. Some of those who find in the ending of the play an affirmation of divine order are Irving Ribner (*Patterns in Shakespearean Tragedy*), John Danby (*Shakespeare's Doctrine of Nature*), O. J. Campbell ("The Salvation of Lear"), Robert Heilman (*This Great Stage*), Virgil Whitaker (*The Mirror up to Nature*), Robert Speaight (*Nature in Shakespearean Tragedy* [London, 1955]), and Paul Siegel (*Shakespearean Tragedy and the Elizabethan Compromise* [New York, 1957]). Wilson Knight, on the other hand, characterized the ending as "the most fearless artistic facing of things in our literature (*The Wheel of Fire,* p. 174), and in one way or another that view is endorsed by Nicholas Brooke ("The Ending of *King Lear*"), John Stampfer ("The Catharsis of *King Lear,*" *ShS* 13 [1960]: 1–10), S. L. Bethell (*Shakespeare and the Popular Dramatic Tradition* [Durham, N.C., 1946], and Jan Kott (*Shakespeare Our Contemporary* [New York, 1964]). The middle ground, which acknowledges the challenge posed by the ending to traditional assumptions but limits its significance, is argued eloquently by Mack (*King Lear in Our Time,* pp. 114–17), Colie ("The Energies of Endurance: Biblical Echoes in *King Lear,*" in *Some Facets,* pp. 116–44), and, most recently, by John Riebtanz (*The Lear World* [Toronto and Buffalo, 1977]).

36. A. C. Bradley, *Shakespearean Tragedy,* pp. 206–7.

37. Colie, "Energies of Endurance," p. 135.

38. For example, George Herndl, speaking of the deaths of Lear and Cordelia, writes: "But an evil, however pitiable its subject, which we can trace to the violation of law may witness at least to knowable order, and without diminishing freedom. An accidental electrocution, a death by freezing in Antarctica, do not move us to fear life or despise the world. The laws of electricity are understood, the lethal cold of the polar regions is known. We are thus not at their mercy. *King Lear* creates to that extent an acceptable world" (*The High Design: English Renaissance Drama and the Natural Law* [Lexington, Ky., 1970], p. 48). Even Mack seems to be tempted toward this position when he writes that "we face the ending of this play, as we face our world, with whatever support we customarily derive from systems of belief or unbelief" (*King Lear in Our Time,* p. 116).

39. For a brilliant exploration of the tragedy as reality's revenge on

dreams of order, see Michael Long, *The Unnatural Scene.* Stephen Booth argues that the greatness of the play lies precisely in its resolute challenging of fixed categories of all sorts, moral, philosophical, esthetic ("On the Greatness of *King Lear,*" in *Twentieth-Century Interpretations of King Lear,* edited by Janet Adelman [Engelwood Cliffs, N.J., 1978], pp. 98–111).

40. *Shakespearean Tragedy,* p. 272. But Bradley's understanding of its significance takes away much of the sting: "The 'gods,' it seems, do *not* show their approval by 'defending' their own from adversity or death, or by giving them power and prosperity. These, on the contrary, are worthless, or worse; it is not on them, but on the renunciation of them, that the gods throw incense."

41. Riebtanz, *The Lear World,* p. 114.

42. John Calvin, *Institutes* III. xxiii. 4, quoted in Herndl, *The High Design,* p. 126. The dismantling of Scholastic thought is surveyed by Herndl and is examined in greater detail by Hiram Haydn, *The Counter-Renaissance* (New York, 1950), and by Herschel Baker, *The Wars of Truth* (Cambridge, Mass., 1952).

43. "We should meddle soberly with judging divine ordinances" (*The Complete Works of Montaigne,* translated by Donald Frame [Stanford, Calif., 1958], p. 160).

I N D E X